CATHOLIC CHARITIES USA

Catholic Charities USA

*100 Years at the Intersection
of Charity and Justice*

Rev. J. Bryan Hehir
Executive Editor

LITURGICAL PRESS
Collegeville, Minnesota

www.litpress.org

Library of Congress Cataloging-in-Publication Data

1	2	3	4	5	6	7	8

Library of Congress Cataloging-in-Publication Data

Catholic Charities USA : 100 years at the intersection of charity and justice / edited by J. Bryan Hehir.
    p.   cm.
    Includes bibliographical references and index.
    ISBN 978-0-8146-3339-7 — ISBN 978-0-8146-3930-6 (e-book)
    1. Catholic Charities USA.   2. Church charities—United States.   3. Catholic Church—United States—Charities. i. Hehir, J. Bryan.

BX2347.C38   2010
259.088'282—dc22   2010017067

Contents

Acknowledgments

Catholic Charities USA offers profound thanks to the following individuals who gave generously of their time and talent in the production of this work.

Executive Editor: Rev. J. Bryan Hehir

Essayists: Sr. Ann Patrick Conrad, Mary Gautier, Mark Gray, Rev. J. Bryan Hehir, Sr. M. Vincentia Joseph, Rev. Fred Kammer, SJ, David J. O'Brien, Rev. Larry J. Snyder, Msgr. Kevin Sullivan, Msgr. Robert Vitillo, and Sr. Linda Yankoski

Readers: Mary DesRoches, Msgr. Charles Fahey, Susan Mundale

CCUSA Centennial Editorial Committee: Brian Corbin, Kathleen Donnellan, Msgr. Charles Fahey, Kathleen Flynn Fox, Patricia A. Hvidston, Rosalinda Lopez, Maria Mazzenga, Kathleen McGowan, Timothy Meagher, Susan Mundale, and Msgr. Joseph Semancik

Additionally, Catholic Charities USA wishes to thank Ruth Liljenquist for the extraordinary skill she brought to this publication in her service as managing editor.

Without the individual and collective contributions of the above individuals this book would not have come into being in celebration of Catholic Charities USA's 100 years.

Chapter
One

Introduction

Rev. Larry J. Snyder
Catholic Charities USA

Introduction

In the year 1866, the Catholic bishops of the United States made the following statement: "It is a very melancholy fact, and a very humiliating avowal for us to make that a very large portion of the vicious and idle youth of our principal cities are the children of Catholic parents."[1]

In these words we glimpse the fact that Catholic immigrants to this country faced a reality that was hardly the American dream as we have come to define it. It may surprise some to learn that for the majority of its history, the Catholic Church in the United States has been primarily an immigrant church. For most Catholic immigrants, the reality that awaited them here was poverty, the struggles of assimilation, and religious and ethnic prejudice.

Another statement, excerpted from an article in the *Catholic Charities Review* of March 1922, attests that the challenges publicly observed by bishops in 1866 continued to plague new immigrants and the church that attempted to welcome and serve them. Catholic social workers pointed to:

> a deplorable percentage of children of Catholic parentage and baptism appearing as delinquents in the courts; to the number of applications by destitute Catholic families to non-Catholic agencies; to the out-of-proportion percentage of Catholic girls in reformative agencies and institutions; to the figures on illegitimacy; and to the number of Catholic women in the police courts.[2]

Even though these conditions were reported in 1922, the church in America had long been responding to the needs of the immigrant church. From the arrival of the Ursuline sisters in New Orleans in 1727 through the nascent efforts in each emerging diocese to respond to the issues and needs found in that local church, the response was not temporary or without vision. The response was systemic in nature and encompassed the areas of education, health care, and social services. Even as communities of religious women and men provided leadership in all three of these areas, local Catholic Charities agencies were established diocese by diocese with spirit and determination.

By 1900, more than 800 Catholic institutions had been organized to provide care for children and for the ill, elderly, and disabled. During the next ten years, a broad consensus formed among the leaders of Catholic charity organizations that a national organization was needed. And so on September 25, 1910, a visionary group gathered on the campus of Catholic University of America to establish a national entity to promote, coordinate, and support these agencies now making a substantial contribution to their local communities and to advocate for the people they serve in the spirit of the Gospel. The new National Conference of Catholic Charities, later named Catholic Charities USA, would eventually become the largest human service network in the United States and the third national organization formed in the world that would eventually help to establish Caritas Internationalis, the international federation of Catholic humanitarian and relief organizations headquartered at the Vatican.

With the impetus of the Second Vatican Council and the social movement that defined the 1960s, Catholic Charities engaged in what became known as the Cadre Study, a process of evaluation and renewal. Adopting the recommendations of the study in 1972, Catholic Charities sought to become an organization that by its mission and mandate would not only serve the poor, but stand with them in seeking economic and social justice. This mission was affirmed by Vision 2000, an initiative of the 1990s to develop a vision for the new millennium, and continues to be the defining vision that focuses the efforts of local Catholic Charities agencies and the national office.

To understand Catholic Charities today, one has to appreciate that since its beginning, it has been defined by two distinct and yet complementary realities. Catholic Charities USA, centered at the national office, first of all functions as a professional trade association, serving the needs of its members through consulting, training, technical assistance, program development, and networking opportunities that allow agencies to share their strength and creativity with others, especially in situations of extreme need or disaster. The national office also acts as a national intermediary for federal grants and coordinates the disaster response efforts of the network throughout the United States and its territories. Participation in this professional trade association is unique to the needs of each member organization.

The second reality that defines Catholic Charities is what I believe truly sets us apart and gives us a clear sense of mission. Throughout its 100-year history, Catholic Charities has been understood as a "movement" committed to social transformation, but a movement also deeply connected to its roots in the Gospel and its Catholic identity and tradition. We find there the clear mandate that we must be of service to our neighbor in need, but in a way that respects the inherent dignity of every human being. The fundamental principles of this movement are found in our seminal documents: the 1910 Charter, the Cadre Study and Vision 2000, as well as in our Code of Ethics, which is based on principles of Catholic social teaching as found in the *Compendium of Catholic Social Thought* and not simply guiding professional principles. Engagement of member agencies at this level is universal.

Professional trade association and movement express the reality of Catholic Charities these 100 years since the founding of Catholic Charities USA. Our history is replete with accounts of heroic service given without consideration for personal gain or recognition. It is filled with champions like Msgr. William Kerby and Msgr. John O'Grady, who championed the cause of "the little ones" in the public forum and put their mark on public policy of their day and beyond.

In this centennial year, 2010, we have, without a doubt, an obligation to look back and recognize those who have preceded us and shown us by word and example that our work is a sacred trust to be discharged faithfully. However, if we look at the strategic directions adopted by Catholic Charities USA for this centennial celebration, we see that our purpose is also to look toward the future. Those strategic directions are:

- *Teach* Americans that poverty is a moral issue destroying the fabric of our communities.

- *Advocate* governmental policy makers to work toward economic justice that empowers all persons to achieve independence, pursue education, access quality health care, safeguard the environment, and enjoy proper nutrition.

- *Record and share* the history of Catholic Charities USA, the national office, supporting the work of local agencies, as it contributes to the social welfare of the country.

- *Celebrate* with liturgy and festivals at the national and local levels the accomplishments of the first 100 years and a commitment to the next century of advocacy and service by Catholic Charities USA and its member agencies.

- *Develop media presence* that celebrates positive advances toward the elimination of poverty and invites the public to civil discourse identifying points of commonality that can bring people of divergent opinions to a table of constructive opportunity.

- *Support* the development of resources that will empower Catholic Charities USA to attain its new strategic directions.

One of these strategic directions is to record and share our history. This book, edited by Rev. J. Bryan Hehir, former president of Catholic Charities USA, is one of our efforts to do so. The essays in this book, both theological and historical, capture aspects of the history and mission of Catholic Charities over the last 100 years, shaped by changes and forces in the church and in the broader society. Let me introduce them briefly.

David O'Brien, noted historian of the Catholic Church in the United States, provides a brief historical work on Catholic Charities in chapter 2, exploring Catholic Charities' development in the context of the reforms and policies of the progressive era in the early twentieth century, the New Deal in the 1930s, and the Great Society in the 1960s. O'Brien comments on the history of Catholic Charities as a case study of the complex methodology of social action: direct service, advocacy, and institutional reform. He concludes with further commentary on the church-state partnership in American welfare history, the government support of Catholic Charities to meet the vast human need in our country, and the work for charity and justice as both Catholic and American.

In chapter 3, Rev. Hehir looks at three moments in the history of the Catholic Charities movement: the founding of the National Conference of Catholic Charities in 1910, the landmark Cadre Study beginning in the late 1960s and culminating with the final report in 1972, and the present moment—the first decade of the twenty-first century. He explores the state of Catholic social teaching and moral vision at each of these moments and how Catholic Charities developed and is developing its sense of identity, mission, and ministry in response to that teaching and vision.

In chapter 4, Srs. Ann Patrick Conrad and M. Vincentia Joseph of the National Catholic School of Social Service at Catholic University of America look at the factors that led to the professionalization of social work and the impact of this process on the Catholic Charities movement in America. The chapter explores how the training of social workers evolved over time, first from apprenticeships to more formal preparation in training institutes and later colleges and universities, including Catholic institutions. The chapter also explores the development of licensing and accreditation standards, the shift in agency leadership from religious to laypeople, and the increasing complexity of human needs and social problems as well as the implications of these shifting patterns for ethics leadership, mission engagement, and service delivery.

Addressing a second topic in chapter 5, Srs. Conrad and Joseph provide a historical snapshot of the development of the unique relationship between Catholic Charities and local parish communities in the American Catholic Church. Dating back to the early twentieth century and the work of the St. Vincent de Paul Societies in the local parish—the basic unit of the church—diocesan Catholic Charities emerged to provide coordination and technical/professional assistance and specialized supports as increasingly complex social problems and issues confronted the church and society. Over time, the various diocesan Catholic Charities structures took on a life of their own, apart from the parish, becoming a voice of the church around human needs and social issues. In the 1970s, however, a groundswell of interest in social services at the neighborhood and church/parish level developed, strengthening the links between parish and diocesan social ministries. From that point on, the parish social ministry movement became a major thrust of Catholic Charities agencies.

Chapter 6, authored by Sr. Linda Yankoski, longtime director of Holy Family Institute (HFI) in Pittsburgh, Pennsylvania, explores the partnership between church and state through a case study of HFI. Founded in 1900 by the Sisters of the Holy Family of Nazareth, HFI was originally an orphanage and an early pioneer in the Catholic social service movement. The agency changed with the needs of the region's population, and its growth is directly tied to its participation in fee-for-service government contracts. Today HFI serves more than 6,000 people annually with services that include alternative and special education, in-home family counseling, and residential care for abused and neglected children. Sr. Yankoski analyzes a century's worth of records from HFI to discover if participation in government contracts affected HFI's Catholic identity and mission, and, if so, how.

In chapter 7, Msgr. Robert J. Vitillo, former head of the Catholic Campaign for Human Development and currently a Caritas Internationalis delegate to the United Nations, explores the roots of empowerment within Scripture and Catholic social teaching and examines the often cited but mistaken tensions between charity and justice in accompanying poor and otherwise marginalized or oppressed people in their own empowerment process. Msgr. Vitillo discusses the unique experiences of the church in the United States through such institutions as Catholic Charities, Catholic Campaign for Human Development, and Catholic

Relief Services in transforming the socio-pastoral work of the church from pure assistance to empowerment models.

In chapter 8, Rev. Fred Kammer, former president of Catholic Charities USA, discusses the mission and identity of Catholic Charities in the context of the long tradition of Catholic social teaching and its emphasis on human dignity, prophetic social justice, the preferential option for the poor, subsidiarity, and solidarity. He also explores the mission of Catholic Charities USA, looking at the Cadre Study of the 1970s, which set forth the mission of service, advocacy, and convening, and the Vision 2000 process, which updated the work of the Cadre Study, with emphasis on empowering services, societal transformation, strengthened church relationships, and organizational capacity-building. In discussing identity, Rev. Kammer underscores the many diverse ways in which Catholic Charities is Catholic and the power of that identity in service of the mission as exercised by staff and volunteers of many faith traditions in a pluralistic civil society.

Msgr. Kevin Sullivan, executive director of Catholic Charities of the Archdiocese of New York, in chapter 9 addresses four interrelated areas: Catholic Charities as an essential and constitutive element of the Catholic Church; the scope of Catholic Charities mission based upon a more traditional and comprehensive understanding of *caritas* as Christian love that includes both justice and compassion; the human rights tradition of the church, most fundamentally the dignity of the human person, as prescriptive for both the justice and compassionate work of Catholic Charities; and how this essential human rights work of the church is currently reflected in Catholic Charities in the United States.

The book concludes with a chapter from Mary Gautier and Mark Gray of the Center for Applied Research in the Apostolate. They draw on statistical information from Catholic Charities USA Annual Surveys as far back as 1970 to provide an empirical overview of Catholic Charities services and programs over the last four decades, with primary emphasis on the last decade. It gives readers a good understanding of who Catholic Charities agencies serve, what services Catholic Charities agencies provide, and how those services have changed over time.

We hope that this book will not only educate and inform but also inspire deep reflection on the legacy of faith, charity, and justice that the Catholic Charities movement has left to us in its first 100 years.

Catholic Charities is recognized as a critical part of the social safety net in this country and an indispensable part of the fabric of local communities. In whatever manner its contribution and presence is recognized, the greatest measure is the calling to which it aspires. In one of his first visits to this country, Pope John Paul II held a special audience in San Antonio in 1987 specifically for the Catholic Charities network. His address was titled The Poor Have a Privileged Place in Christ, and in it he said:

> We have seen how Catholic Charities and all its colleague associations have lent God their own flesh—their hands and feet and hearts—so that his work may be done in our world. For your long and persevering service—creative and courageous, and blind to the distinctions of race or religion—you will certainly hear Jesus' words of gratitude: "You did it for me." . . . So gather, transform and serve! . . . By working for a society which fosters the dignity of every human person, not only are you serving the poor, but you are renewing the founding vision of this nation under God! And may God reward you abundantly![3]

May God who has begun this good work in us bring it to fruition!

Chapter Two

Catholic Charities

A Brief Historical Introduction

David J. O'Brien
University of Dayton

Catholic Charities

A Brief Historical Introduction

The history of American Catholic Charities is well described in many chapters of this volume. Founded in 1910, in the midst of the progressive era, the National Conference of Catholic Charities was an organized effort to incorporate many of the reforms of that remarkable era into the work of the American Catholic Church. At the local level, Catholic charitable work still consisted of a veritable kaleidoscope of projects sponsored by parishes and dioceses, religious communities and dedicated lay men and women, amateurs, and a growing number of professionals. The spreading networks of nondenominational settlement houses drew attention to Catholic counterparts, and some Catholics were attracted to the newcomers' use of social science, case methods, and collaborative strategies for dealing with what seemed an ever growing flood of human need. Across the country, many local Catholics had joined with others to make the distribution of aid to needy families more efficient, effective, and rational, cooperation that would later bring wartime cooperation at the national level and community chest campaigns locally. And long Catholic experience with urban poverty and industrial conflict found expression in support for factory legislation and "bread-and-butter" social reforms in cities and states.

Among themselves, Catholics active in providing social services were more and more likely to meet together, coordinate their work, and cooperate with a new generation of bishops building diocesan offices aimed at making more effective use of the church's limited financial and human resources as the Catholic population exploded. These offices supported cooperation, gradual professionalization of services, and eventually a degree of centralization of fund raising, at least for diocesan and parish-based work. All this was done while preserving room for the spontaneous response of people and communities to the needs they saw around them.

The history of Catholic Charities has been tied closely to the history of American social welfare policy. Catholic Charities leaders at the turn of the twentieth century championed many of the major reforms of the progressive era even while they regarded progressives themselves with some suspicion. John A. Ryan of Catholic University worked to ease those suspicions and build Catholic support for unions, political reform, and social legislation. He and his students provided national leadership to one important cause: minimum wage legislation. Ryan hoped that the emerging organization of Catholic Charities would provide a foundation of clerical and episcopal leadership for social reform. In 1919, in fact, the bishops publicly championed European-style social insurance, producer and consumer cooperatives, and government action to bring about full employment and a greater degree of economic equality. From that time on, the Catholic community was a reliable supporter of labor unions, social welfare legislation, and positive government action to alleviate suffering and correct economic injustices.

In the New Deal years, 1933–39, Catholic Charities leaders backed reform and worked with Ryan's office at the National Catholic Welfare Conference to educate the Catholic public in the basic principles of Catholic social teaching. Catholics backed New Deal era reforms that included not only national legislation like Social Security, with its provision of old-age pensions and support for dependent persons and families, but state and local efforts to ensure that the government would be the service provider of last resort. In its early years, the Great Depression bankrupted private charities and local governments so that almost all those who worked with poor and working-class people were persuaded that a safety net of publicly provided services was essential to the stability of American institutions. Out of that era emerged a uniquely American arrangement in which state provision remained limited. Much still depended on private benefactions, and at the local, state, and national levels, government worked with and through private agencies, including church-sponsored social service agencies.

This pragmatic, cooperative approach, rooted in nineteenth-century provision by local and state governments of per capita support for dependent persons, became fully institutionalized after World War II and found expression in many of the bottom-up, community development initiatives of the Great Society of the 1960s. By then Catholic leaders in combating poverty had won respect and influence in the development and administration of social policy. Sargent Shriver headed the Office of Economic Opportunity, Daniel Patrick Moynihan became a very influential voice on poverty, and Saul Alinsky, with his approach to community organizing backed across the country by Catholic bishops and priests, informed the most dramatic of the projects of the War on Poverty. In that era, the bishops launched their own antipoverty program, the Catholic Campaign for Human Development, which channeled millions of dollars to grassroots self-help organizations among poor and marginalized Americans. By that time, the Catholic Charities movement itself, spurred by racial conflict and violence in American cities, was rethinking its own work, which led to efforts to decentralize service provision, encourage parish-based social action, and empower the poor.

Catholic Charities was and remains among the most important segments of American Catholic life. In an excellent history, Elizabeth McKeown and Dorothy Brown describe in great detail the manner in which Catholic Charities at the diocesan and national levels has interacted in a constructive fashion with other charitable agencies, welfare reformers, and, eventually, the welfare state. Utilizing insider Catholic language, they noted that while "the poor belong to us," they also needed more than "we" could provide. Accordingly Catholic leaders were usually very responsible and associated their efforts with other projects aimed at the alleviation of suffering through relief and reform. This willingness to collaborate with other agencies and cooperate with government demonstrates the complex practice and rich promise of American pluralism and provokes suggestive reflection on the surest route to reforms respectful of cultural and religious diversity.

The history of Catholic Charities also serves as a case study of the complex methodology of social action: direct service, always needed; advocacy, arising naturally from the experience of service; and institutional reform, the concrete answer to the questions posed by the advocates and the poor themselves. The internal politics of Catholic Charities reflected differing emphases arising from these three functions: service providers naturally impatient with reformers, advocates sometimes placing unbearable demands on the systems, and reformers tempted to prefer orderly "scientific" methods to messy efforts to enable the poor to participate. It was not easy to combine the roles of advocate for the poor and partner in government programs, yet Catholic Charities leaders regularly succeeded in doing so. The Catholic Charities movement as a whole did justice to all three responsibilities, especially in the heady days of New Deal reform. But at the same time, the movement became more and more centralized and clericalized, as clerics thought themselves better suited than women religious or laypeople to serve as "protectors of the religious rights of Catholic welfare recipients in order to make a place for their agencies in the new public programs." Eventually a heavy price would be paid for this combination of centralization and clerical control.

One should always remember that Catholics—rich and poor, bishops, religious, and laypeople—are also Americans. The large question in American Catholic studies is always the balance between Catholics as a distinct subculture and Catholics as responsible participants in shaping American culture and society as a whole. This same balancing between Catholic Charities as an expression of Catholic faith and Catholic Charities as a form of shared civic responsibility has informed the rich history of the Catholic Charities movement. And the history makes clear that this tension is not a new phenomenon but has always marked the movement.

There is much merit in the "immigrant outsider to the Americanized insider" interpretation of American Catholic history, but its downside is the suggestion that, until recently, Catholics had little power over and less responsibility for the development and behavior of dominant institutions. But Catholics, of course, were around from the start and in some places became major players quite early. In their vivid and richly detailed description of political battles over welfare policy in New York before and after the turn of the century, in the states during the Great Depression, and in Washington, DC, during the making of Social Security, McKeown and Brown combine attention to the separate work and ideas of Catholics—"the poor belong to us"—and their unapologetic participation in policy making and public welfare administration at every level. This is not just a Catholic story but an important and neglected angle on the American story of public welfare.

Brown and McKeown state that charity became "the chief means by which the church established a public voice." I do not think that is quite right. Education was at least as important in establishing the public voice of the church. Until the late nineteenth century there were many Catholics who spoke about education in a voice similar to the way they came to speak of social welfare, a voice that combined specifically Catholic responsibilities with a larger sense of civic well-being, the common good. In education, in sharp contrast to welfare, after 1900 those voices were no longer heard: Catholics spoke a more separatist language around education and came across consistently as a group that would hold public policy hostage to group interests. In public welfare questions, in contrast, Catholics were regarded as partners with public bureaucracies. In education, lay teachers and administrators were strangers whose opinion and advice were not needed. On poverty, Catholic pastors and social workers were experts whose help was needed to reach public objectives. Unfortunately, I suspect that the public image of the church was shaped at least as much by its fierce attention to its group interests in education as by the collaborative tone of Catholic Charities, and a price in public influence has been exacted.

Out of this history emerge at least three themes for citizens, Catholics and others, to think about. First, faith-based services with public support are nothing new. In the nineteenth century, charity was mostly private, but local governments regularly spent public funds for needy persons served by religiously inspired agencies. Over the last 100 years, public-private partnerships, including partnerships between public programs and religiously based agencies, became more the rule than the exception. To be sure, state and federal officials sometimes worried about church-state questions, so much so that Catholic, Protestant, and Jewish leaders became expert at negotiating pragmatic arrangements for specific projects to abide by legal prohibitions against religious preference or discrimination. It was and remains a complicated system with blurred boundaries, but a system that served public purposes fairly well while allowing for the expression of religious ideals. As many in need of services continue to come from diverse religious and cultural communities, arrangements that recognize the importance of religion, ethnicity, and neighborhood continue to deserve recognition and support.

Second, Catholics should note that Catholic Charities organizations depend very heavily on public support, including government support. While Catholic financial contributions and especially human contributions are crucial, budgets often are heavily composed of public provisions. In specific cases, Catholic charitable organizations can and should avoid their support for programs that contravene church teaching, and they must be ready to take an independent stance when needed to express Catholic religious and moral convictions. But in most cases, the needs of real people for income support, housing, child welfare, health care, and other services are so vast that they require public support. The cooperative structures that have arisen are commendable and in need of theological reflection to complement the quite different experience of Catholic education. In fact, many Americans are convinced that our overall educational efforts would improve dramatically if we had adopted or would adopt the flexible approach to religious and cultural pluralism reflected in American social welfare policy.

Third and finally, Americans should understand that charity and justice are both requirements of American citizenship and Christian discipleship. As the popes keep reminding Catholics, the church reaches out to the poor and needy as Christ did, and that compassion and generosity are marks of Christian faith, integral to any form of discipleship. It is also a feature of American citizenship, revealed in the response of Americans to outbreaks of human suffering across the globe. While elements of American culture, such as individualism and uncritical commitment to free market capitalism, at times obscure the bonds of solidarity, reformers from Thomas Jefferson to Martin Luther King Jr. have always been able to appeal to a sense of unity and shared responsibility. In both cases, Christian and American, response to human suffering is almost always accompanied by an impulse to equal justice. That impulse to equality and justice empowered long excluded groups—African-Americans, women, immigrants, and, in recent years, Latinos, Asians, homosexuals, the mentally and physically challenged—to take their place at the table of American democracy. In almost all cases, charity helped relieve suffering and ease passages, and a gradual achievement of justice was the result.

Chapter
Three

Theology, Social Teaching, and Catholic Charities

Three Moments in a History

Rev. J. Bryan Hehir
Harvard Kennedy School of Government

Theology, Social Teaching, and Catholic Charities

Three Moments in a History

Catholic Charities as a ministry and an institution arose from the Catholic Church, is an expression of the Catholic commitment to justice and charity, and represents the Catholic community in American society. The bond between Catholic Charities at the diocesan and national levels has been tightly maintained for a century. This chapter is designed to explore the theological and moral relationship of Catholic Charities and the wider ministry of the church. Specifically, I propose to examine three historical "moments" in the relationship.[1] At each of these discrete "moments," the chapter will identify the broader *theological setting* of the church at that time, then characterize the state of the *social teaching*, and finally provide a statement of dominant characteristics of the *ministry* of Catholic Charities.

The three moments cannot be easily isolated from the broader narrative of the church's life in the last century, but the limits of a chapter require some line drawing. Hence I will look first at *Rerum Novarum* and the inauguration of the National Conference of Catholic Charities; second, at Vatican II and the Cadre Study; and third, at *Deus Caritas Est* and Catholic Charities in a new century.

Rerum Novarum and the National Conference of Catholic Charities

The inauguration of the National Conference of Catholic Charities (NCCC) took place at the Catholic University of America in 1910. It

29

occurred during the pontificate of Pius X (1903–14), but the theological and social context for the church was still principally influenced by the expansive teaching and ministry of his predecessor Leo XIII (1878–1903). Leo XIII's influence had lasting consequences because he had undertaken a series of broad initiatives in his papacy that moved Catholicism decisively away from dominant nineteenth-century papal positions and established a subtle but significant change of direction for the church as it entered a new century. Leo XIII announced immediately after being elected, "I want to carry out a great policy."[2] Over 25 years, one of the longest pontificates in history, he pursued this broadly defined vision. His influence, which shaped the meaning of being Catholic at the time of the founding of the NCCC, was due to his theological, diplomatic, and social teaching, and the policy decisions that accompanied them.[3]

Theological Setting

The unifying theme supporting Leo XIII's three-dimensional strategy was his deep conviction that the nineteenth-century isolation of the church from the modern world—intellectually, politically, and socially— had to be reversed. Explaining Leo XIII's election, Professor Eamon Duffy says, "Many of the cardinals felt that the apocalyptic denunciations of the world and the political intransigence of Pio Nono had painted the church into a corner."[4] Leo XIII did not entirely succeed in his "great policy," but he made progress on all three fronts, and he provided in each area a foundation for the church to enter a new dynamic century.

Leo XIII recognized that the primary challenge to the church was to find a method of analyzing and addressing a world undergoing profound political, economic, and intellectual change. The consequences of the Industrial Revolution, the emergence of modern democracy, and the impact of a century shaped by Kant, Marx, and Darwin all required that the church renew its address to the world, its presentation of the truths of faith to Catholics and to the wider society. Leo XIII was convinced that the basic resource for the church lay in its history. Specifically, it was to be found in the wisdom of Thomas Aquinas (1225–74):

> Leo was convinced that once it had been revived the wisdom of
> St. Thomas could provide nineteenth century Catholics with the
> resources needed to integrate modern science and culture into a
> coherent whole under the light of the Christian faith.[5]

In the first year of his papacy Leo XIII issued the encyclical *Aeterni Patris* (1879), which mandated the teaching of Thomistic philosophy and theology in Catholic seminaries and institutes of higher learning. While historical scholarship in the twentieth century would draw distinctions between Aquinas's own work and some of his later commentators, Leo XIII did not enter this academic debate. He saw the Thomistic synthesis of philosophy and theology, exemplified in (but not exhausted by) the *Summa Theologiae* as the architecture, the guide, and, on specific questions, the mandated conclusions that should direct the intellectual life of the church. This chapter is not the setting to examine the Thomistic position, but it is possible to illustrate how Thomistic themes exercised long-term impact on Catholic thought and papal teaching. His influence extended beyond Catholic doctrine to the moral and social vision of Catholicism in the twentieth century.

Aquinas lived at a time when both the resources of Roman law and the philosophical corpus of Aristotle became available to medieval Europe. His integration of Aristotle in his work profoundly influenced Catholic moral theology. Theologically, Aquinas exemplified a theme that Charles Curran has described as the importance of the Catholic *both/and*.[6] By this is meant Aquinas's fundamental conviction that faith *and* reason are compatible; that nature *and* grace are complementary; and that church *and* world are distinct but called to collaborate for the good of the human community. All of these themes informed Catholicism's understanding of itself and its relationship to secular thought and secular society. It is possible to trace the influence of these themes in magisterial texts and in the work of Catholic scholars like Jacques Maritain, Etienne Gilson, John Courtney Murray, and others in the last century. There were a variety of Thomisms in the church, and it cannot be said that it was the sole theological influence of the century, but it was the dominant influence, and that in part was due to Leo XIII's espousal of Aquinas.

Social Teaching

While Leo XIII precisely understood that the primary challenge facing the church was the reinvigoration of its intellectual life, he was also committed to reestablishing a role for the Holy See and Catholicism in the political-diplomatic world. The preeminent Leonine scholar, John Courtney Murray, SJ, described the initial challenge Leo faced:

> The Church had entered the decade of the 1850s in close collaboration with all the dominant interests in society; in the 1870s she stood isolated and alone. And the change was related to all the important movements of his time, intellectual, economic and political. Leo XIII made it his supreme interest to end this isolation.[7]

In pursuit of that goal, Leo XIII designed a strategy with multiple tactics. He took the initiative to notify formally the European heads of state of his election. It is understood, but not documented, that he desired to give the initial papal blessing *urbi et orbe*, signifying a new openness to the world, but he was dissuaded by his Vatican advisors. His long-term design (not a realistic one) was to restore the papacy to the medieval role it had as "the great world power with an intellectual and spiritual mission."[8] While that conception was quite at odds with the world of his time, Leo XIII's diplomatic accomplishments were significant. His most prominent one was finding common ground with Chancellor Bismarck, thus ending the "Kulturkampf" in Germany. Less successful was Leo XIII's attempt to bridge the chasm between the French Catholic Right and the French government. He made little progress in addressing the neuralgic "Roman Question," and his desire to play an international role as a mediator found few opportunities. In sum, the long-term effect of his diplomatic efforts was less significant than his intellectual or social policy. Without doubt, however, he did put the Holy See back on the (European) diplomatic map, and in that sense he began a process that his later successors could build upon. His "great policy," to reverse the isolation of the church, was a partial achievement on the diplomatic front. A generous and realistic assessment of it is Oskar Köhler's concluding judgment: "The fact that the election of the new Pope after Leo's death on 20 July 1903 stirred the political powers much more than in the year 1878 was a result of the respect which Leo XIII had gained in the world for the papacy."[9]

The social dimension of his "great policy" was more lasting; it was his magisterial response to the moral consequences of the Industrial Revolution. The response was made in the encyclical *Rerum Novarum* (1891), now acknowledged as the foundation and catalyst for Catholic social teaching in the twentieth century. Leo XIII began a process with this first of the "social encyclicals" that went beyond his teaching in many ways but always maintained a connection with it. Writing a century after *Rerum Novarum* John Paul II dedicated his encyclical, *Centesimus Annus* (1991), in the following way:

> I wish first and foremost to satisfy the debt of gratitude which the whole church owes to this great pope and his "immortal document." I mean also to show that the vital energies arising from that root have not been spent with the passing of the years, but rather have increased even more.[10]

Rerum Novarum addressed the socioeconomic consequences of industrialization in Europe and (by extension) in North America. By 1891, Leo

XIII had authored a corpus of statements on political society, church and state, democracy and freedom. These texts were addressed mainly to rulers, governments, and political philosophers. They set forth Leo XIII's conception of a Christian understanding of the state and civil society. In contrast, *Rerum Novarum* was addressed to managers, owners, and workers, but it did also relate to Leo XIII's conception of the role of the state in the socioeconomic order.

The focus of the encyclical was a national setting; unlike later texts in the social tradition (*Pacem in Terris* in 1963 and *Centesimus Annus* in 1991), Leo XIII did not address international issues. The sources of his thought were Aquinas and Aristotle's theory of justice. The employment of the category of justice was of fundamental importance. It declared the church's conviction that "The Social Question" could not be resolved by charity. Beyond this assertion, the letter grounded its claims for protection of workers in the dignity of the person. To protect the sacredness of human dignity, Leo XIII invoked the language of human rights, but in a much less developed statement than the later teaching of John XXIII and John Paul II.

In the volatile context of socialist and capitalist advocates of the late nineteenth century, Leo XIII set the direction of Catholic social teaching for the next century by offering a critique of both systems, particularly in terms of their philosophical premises, but also in terms of some of their practical policies. While the encyclical was primarily focused on claims of justice, Leo XIII saw an expansive role for charity at the personal level and through organized groups. In many ways, Catholic Charities at this time fit into the category of a religiously based charity at work in the United States. Beyond these specific categories of Catholic teaching, historian David O'Brien captures the broader intent and impact of *Rerum Novarum*:

> [Leo XIII] had decreed the use of Thomistic philosophy in seminary education and encouraged biblical and historical studies because he wished to free the church from an inflexible, doctrinaire dogmatism that isolated it from modern claims of truthfulness. Just as he had tried to free the church from inflexible identification with royalty and with outmoded anti-intellectualism, he tried in *Rerum Novarum* to free it from paralyzing resistance to bourgeois civilization by shifting attention from the intractable problems of church and state to the social question, where a more flexible pastoral and evangelical approach might be possible.[11]

Leo XIII's leadership did not provide all the elements, conceptually or diplomatically, needed for this transformation; both the theological and moral categories of Vatican II moved significantly beyond his ecclesiological

and moral vision. But the social encyclical tradition that has characterized Catholicism in the past century is based in the Leonine teaching. In a
sense, Leo XIII's social teaching is a dimension of the intellectual renewal
he sought to catalyze. Together they established the ground on which the
church could engage a new and very different age.

Catholic Charities

Leo XIII's frame of reference—intellectually, diplomatically, and socially—was the European world. He did not manifest a concrete understanding of American society; indeed, he expressed pastoral concerns
about the way in which the church in the United States was adapting to
its secular context. Nevertheless, the social teaching of *Rerum Novarum* was
warmly welcomed in the United States and its influence coincided with a
time of transition for Catholic Charities. Encyclicals are not designed for
short-term impact. While often addressing concrete issues, their objective
is to establish categories of discourse and perspectives that will influence
the life of the church over time.

Rerum Novarum was promulgated in 1891, but it was still very much
a current resource when the NCCC was founded in 1910. The history of
Catholic Charities in the United States reached into the eighteenth century, but its dramatic expansion coincided with the waves of immigration
in the following century.[12] Throughout the nineteenth century, Catholic
Charities was principally a local—indeed parochial—ministry, a way for
parishes to respond to the needs of newly arrived Catholics.

The transition from a parish-based ministry of charity to a more professionally organized diocesan-wide ministry extended into the 1920s. The
driving force behind the transition was a strong-willed episcopate seeking
to consolidate financial and organizational control over a quite pluralistic
and growing dimension of the church's ministry. Over time, the diocesan
agencies, usually directed by a priest answerable to the bishop, became the
primary locus for the work of Catholic Charities. This more centralized form
of ministry built upon and partially supplanted the earlier work of parish
volunteers, lay leaders, and the Society of St. Vincent de Paul. It also was
complemented by the distinct role of women religious—neither parish- nor
diocesan-based—who staffed an impressive array of institutional agencies
and residences. The transition to diocesan and episcopal control was not a
total change, and it was accompanied by some conflict, but by the middle
of the twentieth century it was the dominant pattern for Catholic Charities.

A key element of this transition was the conviction that Catholic Charities needed a form of national organization to complement the dioceses.
The conviction was a product of several sources. One was the experience

of the diocesan agencies who sought greater recognition within American society. Recognition was not primarily about accolades, but about establishing the ongoing work of Catholic Charities in the mainstream of social work. Participation in the mainstream would also facilitate access to public funding at the state and local levels.

While a desire existed for *some* form of national organization, tight consolidation from the top was never in the cards. The intellectual and organizational leader of the movement for a national presence, Msgr. William Kerby of Catholic University, made clear that the national organization "will invade no field now occupied, it will displace no organization, and will in no way enter the field of actual relief."[13]

Kerby, whose influence would be dominant until he was succeeded by Msgr. John O'Grady (also of Catholic University), set forth the positive services that a national organization would provide for those doing the work of "actual relief" in parishes, institutions, and dioceses. It would:

> explore conditions, renew the inspiration of old ideals, guide wisely in the larger relations of the work, and thus serve in no mean way to make our methods equal to our problems, our aims worthy of our ideals and our achievements worthy of our faith and its noble traditions of charity.[14]

In addition to internal reasons for a national organization, there were broader, secular forces at work that required a new level of capacity for Catholic Charities. These secular forces were precisely the ones that Leo XIII addressed in his encyclical. By the first decade of the twentieth century, the consequences of the Industrial Revolution were clear for all to see. The immigrant population whose immediate spiritual and material needs first sparked the local response of parishes and Catholic Charities were now participants in the historic process of industrialization, which was destined to dominate American economic life through the century. They were now "the workers" whose conditions catalyzed Leo XIII's encyclical; it was their rights he would espouse; it was their situation that he said necessitated moderate but significant state intervention in the economy. It was their lack of bargaining power that brought the papacy to support the right to unionize.

The principal themes of *Rerum Novarum* corresponded powerfully with the issues that the Catholic Charities movement and its national office (NCCC) were addressing in the first half of the last century. The idea of the encyclical set a direction for Catholic Charities as it confronted the challenge of combining the work of actual relief (i.e., charity) with the need to address the social sources of poverty (i.e., justice). The distinction of these two ways of responding to human need was being debated in the wider secular world of social work. Leo XIII's categories provided the NCCC with the conceptual tools to enter the discussion, advocating for social justice (Pius XI's term) but combining it with the continuing work of actual relief.

The deepening crisis of the Great Depression intensified the debate about the moral responsibility of the state and its role in the socioeconomic order. Leo XIII and his successors legitimated a role for an activist state, but set limits on it through the principle of subsidiarity. That idea, in turn, argued for combining an activist state with a pluralism of power in civil society. By mid-century Catholic social teaching possessed a set of ideas—social justice, charity, common good, subsidiarity—that provided the NCCC with the ability to contribute intellectually and institutionally to the changes in socioeconomic life catalyzed by the New Deal and its consequences. By any measure, Catholic Charities was in the mainstream of social service.

Vatican II and the Cadre Study

The founding of the NCCC was in many ways a response to practical and organizational needs of ministry in the United States. The next "moment" in the history of Catholic Charities was principally the result of broad theological themes at work in the universal church. The themes were the product of both continuing development in the social teaching and the enormous theological impact of the Second Vatican Council (1962–65). The council was clearly the dominant influence, reshaping Catholic Charities as it did every dimension of Catholic life.

Theological Setting

The theme of Vatican II was the church itself.[15] Other ecumenical councils had focused on the Trinity (Nicea 325) or Christology (Chalcedon 450); most, like Trent (1645), had been called in response to crises that needed immediate attention. John XXIII (1958–63), who convoked the council to the surprise of almost everyone, envisioned it not as a response to crisis, but as an opportunity to renew the life of the Catholic Church by drawing on its deepest roots of tradition. Over time, his basic insight became the now classical formula of how *aggiornamento* would be the product of *ressourcement*.

The theological setting of this second moment in the history of Catholic Charities was the council and its consequences. The final authoritative product of the council was its sixteen documents; the basic design and dynamic of the council was the distinction between the church *ad intra* and the church *ad extra*. Hence the pivotal texts are *Lumen Gentium* (The Dogmatic Constitution on the Church) and *Gaudium et Spes* (The Pastoral Constitution on the Church in the Modern World).[16]

The calling of the council was a surprise, but the content of its work had in fact been in preparation for much of the last century, and had been the subject of much theological research and reflection since the end of World War II. The principal intellectual resources were found in Europe, and European bishops and theologians were the dominant voices of the council. Many of the theologians (Yves Congar, OP; Henri de Lubac, SJ; Karl Rahner, SJ) had been under suspicion in Rome in the 1940s and 1950s. Their work and the work of others like Gerard Phillips of Belgium became the raw material for the documents of Vatican II.

As summarized by David O'Brien earlier in this chapter, Leo XIII made efforts to transform the church-world relationship. However, his time in history and to some degree his theology made the realization of this change impossible. By the time *Gaudium et Spes* was written, both the times and theology available allowed for major developments in this transformative relationship. The work of diverse scholars—Congar, de Lubac, Gustav Thils, John Courtney Murray—prepared the way for a new chapter in the church-world relationship. The issue is as old as the apostolic church, but the resources for addressing it had been deeply enriched in the decades immediately preceding the council.

Internal ecclesial topics dominated the initial sessions of the council (reflected in the documents on the church and the liturgy), but there were continuing references to church-world relations; these passing references stimulated the conviction that a direct, explicit address to the question by the council was needed. The conviction led to the decision to expand the agenda of the council, and the product was *Gaudium et Spes*.[17] The text has two sections: the first, a theological-ecclesial reflection; the second, a series of chapters that really are an extension of the church's social teaching.

The theological section locates the church in history, as a participant, a teacher, and a partner with other social institutions. The text itself sparked extensive debate about its positive assessment of forces at work in the world. Its fundamental message, however, was the willingness of the church to engage the world as a partner for the good of the human family.

Continuing and expanding the social teaching of the last century, *Gaudium et Spes* principally provided theological grounding and interpretation for social ministry in the church.[18] As part of this theological reflection, it recast the church's approach to several questions. *Gaudium et Spes* acknowledged the legitimate autonomy of secular disciplines and invited a dialogue with modern science and social science. It reflected a distinctively more positive assessment of democracy than the nineteenth-century magisterium and it expressed an understanding of cultural and religious pluralism often absent in earlier texts.[19] These themes had a cumulative effect of establishing a different posture for the church's role in the world.

But *Gaudium et Spes* went beyond posture; it articulated a theological understanding of the relationship of Kingdom-Church-World that provided intrinsic religious meaning to the church's social ministry. In a key sentence, the conciliar teaching document declared: "Far from diminishing our concern to develop this earth, the expectancy of a new earth should spur us on, for it is here that the body of a new human family grows, foreshadowing in some way the age which is to come."[20]

The theology of the council envisions the social teaching and social ministry as Catholic contributions to "developing the earth" and preparing "the age which is to come." For agencies like Catholic Charities, the conciliar text enhances the meaning of the work it does, locating it at the very heart of the work of the church, an expression of its religious mission.[21]

Social Teaching

Gaudium et Spes broke new theological ground for social ministry; it also combined with two other magisterial texts belonging to the social teaching, John XXIII's *Pacem in Terris* (1963) and Vatican II's *Dignitatis Humanae* (1965). John XXIII's encyclical gained a hearing from beyond the church; its subject (peace in the nuclear age), its tone, and its content all attracted the attention of a world that had anxiously endured the Cuban Missile Crisis nine months earlier. John XXIII addressed his letter to all people of goodwill, and his analysis extended to the world as a whole. The heart of the letter was a creative restatement of the Natural Law ethic that has been at the heart of the social teaching. The creativity resided in John XXIII's address to human rights as the key to international order. While his predecessors had invoked human rights in their teaching, John produced the most systematic and expansive statement on the topic in a church teaching document. The crucial contribution of this articulation of human rights is that it provides the middle term between two traditional elements of Catholic social thought: the dignity of the person and the social nature of the person. Human rights are rooted in the unique dignity of the person; rights are moral claims to goods (spiritual and material) needed to protect and promote dignity. The social nature of the person means we require a social setting (multiple communities) in which we grow, develop, and flourish as persons. Rights mediate between dignity and the social fabric of life; they define the conditions needed for each person to develop and flourish.

Pacem in Terris clearly established the protection and promotion of human rights as central to the church's social ministry. It also established a parallelism between Catholic teaching on rights and much of the United Nations human rights regime. More significantly, *Pacem in Terris* provided a foundation upon which John Paul II articulated an even more expansive position on human rights for the church in his 1979 address to the General Assembly of the United Nations.

A second way in which *Pacem in Terris* established the foundation for development in Catholic teaching was its relationship to the Declaration on Religious Freedom (*Dignitatis Humanae*) of Vatican II. Religious freedom is one of the central political-civil rights of the person. But Catholic teaching prior to Vatican II had, at best, a partial and limited understanding of its meaning. John XXIII simply stated a fuller expression of the right but without explanation of its meaning. The council, in turn, after extended debate overwhelmingly adopted a philosophical-theological declaration affirming the church's support for religious freedom in all its dimensions.[22]

Beyond this central affirmation, *Dignitatis Humanae* also contained an endorsement of the secular, democratic state as a sure support for human rights. This recognition of the legitimate secularity of the state and of the value of democracy provides support for the kind of collaboration between Catholic Charities and the state (federal, state, and local levels) that is the pattern across the United States.

Catholic Charities

Virtually every Catholic institution used the period after Vatican II to assess their ministry and the NCCC followed this pattern. Over a three-year period, ending in 1972, the NCCC engaged in a comprehensive renewal process that resulted in the publication of *Toward a Renewed Catholic Charities Movement*,[23] which later came to be known simply as the Cadre Study. Sixty years after the founding of the NCCC, the Cadre Study drew upon themes of the council, the resources of recent social teaching (e.g., Pope Paul VI's *Populorum Progressio* and the emergent "Theology of Liberation" from Latin America) to restate and renew the work of the NCCC. The Cadre document relied heavily on the language of liberation to situate the work of Catholic Charities in the tumultuous decades of the 1960s and 1970s. In addition to the language of liberation, the Cadre Study drew on themes of social justice to specify aspects of continuity and discontinuity in the work of Catholic Charities. To that end, the Cadre Study called Catholic Charities at every level to weave together three dimensions of ministry: the delivery of social services, advocacy for social change (seeking to address the roots of poverty and injustice), and convening the wider ecclesial community to build support and engagement for the work of charity and justice as citizens and disciples. The continuity of a tradition of providing quality care through delivery of social service now shared the agenda with the more recent emphasis on structural problems in the society. The convening work of engaging the broader church certainly reflected the theology of *Gaudium et Spes*. The tone and style of the Cadre document was not sustained in later descriptions of the work of Catholic Charities, but the three basic functions of the Cadre Study continue to define the work of Catholic Charities.

Deus Caritas Est and Catholic Charities USA

Postconciliar Catholicism has passed through three stages of leadership. Paul VI (1963–78) guided the council to completion, and then faced the complex challenge of communicating its vision and implementing its reforms. John Paul II led the church in word and deed for one of the longest pontificates in history (1978–2005). Benedict XVI leads the church today as the heir of both the council and the legacy of John Paul II. To examine the present moment in the history of Catholic Charities, one must have a sense of the continuity of the two papacies of this century: Cardinal Ratzinger's crucial role in the papacy of his predecessor establishes themes of continuity at a substantive theological level, even though this pontificate has its own priorities, style, and purposes.

John Paul II led the Catholic Church in a fashion that powerfully shaped its internal life and produced a major secular influence in the world. A basic theme for him was the work of evangelization, and he brought to that ministry multiple methods. He produced a body of teaching notable for its scope, its way of interpreting Vatican II, and its specific conclusions on matters in the church and the world. He combined teaching with travel, bringing the influence of his personality and his office to bear upon conflicted situations throughout the world, with deep implications for human rights and social justice.[24] And he combined an internal ecclesial discipline that was theologically conservative with an expansive social vision in support of economic justice, human rights, and peace. The choice of Cardinal Ratzinger to lead the church signaled to most an expectation of continuity in substance if not style. In many ways these expectations have been fulfilled, but Benedict XVI's distinctive approach to issues is exemplified in his first encyclical, *Deus Caritas Est* (2008).

Theological Setting

Benedict's background and scholarship have been that of a systematic theologian. He brought none of his predecessor's extensive engagement in the public arena with him. It was a bit of a surprise, therefore, when he dedicated his first encyclical—in part—to the role the church should play in a world marked by suffering and injustice. To be sure, the encyclical has a strong doctrinal foundation. Its basic assertion, drawn from St. John the Evangelist, is that God is love, that he fills our lives with the power of his love, and that we are called to respond in love to God's generosity. From this theological baseline, Benedict pursues his theme in two directions: first, how human marital love is an expression of God's love in the world, and, second, how Christians are called—personally and institutionally—to be agents of God's love to those in need. In one letter, therefore, Benedict XVI cuts across two broad areas of Catholic moral theology: (1) relationships, sexuality, and marriage; and (2) charity, justice, and social ministry in the world.

From the perspective of Catholic Charities, the primary significance of the encyclical is its existence. By raising up the role of charity, and by emphasizing the need for an organized ministry of charity, Benedict ties the daily work of Catholic Charities directly to the essential ministry of the church:

> As the years went by and the Church spread further a field, the exercise of charity became established as one of her essential activities, along with the administration of the sacraments and the proclamation of the word: love for widows, orphans, prisoners, and the sick and the needy of every kind, is as essential to her as the ministry of the sacraments and preaching of the Gospel.[25]

Having established its theological importance, Benedict stresses the need for an organized, institutional ministry of charity; such a ministry, especially in our society, requires professional training as well as compassion. The stress on an institutional presence in society and on the need for professional competence corresponds closely to the evolution of Catholic Charities in this society. The past century was marked precisely by these two characteristics as Catholic Charities moved to the diocesan and national levels of American society.

The most important theological theme in the encyclical is the one captured in the extensive quote above concerning charity and the essential mission of the church. In many ways, the statement builds upon *Gaudium et Spes*, on the document Justice in the World (1971), and on similar statements of John Paul II. But this is the clearest and most authoritative expression of the theme. A second major theological issue in *Deus Caritas Est* may well provoke some extended debate. It is Benedict's analysis of the relationship of charity and justice. The topic is a traditional theme in Christian ethics: how to understand, relate, and implement two distinct ways in which faith takes shape in the service of others. Images of the question are found in the Scriptures: the Hebrew prophets' powerful cry for basic structural reform in society and the Good Samaritan's immediate response to the traveler in need. Charity is characterized by actual relief; justice seeks fundamental changes to ameliorate further patterns of suffering.

Theologically, distinctions are drawn between the two virtues, each with its own object and means of fulfillment. The great Protestant theologian Reinhold Niebuhr defined justice as the approximation of love achieved under conditions of sin. Catholic social ethics usually describes justice as the minimum of charity, in the sense that justice is what is due others by objective standards; charity is the spontaneous response over and above justice.[26]

Benedict XVI does not focus on the nature of justice and charity as much as he does on the proper agent of each. He stresses the distinct and complementary roles of church and state. In an encyclical dedicated to charity, he argues that the primary agency of justice should be the secular state: "We have seen that the formation of just structures is not directly the duty of the Church, but belongs to the world of politics, the sphere of the autonomous use of reason."[27] The complementary prescription for Benedict is that "the Church cannot and must not take upon herself the political battle to bring about the most just society possible. She cannot and must not replace the state."[28]

What, then, is the role of the church in building a just society, in responding to the needs of the poor, the vulnerable and marginalized, in addressing issues of justice and peace? First, the basic assertion of the encyclical is that the church has a right and a duty, in every age and in any political system, to provide for the works of charity—individually and in an organized form. Benedict defines this primary duty with traditional simplicity: "Christian charity is first of all the simple response to immediate needs and situations: feeding the hungry, clothing the naked, caring for and healing the sick, visiting those in prison, etc."[29] Second, the church as a teaching voice and a public advocate in society has an "indirect" contribution to make to the building of a just society. It should provide both intellectual and motivational resources. Intellectually, the church's teaching should contribute to an understanding of the specific meaning of standards of justice: "Faith enables reason to do its work more effectively and to see its proper object more clearly. This is where Catholic social doctrine has its place: it has no intention of giving the Church power over the State."[30] Motivationally, Benedict argues that the church must work "to reawaken the spiritual energy without which justice, which always demands sacrifice, cannot prevail and prosper."[31]

Relating the implications of *Deus Caritas Est* to the work of Catholic Charities in the United States will be the final section of this chapter. Here it is useful to make a more general comment. In this encyclical and in the other statements about public issues, Benedict XVI has brought a distinctive voice to the church's public role. It is less specific and to some degree less engaged than his predecessor. It stresses the theological foundations and precise distinctions embedded in the Catholic tradition of ecclesiology and ethics. The effect of this is to provide secure and expansive religious legitimation for the church's social ministry, but to be less specific about concrete questions of justice and peace and less assertive in the church's role as advocate in the public arena.

Social Teaching

Benedict's great service thus far is to strengthen the foundations of the church's social ministry. In this third moment of the work of Catholic Charities, the social teaching for ministry remains principally that of John Paul II. The scope of that teaching defies simple synthesis here; my purpose is to highlight major characteristics of John Paul's social legacy.

First, the issue of style: From Leo XIII through John XXIII, Catholic social teaching was expressed almost exclusively in the philosophical ideas of the Natural Law. *Gaudium et Spes* was a turning point, relying much more extensively on biblical-theological ideas. John Paul II combined in his teaching the two modes of discourse. He used the classical ideas of social justice, common good, and subsidiarity, but turned to the power of the Hebrew prophets and the social imagery of the New Testament to call the church and the world to address poverty, war, and injustice.

Second, at the heart of his social vision he placed the church in support of an expansive understanding of human rights. Here he built on *Pacem in Terris*, but he brought his own philosophical style to the issues and his hard-won experience of living with a totalitarian ideology and an authoritarian state.

Third, he took Paul VI's idea that the "Social Question" was now global in scope, and he used it to address interdependence and globalization as primary challenges of our era. Within a global perspective, he still affirmed the distinct significance of different national and local questions. Like Paul VI in *Octogesima Adveniens* (1971), John Paul II saw distinctive social challenges arising in advanced industrial democracies. These questions emerged from the complexity of the political-economic system, from a galloping technology, and from a very complex social pluralism.

Fourth, John Paul II made a distinctive advance in the way he articulated the normative relationship of states, society, and the market. While recognizing that this triad would have to be worked out specifically in each national setting, he set out a general conception of the three.[32] He endorsed a conception of a limited but activist state. He clearly believed the state had unique responsibilities in society, particularly to the poor and vulnerable. At the same time, on the basics of Catholic principles and his own Polish experience, he was opposed to an all-encompassing view of the state. He sought to create space in civil society for free initiatives and a pluralism of power. John Paul was more positive about the possibilities of a market economy than his predecessors. He saw a properly functioning market protecting freedom and creativity, offering a certain form of rational allocation of resources and setting limits on the power of the state in the lives of citizens. John Paul's view may be summarized as providing space for the market to fulfill its positive functions, and then surrounding a market economy with public policy to address needs the markets leave unfulfilled.

Catholic Charities

The model of organized charity represented by Catholic Charities USA corresponds remarkably closely to what we have seen in Benedict XVI and John Paul II. Following Benedict, the church in the United States has developed an extensive fabric of social institutions—charities, health care, and schools—that are rooted in the religious ministry of the church, but serve American society as a whole. These social institutions act like bridges between the church and the wider society. For decades they have been committed to Benedict's model of combining professional expertise and compassion.

When one uses John Paul II's triad of state-society-market and locates it in the U.S. context, one finds the role and place Catholic Charities occupies. In comparison to other postindustrial democracies, the U.S. model of social policy expects *less* from the state, *more* from the market, and *a great deal* from nonprofit agencies (secular and religious). Across the country, Catholic Charities plays a major role in that nonprofit sector upon which U.S. society relies for vital social contributions, especially for those in poverty or in socially vulnerable situations like women, children, and the elderly.

The fundamental mission of Catholic Charities, rooted in the Scriptures and Catholic social teaching, has remained constant in the past century. The conception of how the mission should be fulfilled in response to changes in both the church and in American society has evolved over time. From the founding of the NCCC through the Cadre Study to the Vision 2000 statement of Catholic Charities USA, the basic commitment to provide immediate actual relief has been supplemented by increasing public advocacy and outreach to the wider church community for support and collaboration.

The capacity for change and adaptation is a fundamental need for a social service agency in the United States. The context in which Catholic Charities functions is the most complex economy in the world, located in a society of constantly changing technology and shaped by both ethnic and racial pluralism as well as religious and moral pluralism.

The events of the first decade of this new century testify to the need for continuity of mission and capacity for change. The terror attacks of September 11, 2001, and the social and economic devastation of Hurricane Katrina in 2005 tested the Catholic Charities response to domestic emergencies in entirely new ways. The impact of the worst financial crisis and recession since the Great Depression has stretched the financial and personnel resources of Catholic Charities to the limit.

As Catholic Charities begins a new century, its religious motivation, moral vision, and commitment to service of society are all solidly grounded. Yet, each of its basic functional roles faces a future that is not easily defined. Delivery of quality services to those in need will require, in the short- to mid-term, meeting expanding needs in the face of declining or stagnant state collaboration and a difficult fundraising setting. The need for advocacy in support of the social safety net for young and old will require a clear and consistent voice as the country debates health care reform, Medicare and Medicaid funding, and the future of Social Security. Each of these programs is relevant to the constituencies Catholic Charities serves. Convening the church around justice and charity must be seen as one dimension of a larger pastoral strategy in a religious atmosphere where maintaining lifelong commitments of individuals in a single religious tradition is an increasingly difficult objective.

None of these challenges is fully understood because of their contingent character and their complexity. But those who gathered at Catholic University in 1910 to found the National Conference of Catholic Charities stood on the threshold of a century of two world wars and a worldwide depression. They could not see the future, but they knew by faith and reason where they were grounded—in justice and charity—and that was sufficient for them. It should be for us also.

Chapter Four

The Rise of Professionalization

Catholic Charities and Social Work

*Sr. Ann Patrick Conrad
and Sr. M. Vincentia Joseph*

The Catholic University of America

The Rise of Professionalization

Catholic Charities and Social Work

Catholic Charities agencies across the country have evolved over the past century to the point where today they mirror the dedicated service and shared values of volunteers, professionals from many disciplines, and the collaborative efforts of multiple human service organizations on behalf of the poor and disadvantaged. From the earliest days of the Catholic Charities movement, the developing profession of social work played a key role. This chapter will highlight some of the parallel developments in social work and in Catholic Charities, and will consider the impact of social work's professional influence on the Catholic Charities movement in the United States.

From the outset it is important to recognize that with the punitive attitudes of the late nineteenth and early twentieth centuries toward the poor and the increasing social and economic complexity that resulted from expanding industrialization accompanied by the new waves of European immigrants, the early leaders of the Catholic Charities movement in the United States recognized the complementarity of the values of the profession of social work and the social teachings of the church.[1] They adapted the methods of the new profession for serving those in need in the fledgling Catholic Charities agencies.

Simultaneously, and consistent with the development of professions in the United States,[2] social work progressed from a volunteer venture in the mid-1800s to a full-time occupation. Training schools were established and affiliated with institutions of higher learning, professional associations were formed at local and national levels, legal sanction was sought, and a formal code of ethics was created. Catholic Charities' emergence as a national organization paralleled and was influenced at times by major

49

developments in the field of social work. Interestingly, key leaders in the early Catholic Charities movement were also active participants in the developing field of social work. In the account that follows, attention will be given to the influence of some of the major milestones in these parallel developments such as ethics leadership, the nature of service delivery, and the shifting patterns of mission engagement that both strengthen and challenge Catholic Charities in the twenty-first century.

Concern for the Poor and Disadvantaged in Early America

Attention to addressing the needs of the poor and disadvantaged in America took the form of a localized focus on the needs of particular groups—predominantly immigrants, either by local government jurisdictions or by volunteer groups that were often sponsored by faith-based organizations. As the social problems and needs of the early twentieth century intensified, collaboration and cooperation among human service organizations became the norm. Interestingly, both Catholic Charities and the profession of social work developed within this context and made important contributions to American society.

Volunteer Roots

Rooted in humanistic and religious/spiritual motivation, concern for the poor and disadvantaged in early America was typically a volunteer effort. There were no social service agencies as we know them today. In spite of the social Darwinian attitude of the time that espoused "survival of the fittest," even Herbert Spencer (who coined the term) admitted that voluntary charity could be tolerated because it encouraged the development of altruism, a Christian virtue.[3] Thus, the charitable and humanitarian efforts of philanthropic and faith-based groups were supported and independently financed by their sponsoring organizations. As Amos Warner, author of the first U.S. social welfare text, pointed out, "Of all the churches the one that probably induces the largest amount of giving [to charity] in proportion to the means of those who give is the Roman Catholic."[4]

Alternately, early public sector leadership in meeting human needs became the responsibility of county agency administrators. "Deserving poor," such as the disabled, elderly, and young children, were seen as a public responsibility, though the style of public service delivery in that period accepted child labor as a norm, expected adults in need to "pull themselves up," and viewed poverty as a moral weakness. Available services varied by legal jurisdiction and regional resources were minimal in nature.

Social work in the early years evolved from the impetus of Charity Organization Societies first established in Buffalo, New York, in 1877.[5] These
groups coordinated the efforts of the many charitable bodies that were
sponsored by independent faith-based groups operating in local communities and the public sector efforts of local jurisdictions. In many instances,
the pioneer social workers of the late nineteenth and early twentieth
centuries—many of whom were financially comfortable women—began
as volunteers who were deeply concerned about the plight of the poor and
disadvantaged.[6] As they developed skills and ongoing commitment to this
form of service, they began to see their work as a career. Although early
social work was later criticized by some because of what was viewed as
a "preoccupation with methods and treatment," social work came to be
viewed as an appropriate and acceptable career for women.[7]

As detailed elsewhere in this publication, the Catholic Charities movement in the United States emerged largely from grassroots concerns at the
parish level for both the social needs of people as well as for the preservation of their religious/spiritual heritage. Thus, the local Catholic parish was
not only a place of worship and sacramental life for the rapidly increasing
ethnic immigrant populations who arrived in the new world, but also a
center of cultural and social life. Additionally, parishioners looked to their
local church for help with their social, economic, and health needs. In
those early days, basic survival needs, such as food, clothing, housing, and
employment, were addressed by lay volunteers in the parish, particularly
members of the St. Vincent de Paul Societies (the Vincentians). As time
went on, the Vincentians and others at the parish level were faced with
an increasing complexity of "charity work" and came to the conclusion
that it was inevitable that full-time paid workers were necessary and
that the developing methods of "scientific charity" had much to offer in
their ministries.[8]

As more specialized needs arose, such as for the care of orphaned children and the elderly, service was provided in specialized settings affiliated
with particular ethnic groups, Catholic dioceses, or religious communities.
For example, the first reported formal Catholic charity in the new world
was a special unit for the care of children whose parents had been slain
in an Indian raid. This early "orphanage" was established in 1727 in New
Orleans by the Ursuline Sisters in their convent.[9]

From Independence to Collaboration

By the end of the 1800s, there were over 800 Catholic charitable institutions providing care to orphaned and delinquent children, the aged,
and infirm. However, as Msgr. William J. Kerby, professor of sociology at

The Catholic University of America (CUA) and the first executive director of the National Conference of Catholic Charities (NCCC), pointed out:

> The intense individualism of institutional and geographical units of the Church's life has exerted a marked influence on the development of her charities. It has led to a variety and resourcefulness that have been admirable. But it has resulted in a mutual independence and lack of coordination that have undoubtedly interfered with progress in certain ways, ways that are particularly dear to the modern world.[10]

Kerby was referring to the developing trend toward collaboration among sectarian social service providers. For example, the National Conference of Charities and Corrections dating from 1874 was the outgrowth of attempts to organize boards of public charities on a national basis. That secular organization continued under the aforementioned name until 1917 when it became the National Conference of Social Work.[11] The trend toward collaboration continued among both private and faith-based organizations. Interestingly, in 1899 Thomas M. Mulry, then head of the St. Vincent de Paul Society and actively involved in the National Conference of Charities and Corrections, presented a paper on child welfare at the Charities and Corrections annual meeting in which he advocated for the preservation of home life and safeguards for the spiritual heritage of children.[12] In 1909, the Bureau for the Exchange of Information Among Child-Helping Agencies, which later became the Child Welfare League of America, was organized. Other national organizations such as the Family Service Association of America (now known as the Alliance for Families and Children), the Children's Aid Society, and the Salvation Army were also founded in the early 1900s. And, as we celebrate with this volume, it was in 1910, through the initiative of Br. Barnabas McDonald, FSC, and Kerby and at the invitation of the Catholic University rector, Bishop Thomas J. Shahan, that The Catholic University of America in Washington, DC, hosted a meeting of all those who were involved in the work of Catholic charities to form the National Conference of Catholic Charities (NCCC).[13] Brother Barnabas, a member of the National Conference on Social Work,[14] was internationally known for his work with orphans, abandoned children, and delinquents and shared Kerby's interest in coordination. More than 400 clergy and lay delegates from 38 cities in 24 states attended. The mission of the National Conference of Catholic Charities was to bring professional social work practices to the agencies and to promote the establishment of diocesan Catholic Charities bureaus.[15]

Clearly, the volunteer spirit in the United States provided a foundation for the development of both the social work profession and the Catholic Charities movement. Yet, as philanthropic volunteerism and Catholic charity expanded, the need for coordination and training became clear to the pioneer leaders.

The Apprentice Approach to Training

Typically, early social agencies, both private and public, were staffed by a combination of paid and volunteer workers. Early training of social workers, usually referred to as caseworkers, was carried out utilizing an apprentice system. In this system the workers modeled their professional approach after the style of their supervisors or administrators.[16] Thus, their skills and abilities were developed while on the job. As Walter Trattner described, "By watching older members, by talking to executives, and by attending staff meetings and the National Conference [of Charities and Corrections], new workers learned something of the art and science of helping those in need."[17]

In public agencies, apprentice training focused primarily on the legal standards of the jurisdiction in which service was provided. In lieu of attention to mission engagement, ethics, and the human dignity of the persons they served, workers were expected to engage in organizational/legal compliance within the established policies and procedures of their employing organization. This approach was criticized by some in the developing social work field and by Catholic Charities leaders for what was viewed as an exclusive attention to economic and material resources while neglecting the psycho-social-spiritual dimensions of the persons they served. Consequently, investigation, record keeping, and moralizing were sometimes reported as taking precedence over interpersonal and human relationship skills.[18]

As early diocesan Catholic Charities agencies developed, they were administered by diocesan directors. Typically, the directors were priests, who had parish or other diocesan responsibilities as well, although dedicated lay workers or women and men religious also served in this role. Staff received on-the-job training provided by the director, by colleagues, or by the local superior in diocesan agencies staffed by women or men religious. The content of training was based primarily on the practice wisdom—the practical experience—of the administrators and supervisors as well as the formal social work methods and techniques that were being conceptualized and developed.

Motivation for service in Catholic Charities agencies was grounded in the Gospel's concern for the poor and disadvantaged. The moral imagination of the workers drew on images of love and service evident in Scripture and the lives of the saints. The Good Shepherd who "laid down his life for his sheep," the Good Samaritan who provided for the stranger, and Jesus' Sermon on the Mount provided a vision of Christian humanism. The lives of saints such as Vincent de Paul, Louise de Marillac, and others provided models of Christian service and social action. Additionally, the principles of Catholic social thought shared in papal encyclicals provided impetus for the social reform initiatives undertaken by the fledgling Catholic Charities movement. Pope Leo XIII's 1891 encyclical *Rerum Novarum* called attention to the working conditions of the poor, the need for fair wages, and the rights of workers to organize.

Although to some extent parallel styles were evident in both the public sector and in the early Catholic Charities agencies—such as volunteer/paid staffing arrangements and apprentice training—the religious and spiritual traditions of the diocesan and religious community leaders provided a distinct basis for mission engagement in Catholic Charities. Although controversial because of their "scientific" and sometimes "moralizing" nature, the developing skills and techniques of social work were beginning to be embraced as well.

From Training Institutes to Professional Degree Programs

The academic preparation of social workers can be traced to the early developments in the field of sociology or "the science of society" that became a popular course of study in colleges and universities across America beginning in the 1890s. Early twentieth-century sociology instructors emphasized that while both sociology and the emerging area of social work were distinct fields, there was a complementary relationship between the two. The sociological domain focused on the general laws and principles governing human behavior and social structures. Social work focused on the application of these principles. Interestingly, the first sociology faculty in prestigious public universities such as the University of Chicago and Columbia University were also associated with social work as well as with the Charity Organization Society.[19]

In the public domain, stirrings toward the establishment of explicit social work education began as early as 1893 at the annual meeting of the National Conference of Charities and Corrections, when the lack of opportunity for training of new workers was raised as an issue. By 1897, Mary Richmond, of the Baltimore Charity Organization Society, later to be widely known for her early formulation of social work practice theory, presented a comprehensive plan for a training school in "Applied Philanthropy." She pointed out that it should be located in a large city and affiliated with an institution of higher learning. The curriculum should emphasize "practical work," particularly field experience. Moreover, she held that the school should be in close touch with public and private community agencies so that students could work under the supervision of experienced practitioners. The next year, the New York Charity Organization Society initiated an annual six-week summer program based on Richmond's design and in which she taught. Similar initiatives were implemented in other cities; and with time, the programs were expanded to one-year graduate programs affiliated with universities and colleges. By 1910, America's five largest cities had sectarian schools of social work.[20] This was a decisive move as it placed social work in academic settings consistent with other professions.

Within the Catholic Charities movement, there was diversity of opinion on the acceptability of the scientific methods and professionalization. At the first meeting of the National Conference of Catholic Charities in 1910, the relative merits of the volunteer versus the trained and paid worker were raised. Vincentian leader Robert Biggs pointed out that the Vincentian mission was to bring one's education, intelligence, and knowledge of life into ministry with the poor. He held that this ideal had been picked up by trained social workers but was being lost in Catholic charity. Others felt that discussion of trained workers represented an attack on the volunteers. Biggs countered that the progressive agenda of the Catholic Charities movement could not be addressed with respect to the causes and extent of poverty and related social ills without trained workers. As Donald Gavin, in an early history of the Catholic Charities movement, summarized:

> One of the basic difficulties in the controversy over the trained worker and the volunteer appeared to arise from the failure of a majority to realize the preventive aspects of charity. Many could not see why relief, which had seemed adequate to them up to now, was not a sufficient solution to the social problems of the early twentieth century.[21]

Kerby urged that "modern charities have produced experts in every field of social service and have used them to good advantage. We [in Catholic Charities] have much to do still in the training and use of them."[22] Mrs. P. J. Toomey, a member of the board of directors of the St. Louis School of Social Economy, added that "the fact of calling a National Conference of Catholic Charities seemed logically to suggest the need of a School of Social Study under Catholic auspices."[23]

Like Mary Richmond in the secular movement, Catholic Charities leaders designed and implemented a response. The first school of social work at an American Catholic institution was developed at Loyola University in Chicago in 1914 by Rev. Frederic Siedenburg, SJ, who was active in the social movements of the time, including the early work of Catholic Charities. The school, initially the School of Sociology, was the first school at Loyola to routinely admit women. Fordham University in New York City followed in 1916, offering courses in social work through the Department of Sociology.[24]

Emerging through a complex set of circumstances and with a combined global and domestic outreach from its initiation, the National Catholic School of Social Service in Washington, DC, became the third Catholic school of social work, cofounded by Rev. John J. Burke, CSP, and Kerby.[25] In his role as a sociologist and faculty member at Catholic University, Kerby worked closely with Rev. John Ryan—the framer of the American Catholic Bishop's Program of Social Reconstruction.[26] At that time, Ryan, a fellow CUA faculty member, also headed the Department of Social Action of the Bishops National Catholic War Council—a council on which Kerby also served. The War Council was formed in 1917 to devise an official Catholic response to World War I and to lobby for Catholic interests with the federal government.[27]

A particular interest of the War Council was "the development of a program focusing on the welfare of women and girls employed in the war effort through the establishment of community houses and residence clubs in various centers of war activity."[28] Kerby and Burke recognized immediately that such an initiative would require specialized training in the social services. Thus, they took an active role in curriculum development and course instruction, and established the National Service School for Women in 1918. The school was financed by the War Council and was designed to provide a training program that prepared and deployed graduates for social work on the domestic front and abroad. During the next two years, the school's curriculum content and length of study gradually expanded, and by 1921 the school provided a full two-year graduate program of academic and professional training. Renamed the National Catholic School of Social Service (NCSSS), the school's sponsorship and direction was transferred to the National Council of Catholic Women, but by 1930, NCSSS became an affiliate of Catholic University—consistent with the structures of other secular and Catholic schools of social work of the time.

In 1934, however, at the request of the Catholic Charities diocesan directors, Catholic University established its own school to prepare both clergy and laypersons for the field of social work, with Msgr. John O'Grady, CUA faculty member and executive secretary of the National Conference of Catholic Charities, as dean.[29] (Importantly, at that time, O'Grady was an active collaborator with President Franklin D. Roosevelt on national issues such as the Social Security Act.) Only men were admitted to the newly established School of Social Work until the Catholic Charities directors complained and this policy was reversed.[30]

As might be expected with two similar programs affiliated with the same institution, a complex series of academic and professional consequences unfolded. In 1943, an Advisory Committee of Diocesan Directors of Catholic Charities recommended a merger of the women's school (NCSSS) and the School of Social Work within Catholic University. Full details of the merger were worked out by 1947 and the title National Catholic School of Social Service was retained.[31] Simultaneously, during O'Grady's 40-year leadership of the Catholic Charities movement, the number of diocesan agencies expanded from six "bureaus" located predominately in the larger dioceses to 140 across the country.[32]

Over the years, social work programs affiliated with Catholic universities and colleges across the United States have continued to be established for the purposes of preparing trained and qualified professionals at the baccalaureate, master's, and doctoral levels. Graduates serve in both secular and faith-based settings, including Catholic Charities agencies, and in a wide range of practice specializations. Additionally, due to the profession's emphasis on field work—referred to in contemporary terms as its signature pedagogy[33]—many social work education programs partner with local Catholic Charities agencies and programs in the field training of students. Thus, although they may not pursue employment in Catholic Charities, today many professionals throughout the country are exposed to the values, the mission, and the services of Catholic agencies.

Moreover, specialized training institutes have continued to play an important role in the professionalization of agency staff. For example, in the mid-twentieth century, child care workers in Catholic institutions enhanced their practice and policy development skills through enrollment in the University of North Carolina Child Care Institute conducted by Dr. Alan Keith-Lucas of the university's School of Social Work. From the 1980s and beyond, social ministry planners and workers partnered with professional programs in various parts of the country, such as NCSSS and Loyola University of New Orleans, for training and certification of workers. More recently, leadership institutes affiliated with academic institutions such as Regis University and the University of Notre Dame have provided advanced training as well as a sense of collegial bonding among agency directors.

The Impact of Agency and Social Worker Licensing

Obviously, although controversial, the early professionalizing influences of social work had a direct and stabilizing effect on the expansion of the Catholic Charities movement and its mission of service and advocacy for the poor and those in need. Most likely, this was enhanced by the profession's traditional twofold mission to "help people in need" as well as to "work for social change"—a mission consistent with the Catholic Charities movement.[34] However, as greater responsibility for social services was assumed by federal and state governments following the Great Depression of the 1930s, licensing of service agencies became a norm. Within this context, many states required that Catholic Charities agencies employ trained directors and professionally qualified staff, particularly in child and family services such as adoption, child care institutions, and foster care. Moreover, in many jurisdictions third-party reimbursements for service provision required licensing. Importantly, Catholic Charities agencies and institutions, although able to provide needed services, became increasingly dependent on contractual arrangements with legal jurisdictions. This trend continues to this day. The 2008 Catholic Charities USA Annual Survey indicates that over half of the participating agencies' funding in 2008 came from federal, state, and local governmental sources.[35]

Additionally, by the 1970s the social work profession began to seek formal public sanction for social workers through state licensing. This came about because in many instances social workers' unique skill sets were not recognized or reimbursed on a par with peers from other professions such as physicians, psychiatrists, and psychologists. The move toward licensing came particularly in reaction to the practice in many child welfare agencies that college graduates with degrees in unrelated fields were hired to carry out social work responsibilities. For example, literature majors were assigned to provide highly specialized services such as counseling and social casework.

By the 1980s, the National Association of Social Workers had succeeded in passing legislation that achieved licensing of social workers across most states. Typically, this legislation is a "title protection act," which specifies that the title "social worker" is reserved for those who have graduated from an accredited school of social work and have passed a state licensing examination. This was a much needed achievement for social workers and has helped to enhance and ensure quality service. Although this contributed to service accountability and reimbursement eligibility, it did in some ways increase the gap between social workers who were trained through on-the-job experience and those who were educationally trained.

The Influence of Vatican II, the Renewed Role of the Laity, and the Cadre Study

By the 1960s and into the 1970s, many social service agencies experienced a crisis of identity, including Catholic Charities. Interestingly, but problematic for the Catholic Charities movement as well as for the social work profession, researcher Irwin Epstein found that social workers in agency leadership positions and social caseworkers were less likely than their group work or community organizer colleagues to engage in social change activities.[36] This was in sharp contrast to the mission of social work, which included both social service and social change, as well as the social teachings of the church as presented in church documents. This body of social teaching includes the documents of the Second Vatican Council, subsequent social encyclicals, and the statements of the U.S. bishops that emphasized that the church should take a proactive role in the world with respect to moral, social, and economic issues, including concern for the poor. During this period in the United States, the Civil Rights movement and the War on Poverty were underway. There was strong public reaction to the Vietnam War, and the women's rights movement was at its peak. These social movements drew attention to the plight of the poor and disadvantaged as well as to the economic and social discrepancies in society.

In schools of social work, curriculum from the mid-1920s through the first half of the twentieth century drew heavily from the theoretical views of the developing field of psychiatry and psychoanalysis, particularly for the training of caseworkers. This was understandable at the time because knowledge and interpretation of unconscious forces and drives provided some explanation for the unexplainable and sometimes illogical desires and behaviors of persons of all ages and cultures.[37] Consideration of unconscious motivation helped workers to understand why an abused child would desire to return to an abusing parent, or what would motivate a woman to return to a violent marital relationship. Early Freudian psychodynamic theory and ego psychology provided beginning tools for explaining the unexplainable within a professional context. However, these approaches were not sufficient for dealing with the social problems and issues of the 1960s and beyond. Harry Specht and other critics, consistent with the climate of the time, called the social work profession to accountability for mission effectiveness, particularly in the area of social advocacy for the poor.[38]

Social work practitioners and educators began to search for new ways to conceptualize the experience of persons within the complex social structures of the mid-twentieth century. Social systems thinking that simultaneously analyzed the person in their social environment and later practice models such as the strengths and resilience perspectives were developed and articulated for use in social service agencies.[39] Professional social workers were urged to use a range of interpersonal, group, community, and social advocacy skills as part of their practice repertoire. Social work renewed its traditional commitment to interdisciplinary collaboration.[40] By the 1980s with the development of the North American Association of Christians in Social Work and the Society for Spirituality in Social Work, there was an emphasis in the profession on integrating a bio-psycho-social-spiritual perspective in professional practice.

In Catholic Charities, there was a parallel concern that the agencies had become over-professionalized to the neglect of the larger social issues facing dioceses and parish communities. The difference between Catholic Charities and other social service agencies was questioned. Discussion of identity led to the NCCC's three-year Cadre Study that took place between 1969 and 1972.[41] Included was a reexamination of some of the parallel social ministries that had developed within dioceses but separate from Catholic Charities. For example, in reaction to what some perceived as an overemphasis on counseling and family therapy in Catholic Charities, specialized ministries addressing very basic needs of some communities for food, clothing, and shelter had been developed by indigenous/nonprofessional volunteers and some religious communities. Other groups, often led by community organizers and social activists, became involved in community development and political change efforts at the local, regional, and national levels.

The Cadre Study strove to be responsive to these critiques and alternative developments. It was deeply influenced by the Second Vatican Council, with its emphasis on the engagement of the church in the affairs of the world as well as the participation of the laity in the ministries of the church. At its annual meeting held in Florida in 1972, the National Conference of Catholic Charities affirmed the three roles of direct service, advocacy, and convening of Catholic Charities and other concerned people, with a renewed interest in outreach and involvement of Catholic Charities agencies at the local parish level. It became clear that the social ministries of the church required persons with a range of professional and volunteer skills supported by a rich spiritual motivation. It also called for parish outreach—a long neglected area—that involved partnering with parishes in the development and implementation of models of parish social ministry, stressing both personal/direct services, advocacy, and collaboration with the broader community in these areas.[42]

Although each diocesan Catholic Charities agency has implemented the directions of the Cadre Study in its own way in response to the local context, Catholic Charities agencies of the early twenty-first century are characterized by an extensive array of programs and services, such as emergency services, housing-related services, disaster response, domestic violence intervention, and child welfare services, as well as programs that build strong communities, often in partnership with affiliated parish social ministry programs; strengthen families; and assist special populations (i.e., developmentally disabled, refugees, former prisoners, etc.).[43] Current advocacy initiatives include immigration, affordable housing, hunger, economic security, and health reform. Convening takes place locally, regionally, and nationally with other Catholic organizations such as the United States Conference of Catholic Bishops and the Catholic Health Association; with other faith-based organizations such as Lutheran Social Service and Jewish Social Services; as well as with other groups such as the Child Welfare League of America, the Alliance for Families and Children, the Independent Sector, the Annie B. Casey Foundation, and many others. Staffing patterns reflect an impressive expansion of interdisciplinary personnel within the agencies such as the inclusion of lawyers, nurses, management professionals, organizational and funding development specialists, and many others. Importantly, and consistent with the urging of Vatican II, "volunteers make up 77 percent of the Charities workforce" nationwide as reported in Catholic Charities USA's 2008 Annual Survey.[44]

Accreditation as a Tool to Enhance Best Practice

In order to more fully appreciate the reciprocal influence of renewal in the Catholic Charities movement as well as in the profession, it is useful to briefly consider the influence of voluntary human service accreditation and the convening role of Catholic Charities. There are multiple professional human service accrediting organizations in the United States, and Catholic Charities agencies, depending on the services they provide, may interact with more than one accrediting body. However, emphasis here is placed on the unique relationship between Catholic Charities and the Council on Accreditation for Children and Family Services, Inc. (COA) based in New York City.

In response to a concern in the early 1980s among nonprofit social service providers that the federal government intended to require that all social service organizations who received federal funding be accredited by the well-established Joint Commission on Hospital Accreditation, the leaders of the Child Welfare League of America and the Family Service Association of America joined together to explore the establishment of standards and an accreditation process appropriate to the unique needs of social service agencies.[45] Under the leadership of Msgr. Lawrence Corcoran, then director of the NCCC, and Dorothy Byrd Daly, NCCC director of social services at the time, Catholic Charities joined these colleagues as the third sponsoring organization of COA. Thus it was possible to tailor the standards to both the clinical and community-based aspects of the social service field and to develop a peer/collegial model of accreditation. In the early years of COA, accreditation was voluntarily sought by private agencies and was viewed as evidence of the credibility of the service provider. In more recent years, accreditation has been sought by the public/governmental sector as well. Some states require accreditation in order for private agencies to become eligible to engage in state purchase of service arrangements. Other states have sought accreditation of their state systems as a corrective measure when child welfare scandals have become public and as a way to offset court monitoring. Interestingly, some grant making foundations have begun to consider the usefulness of accreditation as a requirement for funding applicants.

For Catholic Charities, sponsorship has afforded a place at the table in the formulation of accreditation standards, including administrative and infrastructure standards as well as a range of service delivery standards. Participation in standards development has assured that the unique moral principles influencing Catholic Charities service delivery that stem from Catholic social teaching, such as pro-life and pro-family principles, are respected and accreditable. Beyond these particular concerns, the standards are revised regularly in response to COA's view that best practice requires more than the minimal provisions reflected in government licensing requirements. Further, COA holds that standards must respect the dignity and worth of the persons being served and should be sensitive to relevant research findings. In addition to participation in standards development, Catholic Charities members also serve as accreditation peer reviewers and site team leaders, as commission members and chairpersons who review especially complex accreditation applications, and as board members in various leadership positions. Catholic Charities members who serve in these roles make important contributions to best practices in human service delivery, and they also acquire valuable insights from their cross-disciplinary colleagues that can enhance their local agency services as well as the Catholic Charities movement.

Importantly, sponsoring organizations are expected to have an organizational code of ethics that identifies the mission, values, and core principles of their agency's approach to service delivery. Through the leadership of Corcoran and Daly, Catholic Charities was among the first groups to develop an organizational code, which was adopted in 1983. That code was extensively updated in 2007 and has become a document of interest to both faith-based and secular human service organizations. As presently formulated, it provides a focus for interdisciplinary collaboration among professionals in the agency as well as a guide for the numerous volunteers—both lay and professional—who share in the mission of Catholic Charities.

Facing the Increasing Complexities of the New Millennium

When viewed in broad strokes through the highlights presented above, Catholic Charities in the United States enters its second century of service to the people of God both strengthened and challenged by historical experience and by the complexity of contemporary social change. The footprints of professionalization were clearly evident throughout the journey as Catholic Charities evolved from a volunteer venture in parishes to one of the largest and well-respected faith-based service delivery networks in the United States. Formal training for the various ministries was established, often affiliated with institutions of higher learning. Collaboration with other ministries within the church, with other faith-based organizations, and with secular organizations, such as with governmental agencies and funders as well as with the Council on Accreditation, was formalized. Legal sanction was acquired where appropriate for service delivery and purchase of service arrangements, and a formal code of ethics was created and recently revised. Throughout this growth, the profession of social work has played a key role in the process.

For Catholic Charities agencies today, few priests and religious are available for leadership and direct service, as in the early days. However, the church is blessed with an impressive body of committed lay and professional volunteers who carry on the ministries of Catholic Charities. Recall that volunteers now make up over 75 percent of the Catholic Charities workforce. Further, agency leaders and line staff come from a wide range of interdisciplinary, religious/spiritual, and cultural backgrounds, including the staff of the national office. Multiple and sometimes parallel ministries under diocesan sponsorship have frequently been merged into a single nonprofit corporation under Catholic Charities auspices necessitating new leadership skills.

New and complex issues continue to confront Catholic Charities and challenge its mission and foundational beliefs. For example, local governments have recently begun to question the validity of conscience clauses based on the sexual/morality tenets of Catholic social teaching that exempted Catholic Charities from particular organizational or service delivery requirements for purchase of service contracts. Thus, the ability of Catholic Charities to serve in customary ways is becoming threatened. The current economic downturn is requiring agencies, both faith-based and secular, to meet greater needs with fewer resources.

Although professional competence has been central throughout the development of Catholic Charities, the Cadre Study spurred a renewed emphasis on such competence, combined with spiritual motivation for ministry and fidelity to implementing the tenets of charity and justice inherent in Catholic social doctrine that continues to the present time. As Pope Benedict XVI pointed out in *Deus Caritas Est*:

> The Church's charitable organizations, beginning with those of Caritas (at diocesan, national and international levels), ought to do everything in their power to provide the resources and above all the personnel needed for this work. Individuals who care for those in need must first be professionally competent; they should be properly trained in what to do and how to do it, and committed to continuing care. Yet, while professional competence is a primary, fundamental requirement, it is not of itself sufficient. We are dealing with human beings, and human beings always need something more than technically proper care. They need humanity. They need heartfelt concern. Those who work for the Church's charitable organizations must be distinguished by the fact that they do not merely meet the needs of the moment, but they dedicate themselves to others with heartfelt concern, enabling them to experience the richness of their humanity.[46]

The Parish Comes
Full Circle and Beyond

The Role of Local Parishes
in the Work of Catholic Charities

*Sr. M. Vincentia Joseph
and Sr. Ann Patrick Conrad*

The Catholic University of America

The Parish Comes Full Circle and Beyond

The Role of Local Parishes
in the Work of Catholic Charities

Parish-based service programs are by no means new. Over the past few decades, however, both the climate in the post-Vatican II church and trends in the public sector have led to a new emphasis on social ministries at the parish level. The mission of the early Christian community, and later the local parish, included responsibility for providing for those in need in material as well as spiritual ways.

As society grew more complex and as the needs and rights of the person became more clearly articulated, many of the parish's roles were assumed by other societal institutions. Church-related agencies, crossing parish and congregational lines, evolved with many specialized functions to supplement and extend the services of the parishes. Dating back to the early twentieth century and the charitable work of the St. Vincent de Paul Societies in the local parishes, Catholic Charities emerged to meet the new and pressing needs that could not be met at the parish level alone. Over time, many of these agencies became isolated from the parish and took on a life of their own, becoming a voice of the church around human needs and social issues.[1]

In the 1970s, however, there was a groundswell of interest in social services at the neighborhood and parish or congregational levels. The time was right to strengthen the links between diocesan social ministries and the parish. Parish social ministry, then termed parish outreach, became a new and organized thrust of Catholic Charities agencies. As various models of parish social ministry have developed, the link between parishes and Catholic Charities has strengthened and has been in the process of coming full circle and far beyond. Through this collaboration and the creative programs that have evolved, the enormous potential for social ministries, both personal services and social advocacy, is clear.

This chapter will provide an overview of parish social ministry programs affiliated with Catholic Charities agencies within a historical-developmental framework. The purpose is to explore the roots of parish social ministry—social service programs and social change efforts—that have led to the current relationship between the Catholic Charities agency and the local parish and to the establishment of parish social ministry as integral to the Catholic Charities movement. The development of models of parish social ministry and the critical milestones in their evolution also will be presented. Finally, implications for the future in light of rapid social change and current trends within an environment of shrinking funding sources will be considered.

The Roots of Parish Social Ministries within the Catholic Charities Movement

The Catholic Parish in the New World— the Nineteenth and Early Twentieth Centuries

The parish, then as now, was the basic unit of the church, a socio-religious structure, generally with geographic boundaries. The word is derived from the Latin term *parochia* which refers to a neighbor or a people in sojourn. In the mid-nineteenth and into the twentieth centuries, with the growing immigrant population in the United States, there were many national churches composed of and often set up by specific ethnic groups. Catholic parishes were very diverse, especially in the cities. They were relatively autonomous but generally parochial and isolated from the larger church and social environment.[2] They were not only religious centers, however. It was expected that they would carry out the charitable works needed for the care of the poor, the sick, the elderly, and new immigrants and also meet the educational needs of their people. Moreover, they were social and cultural centers and served as the key source of Catholic identity.

Attitudes toward the poor at this time were highly punitive, being strongly influenced by the English poor laws. Public supports for those in need were extremely limited and generally dehumanizing. Within this social climate, the parish attempted to carry out its charitable works. It was assumed that this important work could be conducted through the ordinary mechanisms of the parish and the shared responsibility of the parish priest and the St. Vincent de Paul Society.[3] However, the economic and social stresses of the new world took their toll on the quality of both family and parish life. With the growing number of poor and the separation of many ethnic groups from their extended families, it soon became clear that special forms of help were needed. Msgr. John O'Grady, executive director of the National Conference of Catholic Charities (NCCC) from 1920 to 1961, stated that there was an inverse relationship between the number of poor and the resources of the parish. Interestingly, he saw this as "the most serious obstacle in the development of parish social work in the United States." It meant that the poor parishes needed some outside resources for assistance in their charitable work.[4]

It should be noted that prior to the Civil War and after, women were the pioneers of parish charitable organizations.[5] Some of the first were established in the mid-1800s in Brooklyn, Baltimore, and Washington, DC. Due to the isolation of parishes, however, no national movement was formed until later when the Ladies of Charity began to work with the St. Vincent de Paul Society. In the 1890s and into the 1900s, as leadership among women grew, they crafted important programs outside of the parish to meet emerging needs at the community level.[6]

The Rise of City-wide Services to Supplement Parish Charities

With the emergence of social work, in its early stages as a profession, the pioneers of Catholic Charities and the St. Vincent de Paul Society recognized that more technical services were needed to meet the increasingly complex needs of the people.[7] Secular organizations, staffed by social workers engaged in charitable activities, began to develop, and their new methods of service gained acceptance.[8] As referral systems were established between the parishes and these newly formed institutions, the value of these institutions as an extended resource for parishes became apparent. Some leaders in parish social work, in the church and the St. Vincent de Paul Society, saw the need for central clearing bureaus that could assist parishes in accessing such services as relief, legal aid, employment, and other forms of assistance. Thus, the Society set up bureaus in "Catholic social work" in various cities to connect the parish with these community programs. Through this experience they saw the need for city-wide programs of Catholic Charities staffed by social workers to carry out more effectively the pastoral responsibilities of the church. At the same time, these new institutions saw the parish as a means to enrich their service provision.[9]

A more definitive move toward supplementing the role of the parish in social services was made when steps were taken toward meeting the needs of not only the parish but those of the broader Catholic community that could not be met by the parish alone. The first such organization was the Catholic Home Bureau in New York, established for child placement in 1898 by the St. Vincent de Paul Society. Similar bureaus were created soon thereafter in various cities in the country.[10] This was in response to the growing need for child care and a concern that some secular groups were placing children in homes without regard to their faith. The Central Bureau of Baltimore, organized in 1907 by the Society, was more than a clearing house for parishes. It was a pioneer city-wide family social work program that aimed to supplement the work of the parish with the experience and skills of full-time social workers.[11] The Bureau established a coordinated program of relief, family work, protective services, home finding and child placement, and later, immigrant welfare. The significance of this program for the growth of Catholic Charities and the role of the parish is clear in O'Grady's statement below.

> It may be said in truth that the Baltimore organization was the first Catholic organization in the U.S. to develop a coordinated program of Catholic social work . . . in family work it launched out into a new and uncharted field. It marked a most important step toward a coordinated program of Catholic Charities in the U.S.[12]

Thus, it is clear that the early roots of parish social ministry are closely associated with the roots of the development of Catholic Charities agencies.

The Role of Religious Communities in Parish Social Ministries

Around this time a few religious communities were founded that engaged in what we know today as parish social ministry. The Mission Helpers, Servants of the Sacred Heart, established in Baltimore in 1894, worked exclusively in missionary work with the black population. Later they served those in need, regardless of race or ethnic background. The sisters worked in a number of ministries, in schools, almshouses, jails, and hospitals. They always associated their work with home visitation and emphasized assisting parents with the needs of their children. They later became involved in parish census-taking as a means to reach those in need.[13]

The Missionary Servants of the Blessed Trinity, commonly known as the Trinitarians, was founded in 1912 by Thomas A. Judge, CM, for the care of the poor and abandoned. This community, which grew out of a lay movement that Judge had established in Brooklyn, New York, in 1909, became active early on in religious and social ministries in the parish and in the formation of lay apostolate groups that participated in their mission work. All of the ministries of the sisters had a social dimension. By the 1920s, they became involved in social services in Catholic Charities agencies. As the parish ministries evolved, many developed networks of physicians and other professionals to offer needed services as well as make referrals to local secular and Catholic Charities agencies.[14]

The Society of the Missionary Catechists, Victory Noll, in Huntington, Indiana, was founded in 1917 by Rev. J. J. Sigstein to focus on the neglected mission fields in the southwestern region of the United States. The sisters worked with the people to keep doctrines of faith alive and active. Many forms of social ministry, including ministries at the parish level, grew out of their work as catechists. They also opened many medical clinics in areas such as New Mexico and California.[15]

The Parish Visitors of the Immaculate Heart of Mary, founded in 1920 by Julia Tallon in New York City, developed a program similar to that of the Missionary Servants. They grew out of a small lay group engaged in parish visitation and worked in a number of parishes in New York.[16]

An Exemplar of Parish Social Ministry in Europe— The Harbrecht Study

A striking work in regard to parish social ministry was a study by Rev. John Harbrecht, a sociologist, on the lay apostolate. In 1929, he studied social work programs in Germany and considered their implications for the United States. He found over 100 paid social workers placed in parishes as well as a number of schools to train the workers. Notable among the schools was the School of Charity at the University of Freiburg in Freiburg, Germany, which offered a two-year program for parish social workers. In 1926, the school enrolled 80 students and the "demand for its graduates" was great.[17] Harbrecht recommended that the local church join with Catholic Charities agencies in this country and envisioned the profession of social work as providing the appropriate knowledge and skills for parish social ministries. Also, he looked to the emerging Catholic schools of social work to develop the curriculum that would include both religious and ethical content.[18] Harbrecht's vision, however, did not take hold in the United States at the time and, as we know, took several decades to be realized.

The Emergence of Diocesan Charities and Its Impact on the Parish

With the prophetic vision of church leaders such as Msgr. William J. Kerby, O'Grady, and Most Rev. Thomas J. Shahan of Catholic University, and leaders of the St. Vincent de Paul Society such as Thomas Mulry and Edmund Butler, and with the new structures of social ministry beginning to develop around the country, the need for more unified and systematized programs of charity became apparent. This led the way to the development and growth of Catholic Charities agencies.[19] Both Mulry and Butler played important roles in the development of organized Catholic Charities.[20]

Rooted in Catholic social teaching and informed by a developing understanding of the social and behavioral sciences, the agencies focused on meeting the specialized needs of families and children, developing linkages with the public sector for funding, and advocating for social policies to address regional and national needs. A critical moment in the development of the Catholic Charities agencies movement was the invitation of Bishop Shahan to hold a national conference of Catholic Charities agencies at Catholic University. The formation of the National Conference of Catholic Charities (NCCC) in September 1910 was a significant event in unifying the movement and, as Kerby observed, it created an opportunity for the national consciousness of Catholic Charities to come to expression.[21]

Gradually, through the years, many works of the parish were transferred to the diocesan level. Although the parish remained the heart of the church, service functions were largely reduced to contributions to a Catholic Charities drive and the monies distributed to diocesan agencies staffed by professionals.[22] Tensions sometimes arose when parishes that were tapped for financial support perceived that agencies neglected the needs of their parishioners. There was not only a disconnect between the parish and Catholic Charities, but a general inertia in most urban parishes, due largely to the changing population and a directive leadership style.[23] At the same time, there was a great rise in the Catholic Action movement with many groups working outside the parish in spiritually oriented service and action programs. In the late 1960s and 1970s, with the impact of the Second Vatican Council, many parishes as well as Catholic Charities agencies began to question their relevance to a sharply changing society. At this time, the Catholic Charities movement began looking at its relationship with the local parish.

Rediscovering the Natural Parish-Agency Partnership

By the 1970s, a number of trends occurred within the church and society that created a climate for the development of parish social ministries. Social scientists were identifying the rich potential of mediating structures and natural helping networks, those structures close to the life of people, in addressing the social problems of persons and families and in re-developing a sense of community. Likewise, social work was beginning to develop practice models appropriate for work in the natural life space of the person, the neighborhood community. It was recognized that such forms of helping offered opportunities for creative and expanded service provision, especially when coordinated with other service providers in the larger community.[24] Also, in this period—the late 1960s and early 1970s—Catholic Charities, similar to the experience of many societal institutions and influenced as well by Vatican II, started the process of organizational renewal. It began by examining its own identity and seeking to conceptualize the distinct roles of the public sector and the church in addressing social needs. In the process, the natural partnership between parish and agency became obvious. It was at this time that a groundswell of interest emerged within the Catholic Charities movement around reconnecting with the local parishes.

A Postconciliar Theology of the Parish

The impact of Vatican II on the parish movement cannot be overstated. The council's theology of the role of the church in the modern world placed the parish in a pivotal position. The Constitution on the Church explicitly states that the local parish-community is the concrete reality of the church, the presence of Christ in which it achieves its fullness.[25] Worship is continued in service, and both are integrated in its communitarian life. The mission of the parish, as a ministering community, is to incarnate Christ in all of its relationships within its boundaries and beyond. As a community of God's people, the parish is the focal point of the actualization of the world church. Not only is it necessary to love God and others, but service is a distinct condition of discipleship. Fundamentally, then, the theological base of parish ministries was incarnational in nature, recognizing the integral unity of the person, one's relationship to the world and one's responsibility to others.

Thus, social ministry was no longer seen as peripheral to the role of the church, but was recognized as an integral component of its mission. Karl Rahner held that social work (in the broad sense) and social services were essential to the church's mission. Furthermore, he held that parish social work was a form of ecclesial social work, which is hardly recognized as such but is extremely important. Furthermore, it cannot be achieved by "preaching, in the normal sense," or by the "spiritual element alone."[26]

The Emergence of Agency-affiliated Parish Programs

The theology of the council and the institutional changes in society caused many to express concerns about the directions of Catholic Charities.

Some questioned the uniqueness and vitality of the movement as well as its adequacy to respond to the changes in society and in the church. With the rise of new public and private agencies, some questioned its very existence. Clearly, it was the time to seriously examine the mission of Catholic Charities and its future role.

At the same time, there was a growing interest in parish social ministries affiliated with Catholic Charities and an accompanying concern that many parishes were engaging in social ministries independent of any social agency.[27] However, a few programs affiliated with Catholic Charities were beginning to develop. The first significant report of such a program was of an inner-city project in St. Paul, Minnesota, which involved three parishes.[28] An agency staff person combined both casework and community organization to address social issues and service needs. From 1970 to 1971 a series of articles described a team approach used by Catholic Charities in a Baltimore parish. A direct service worker provided social services in the parish and coordinated activities with a community organizer.[29] It was concluded that the program bridged the gap between agency and parish and provided a natural network for planning social interventions. In 1971, Sr. Vincentia Joseph presented a comprehensive model for human services at the parish level that involved three contiguous parishes as a part of a technical assistance program through a central agency. The program involved both services and action and utilized a direct service worker based in each parish and a community organizer who served the three parishes. This model was used by several dioceses and adapted to their needs.

Although some questioned the parish as a viable base for sustained social ministries, others viewed it as a vital structure, particularly as the laity assumed greater responsibility in the church's mission. Clearly, the Vatican Council emphasized the role of the laity in the temporal order. However, despite a rise in the development of programs, there seemed to be little indication of a unified effort. Thus, efforts emerged within the Catholic Charities movement to advocate for systematic agency involvement in parish social ministry. A few leaders among the directors, lay members, and the NCCC's Conference of Religious called for a formalized parish outreach program at the national office. The Conference of Religious had a special concern because many religious were moving into parish ministries with little or no preparation. As religious communities were responding to the Vatican Council's call for renewal and a return to the founding charism, many religious looked to the parish as a focus for new ministries. A study of the Sister Formation Conference verified the striking increase in new ministries of sisters in both social work and parish work.[30] As many priests and religious began to work in inner-city parishes, the Conference of Religious began to present programs in preparation for work in parish social ministries at annual Catholic Charities conferences.

It seems important to note at this point that the Conference of Religious was a constituent body of Catholic Charities, founded in 1920 at the NCCC meeting at Catholic University. O'Grady, who became executive secretary of the NCCC that year, recognized that nearly 75 percent of all charitable work was done by religious. However, due to the semi-cloistered atmosphere of most of the communities at the time, the sisters were very isolated from the outside world and from each other. O'Grady saw the need of bringing them together for mutual sharing and communication. Thus, a "Special Conference of Religious Engaged in Social and Charitable Work" was held at the NCCC meeting.[31] As a result, an Organizing Committee of sisters was set up to direct the work but was later replaced by a Standing Committee in 1947.[32] Over the years, consistent with its original role, the Conference of Religious was engaged in coordinating the work of religious in social service, offering consultation and educational programs, and encouraging professional education to enhance service effectiveness. With religious pursuing the study of social work and related professions and as they were becoming more involved with the work of Catholic Charities, it soon became clear that the need for a distinct body of religious was no longer necessary. Eventually, soon after the work of the Cadre Study, the conference was dissolved.

With continued concerns expressed by the membership about the relevance of Catholic Charities and a call for a study to examine its role and explore new directions, the Cadre Study, a comprehensive study of the Catholic Charities movement, was conducted. This study was a highly significant step in the growth of the movement and in the establishment of agency-affiliated parish programs. The Cadre Study report, *Toward a Renewed Catholic Charities Movement*, gave impetus to parish social ministry as an important new direction of the movement. The report not only emphasized the parish as the basic instrumentality through which the needs of people are met but it also moved the agency toward an approach of collaboration, consultation, and facilitation to assist the parishes in meeting their own needs.[33]

The Cadre report defined three roles of a renewed Catholic Charities— personal services, social change efforts, and conscientization, the process of raising social awareness.[34] A forward-looking conference should reach out to people and mobilize them to be mutually supportive in approaching human problems of the day. At times, in social work and in Catholic Charities, there had been a tension between the service role and social action roles. During the 1960s, this tension escalated. Some held that there was no place for personal services as the roots of social problems resided in social structures. The Cadre report, however, clearly emphasized the interdependence of both approaches as well as that of raising social consciousness. It viewed all three as important at both the agency and parish levels. The report also emphasized that renewal and discernment should permeate all works.[35]

Forging a New Partnership

During the mid and late 1970s, there was an impressive growth in parish social ministry programs, both those affiliated with Catholic Charities and those that were established independently of any social agency. The development within the Catholic Charities movement was influenced considerably by the Cadre report but also by the later establishment of the Parish Outreach Office at the national level. It was also influenced by the growing interest in society in mediating structures and natural helping networks at the neighborhood-community level for service provision. A 1978 report on research conducted by the U.S. Department of Health, Education, and Welfare's Administration for Children, Youth, and Families concluded that mediating structures were among the most important in modern society. It recommended research and demonstration to identify service provisions and strategies as well as training, supervision, and consultation needs appropriate to those structures.[36] Peter Berger and Richard Neuhaus, in their work related to public policy research, identified four critical natural structures—neighborhood, church, family, and voluntary associations—and suggested that they be recognized in the formation of public policy and utilized for social purposes.[37]

The Parish Outreach Program started in 1973, and a special department was developed at the national level to facilitate this effort. Another significant event that furthered the development of parish-agency linkages occurred at the Annual Membership Congress of the NCCC in 1976. A resolution was passed that proposed that the NCCC "assist parishes in establishing ministries of service and encourage local agencies and other related organizations within the diocese to make their services known and available to the parishes."[38] In 1976, the NCCC launched the Parish Outreach Project, partially funded by the Lilly Endowment, to further strengthen social ministries at the parish level. *The Parish Outreach Review*, a newsletter, also was instituted at this time. In 1979, the Parish Outreach Project was renamed Parish Social Ministry, and the Parish Social Ministry Advisory Committee was formed at the national office "to assist the Christian community in developing the service and justice dimensions of our faith" and to further the growth of parish social ministry throughout the country.[39] It soon became active in providing consultation and assistance to a number of dioceses in starting parish-agency partnerships. These events did much for the integration and stabilization of these programs within the Catholic Charities movement. The establishment of the Parish Renewal Project of the United States Catholic Conference, in this period, gave even a deeper understanding and fuller expression of the mission of the parish.[40]

In the 1970s, there was an impressive growth in literature that presented new models of parish programs from the perspective of both the parish and the agency. Our focus here is on the literature of Catholic Charities, but it is important to note that there was considerable literature on parish programs developed by other denominations such as the Lutheran and Methodist churches and the Jewish community. In 1973, Donna Preston gave an account of a parish-agency modality that placed women religious in parishes as program coordinators.[41] The diocesan Catholic Charities agency provided budget, training, and consultation, and the parishes assumed financial responsibility for the coordinator and professional training for religious to supervise workers in parish clusters.

A landmark work in this area, the second issue of *Social Thought* in 1975, copublished by the NCCC and the National Catholic School of Social Service at The Catholic University of America, was an important contribution to the theoretical and practical development of this emerging ministry. It brought together a number of articles that focused on the theme of parish-centered social service and social action programs from a multidisciplinary point of view. One article explored the theological understanding of the modern parish as a community of people and highlighted the social dimension as a natural development.[42] Another article discussed findings of sociological research on the religious and social attitudes of parish members and provided important insights into the various views of staff, the parish council, and parishioners on service-action programs at the parish level.[43] A third article examined the organizational components of a parish social service and action center, its role and operation, within an ecological systems framework.[44] Also included was an application of *management by objectives* (MBO) to parish programs. Based on the experience of several models of parish ministry in one diocese, the author looked at the problems specific to MBO and the differences in its use in industry and social services.[45] A case study on social action was provided and showed how Catholic Charities could be a force for political citizen action.[46] A final article on the St. Vincent de Paul Society in modern society highlighted the key role of the volunteer.[47]

That same year, in an issue of *Charities USA*, the magazine of the NCCC, Vincentia Joseph discussed a service and action model that joined the efforts

of Catholic Charities and the Office of Social Development both of the Archdiocese of Washington and the National Catholic School of Social Service at
Catholic University in reaching out to parishes.[48] Based on a diocesan-wide
survey to identify parish needs and locate parishes with social service staff,
a social ministry network was set up for training, sharing, and support.
Consultation and supervision was provided by Catholic Charities. Information on social issues emerging at the parish level was used for advocacy. For
example, based on data provided by the parishes network, a bill detrimental
to low-income families and the elderly was vetoed by the governor and new
legislation was passed that supported the disadvantaged.

The first comprehensive research on parish programs affiliated with
Catholic Charities included 40 agencies and provided important descriptive data as well as a theoretical base for further program development.[49]
The agencies reached out through support, consultation and training,
and financial help. Three broad social ministry models were identified:
personal social services, social action, and a combination of both. Over
80 percent of the programs used a combined model. The data clearly
supported the literature and the Cadre report, which held that there was
a dynamic interdependence between these two approaches. Despite the
view of some that social action and social services are incompatible based
on a divergent ideology, these activities were seen as integrated in this
research. In some of the dioceses included in the study, tension was reported between social development and Catholic Charities and the tension
often flowed over into the parish. However, others reported collaboration
at both agency and parish levels.[50] Many staff members in the parishes
were social workers or persons in a related field and the position title was
most often parish social ministry worker or coordinator. Respondents were
generally enthusiastic about parish outreach and viewed such programs
as a "wave of the future." A number saw them as the most viable instrument for long-range systematic social change.[51]

During the latter part of the 1970s, workshops and training programs began to develop a parish social ministry curriculum. The National Catholic School of Social Service (NCSSS) and the national office of
Catholic Charities co-sponsored national workshops and conferences for
agency directors and parish ministry staff. NCSSS also developed a social
ministry concentration in their program of study that included a course
on parish social ministry and the integration of religion and spirituality
in practice. Other courses were available through the School of Religious
Studies. Eventually, as dioceses developed their own social ministry training programs, some in conjunction with local colleges and universities,
the concentration was dissolved.

One of the early parish programs—at Catholic Charities in Rockville Centre, New York—developed a team approach in which staff reached out to support and assist parishes in the development of social ministries. From the beginning, the agency provided training programs for agency and parish staff. The parish program affiliated with Catholic Social Services in Philadelphia and established in 1976 began a comprehensive summer training program for religious and lay persons which drew some faculty from the National Catholic School of Social Service as well as staff from the parish program at the national Catholic Charities office to conduct some of the sessions. Similar summer training programs were developed in Chicago and Pittsburgh and in other parts of the country. The Washington Social Ministry Network in Washington, DC, evolved into parish clusters that included church programs of other denominations. Training programs continued as an essential component of the network and the clusters.

The Growth of Parish-Agency Collaboration: The 1980s and Beyond

The evolution of the parish-agency affiliation saw the continued strengthening and maturing of the programs. Models of parish social ministry were refined and newer models developed to adapt to changing needs. Workshops and conferences were offered at national, regional, and local levels. At the same time, concerns were raised about the future direction of the programs. In a 1982 article in *Social Thought*, Jerome Ernst, then director of the Parish Social Ministry Program at the national office, discussed a key question that arose in the movement regarding what it meant to provide social services within the framework of a Vatican II ecclesiology.[52] Ernst showed how this question moved the parish program to define itself less in secular terms and more in terms of church ministry. The notion of building a caring community became a central theme in the development of parish outreach. It was strengthened with the policy statement passed at the 1978 Congress of Catholic Charities, which stressed the concepts of convening a caring community and renewal in parish outreach. In 1979, the NCCC's Parish Social Ministry Advisory Committee emphasized these concepts as essential to the mission of parish social ministry. The national office with several diocesan outreach staff formulated a values-based parish-community model that included a reflection process on the meaning of ministry in the parish and a parish-community needs assessment process. This was followed by intensive regional training programs in the use of the model.

In the same issue of *Social Thought*, Vincentia Joseph addressed the changes in parish programs at the agency-parish levels over a decade and presented a generic six-phase developmental model that considered phase-related growth as well as crises.[53] For example, as the program expands, often challenges emerge around staff needs and funding. The implications of the use of the phases to offset problems and to utilize the rich resources available through the parish linkage were stressed.[54] Some ethical issues had begun to surface as parish programs continued to develop, especially around confidentiality and the privacy of persons seeking help. There were concerns about the protection of records and the organizational and physical arrangements of the facilities in which services were provided. Also, questions arose about staff competency and the selection and training of volunteers. Some of these issues became more compelling as the programs evolved into the new millennium. In response, some handbooks and manuals began to appear to assist the development of programs. These included specialized ministries, such as the aging ministries,[55] and resource books on social ministries in the parish geared to religious as well as the laity and volunteers.[56]

A number of church documents and NCSSS publications gave further impetus to parish social ministry, especially in regard to the prophetic role of the laity in the transformation of our culture. The vision statement of the U.S. bishops, *The Parish: A People, A Mission, A Structure*,[57] and *The Parish Self-Study Guide*[58] influenced the extensive Notre Dame study on parish life since the Second Vatican Council. The research was an interdisciplinary work that addressed the structure, leadership, and priorities of the parish in a socio-religious context. Interestingly, the most striking finding in the first phase of the study was the expanded role of the laity in important parish ministries and an expressed need for parish social ministries.[59]

A notable publication, a 1987 issue of *Social Thought* on the occasion of Pope John Paul II's visit to the United States, included a collection of articles that reflected on the pope's call for renewal, redevelopment, and transformation of society as constituent tasks of the church and to address developments in the social teachings of the church. Included was Steven Gratto's article on the pope's teaching on parish social ministry. It spoke of the specific task of the laity in renewing the temporal order and the importance of the local church's volunteer and professional ministries.[60] The pope referred to social ministry as "social love." He interpreted it as a constituent apostolate of the local church that is to mirror the mission of the whole church.[61] John Holland in another article discussed the pope's teaching on the role of the laity in society and his claim that modern society is in crisis and looking for a post-modern culture to be born. Thus, the pope saw the laity's social role as a strategic response to this crisis. Clearly, this stance highlighted the important role of convening and consciousness-raising at the parish level.[62]

In the 1990s and into the new century, there were diverse developments in parish agency models. Many agencies refocused or expanded their programs. There was a striking growth in creative educational programs, some offering parish social ministry credentials such as certification. In 1994, a special issue of *Charities USA* was devoted to the developments in parish social ministry. It featured an interview with Most Rev. Joseph Sullivan, who, as director of Catholic Charities of the Diocese of Brooklyn and Queens, had started a program of parish outreach. Over the years, he had done much to advance social ministries at the parish level. In the interview, he emphasized that the parish movement is more than providing services but it involves a whole understanding of the dignity of the person and the mutuality of the support system.[63] He stated that the fundamental purpose of all social work, particularly in the parish and the wider church, is to build community and social awareness, which can be liberating when it opens people up to reality. Bishop Sullivan also addressed some of the issues facing PSM programs, including the need for more cultural diversity in the parish programs and funding issues. He brought out some of the central issues that agencies faced, such as changing financial concerns with the increasing dependence on public and private sources, some of which may be in conflict with the agency's values.[64] This issue, of course, continues at this time.

A number of other articles included in that 1994 issue of *Charities USA* showed the wide range of parish programs that provided personal services as well as a variety of social change efforts. These included legislative action, coalition building on pressing social concerns, involvement in disaster relief, and sponsorship of refugee families. Msgr. John Gilmartin, then director of Catholic Charities in Rockville Centre and someone who had been in the forefront of the parish social ministry movement, discussed the evolution of their parish program. Parishes hired outreach coordinators and engaged in both personal services and advocacy. At that time, the parish social ministry network of 134 parishes extended across Long Island and was working with other faiths to build a power-based organization to address social needs. Gilmartin felt that although much has been accomplished, Catholic Charities would have to radically re-think parish social ministry in the years ahead. He suggested closer collaboration with other diocesan and church-related agencies to more seriously work toward the transformation of society.[65]

New Challenges in a Changing Milieu

Parish social ministry programs today are well established within the community as well as in Catholic Charities. The expansion of resources available through the agency-parish linkage is clearly recognized at both levels. In the parish, services are more visible and accessible and more readily individualized. The joining of the technical skills and experience of the agency with the natural helping structures and volunteer resources at the parish level is especially powerful in times of diminishing resources. Moreover, the rich data available through the parish experience can be invaluable in efforts toward social change and relevant social policies. Increasingly, the social minister is a member of the parish team, working with other team members to integrate the social dimension in their work through raising awareness of social justice concerns in the school, the liturgy, and in other educational programs.

Parish social ministry now has a distinct section within the organizational structure of Catholic Charities USA, with its own leadership team and subcommittee structure that address timely issues. Its mission is clear, defined as "a network of people . . . working for social justice and serving those in the Church, our communities, our nation, and our world." Catholic Charities USA provides training programs, co-sponsored with dioceses, as well as workshops on parish social ministry and networking and skill-building opportunities at CCUSA annual gatherings. Communication processes include an up-to-date webpage that links members to resources relevant to their work and an e-mail network for member sharing. *Koinonia*, the PSM Section quarterly newsletter, keeps members informed on best practices around the country.[66] In addition, *Charities USA* occasionally publishes articles specifically related to the work of parish social ministry. These developments clearly reflect the evolution of the parish movement within Catholic Charities and the serious efforts to respond to changing service structures and advances in technology and to take a prophetic stance on social justice.

The contemporary scene today in American society as well as in the church, however, presents a number of new and difficult challenges. Funding parish programs continues to be a concern, especially in difficult economic times, when donations to voluntary organizations and other sources of income decrease. This kind of environment requires a reevaluation of priorities at both the parish and agency levels. Leaders are forced to give particular attention to funding sources without compromising the values of their organization, while staff members of necessity must attend to their own career paths and economic stability. The impact of economic downturns and social change can diminish parish social ministries, but also lead to a creative renewal and prophetic stance. Clearly, funding shortages call for parishes to re-focus and design social ministries that respond to the upsurge of basic needs and emerging policy issues. The Cadre report was clear on the importance of on-going renewal and the reformulation of priorities at all levels of Catholic Charities. It is therefore imperative to continually evaluate parish social ministry programs to assure their relevance today. This was stressed very clearly by Tom Ulrich in his 2001 book on parish social ministry, in which he discussed the importance of an annual evaluation of what was accomplished and what has yet to be accomplished and why.[67]

Much attention has been given to the spiritual development of staff engaged in social ministry. There are many opportunities at both the agency and parish levels to enhance theological understandings and to contribute to the spiritual life of the person. With the many stresses currently on families and workers, this is an area that requires continued attention.

Issues related to confidentiality change over time, especially as our understanding of the dignity and the rights of persons deepens. Today there are specific issues concerning client protection and the various ways our verbal communications and information technology are used. This is especially important at the parish level due to the informality of many neighborhood structures. It is also important to keep up to date with the changing ethical challenges related to the competencies and training needed by paid staff and volunteers, especially when it comes to sharing information with outside sources and handling values issues related to the mission of the agency.

Many new and changing competencies are required in times of change for effective service provision. There is much emphasis at this time on evidenced-based practice. This requires research skills to evaluate approaches to both service delivery and social action. Funding sources seriously consider the data available to assure service effectiveness, especially in times of economic constraints. This underscores the importance of linking with other organizations and university faculty to conduct sound evaluation processes. Attention also must be given to the ethical implications of both the service models and how research and technology are used in the evaluation process. This is especially relevant today when there are so many pressures on staff.

Career development for parish staff has been a concern in the past and could be increasingly important today. In the initial period of the developing programs affiliated with Catholic Charities agencies, it was not unusual for staff members, motivated less by job dissatisfaction and more by salary, to leave parish jobs for further education or other job opportunities. Some have left parish ministry for career development and professional competence in areas of social work or law in order to more effectively serve those in need. Many have discussed the need to give more attention to the career ladder for parish staff as staff turnover has serious consequences for effective service delivery. Then too, there continues to be the concern about job security when there is a change in pastor or when there is a consolidation of parishes.

Importantly, the role of Catholic Charities USA, through the dissemination of the Vision 2000 document with its emphasis on partnership development and cultural competence, highlights the potential of parish social ministry to implement an inclusive and ecumenical witness that is faithful to the charity and justice values of Catholic social teaching.[68]

Despite all of the societal issues confronting parish social ministries at this time, the parish-agency movement has clearly demonstrated its relevance to our time and its important place in Catholic Charities. It has contributed much to caring and ministering communities not only at the parish level but at all levels of society. With the personal charisms of its members, the parish can even more fully carry out the mission of the church in the modern world.

Conclusion

Parish social ministry today, indeed, has come full circle and has moved beyond in a more expanded and strengthened role. In response to the call of Vatican II, it is more closely the church in microcosm, carrying out an essential component of the church in the modern world. Moreover, it is positioned for continuing renewal and response to the needs of the time. Its emphasis on social justice efforts at all levels of society and globally in both its mission and its action is in keeping with the call of Pope Benedict XVI in his encyclicals. Its partnership with Catholic Charities empowers the parish-community to carry out its ministries more fully and effectively, while at the same time providing an important resource at the service, social justice, and social change levels. The parish provides a matrix for the more authentic role of the laity in the temporal order. The laity not only participates in the mission of the church but is providing significant leadership roles in building a caring parish-community and in the global church-community. The parish movement has clearly demonstrated its value and that its potential for the future is enormous.

Chapter Six

Common Ground for the Common Good

A Case Study of Church-State Partnership

Sr. Linda Yankoski
Holy Family Institute

Common Ground for the Common Good

A Case Study of Church-State Partnership

When President Bush established the White House Office of Faith-Based and Community Initiatives in 2001, many saw the move as a bold new approach to providing welfare services, despite the fact that government had given funding to religiously affiliated organizations for more than 100 years. This chapter provides an overview of federal funding for social services and an historical case study of the impact of government funding on the Catholic mission and identity of Holy Family Institute (HFI). Founded in 1900 by the Sisters of the Holy Family of Nazareth, HFI was originally an orphanage and an early pioneer in the Catholic social services movement. The institute served a need rooted in the industrial heritage of the Pittsburgh region. The earliest clients were children of Polish workers killed in industrial accidents and urban catastrophes. Over the past 110 years, the agency changed with the needs of the region's population. Today HFI is a fully accredited social services agency serving more than 6,000 children and families with an annual budget of approximately $32 million, with 78 percent deriving from government. Services include alternative and special education, in-home family counseling, and residential care for abused and neglected children. While the partnership with government resulted in the growth and professionalization of the organization, similar to secular social service organizations, this chapter describes how Holy Family Institute was able to maintain its Catholic identity and mission.

Providing charity to the poor and disadvantaged is a tenet of most religions and has prompted the founding of countless religious organizations designed for that purpose. These organizations have played an essential role in American social welfare history.[1] Many of the first schools, hospitals, and social service organizations in the United States were established under religious auspices. "At their founding and through their early lives, these church institutions were often controlled and almost always pervasively influenced by a . . . Christian understanding of human flourishing."[2] Catholic social service organizations were and are still among these institutions. In 2008, Catholic Charities USA reported that the Catholic Charities network of agencies served more than 8.5 million people (unduplicated) with approximately $3.9 billion in income, 67 percent of it coming from local, state, and federal governments.[3]

Historically, Catholic social service organizations were founded by religious orders of men and women to serve primarily (but not exclusively) a Catholic clientele. As the charitable organizations developed, they became more professional and aligned with the social work occupation. Many of these charities organizations became licensed. They participated in voluntary professional associations and adhered to professional regulations. Government funding caused these organizations to proliferate. Internal developments within Catholicism (changes resulting from Vatican II) and increased government funding occurred simultaneously and resulted in dramatic changes in Catholic social service organizations. As Cardinal Joseph Bernardin explained:

> Catholic colleges and universities, health care institutions, and social service agencies already live with one foot firmly planted in the Catholic Church and the other in our pluralistic society. It should come as no surprise, then, when the competing vision and value systems of the "tectonic" plates on which they stand are in tension with one another. The Fathers of the Second Vatican Council clearly pointed out that the Church has to pay closer attention to the fact that it exists in a modern world. It does not go to the world, as though it were a fully separate entity. The Church is a community of Jesus' disciples in the midst of the human family. At the same time the Council acknowledged there is a legitimate secularity in the political, social and economic orders.[4]

Most Catholic orphanages were created in the nineteenth century, as part of a movement to preserve the faith of poor Catholic immigrants marginalized in a predominantly Protestant country. As Dorothy Brown and Elizabeth McKeown state in their history of Catholic Charities, "From its inception American Catholic social provision was anchored in child-care."[5] The abundance of women and men in religious orders was one factor that allowed the Catholic Church to establish numerous institutions, including orphanages, hospitals, schools, and nursing homes. These women and men dedicated their lives to the church, and they staffed church-affiliated institutions. By the beginning of the twentieth century, more than 40,000 sisters worked in such institutions.[6] Another factor contributing to the growth of these institutions was the availability of government monies through grants, loans, and contracts.

In 1910, the National Conference of Catholic Charities was established by lay volunteers to help Catholic social workers adapt to the emerging social service profession and was the precursor to the consolidation of Catholic charitable works by diocesan bishops.[7] This consolidation resulted in new central bureaucracies of charity. These diocesan Catholic Charities agencies were initially administered by priests. Today, however, 80 to 90 percent of the diocesan charity organizations are led primarily by lay administrators.[8]

The Second Vatican Council (1962–65) had a profound impact on the church, its people, and its institutions. The council initiated a renewal and adaptation of vowed religious life; redefined the role of the laity, asserting that the apostolate comes from baptism and all are called to share and collaborate in the ministry; and reaffirmed the church's role in social justice.[9] On this premise, the church—through its various structures, organizations, and associations—is involved directly in the economic, political, and social action of the world. Religiously affiliated nonprofit corporations are one means by which the church fulfills its role of living the Gospel.[10]

The social, political, legal, religious, and economic environments within which Catholic nonprofit social service organizations operate have changed dramatically over the course of the past 100 years. The religious mission to serve the poor and needy has grown more complex. Enormous challenges have been imposed by declining numbers of sisters and clergy, involvement of the laity, professionalism, and competition from other organizations. Politicians, practitioners, and researchers are beginning to give significant attention to the impact of government funding on the religious mission of religiously affiliated social service organizations.[11]

The central problem facing religiously affiliated social service organizations is whether accepting government funding inherently leads to secularization. The identity of an organization cannot stand apart from the environment in which it exists. Certainly, changes in the environment will affect an organization's identity, conduct, and formal and informal processes.[12] "When public funds play so vital a role in private agency budgets, it is disingenuous to think that the nonprofit sector would not be in danger of losing its separate identity," state researchers Steven Smith and Michael Lipsky.[13]

To investigate these issues, and as a partial fulfillment of the require-ments for a doctoral degree, I undertook a historical case study covering the period from 1900 to 2002 to trace government funding and changes in the institutional identity, structure, and culture of Holy Family Institute (HFI), a Catholic social services organization in Pittsburgh, Pennsylvania.[14] The goal of this study was to answer these questions: (1) who defines the Catholic identity and mission of HFI, and how are such constructs measured? (2) what was the amount of government funding compared to other income sources? and (3) what were the effects of receiving govern-ment funding on the Catholic identity and mission of the organization?

Eras of Government Funding of the Nonprofit Sector

A review of the history of government funding of nonprofit organiza-tions demonstrates that nonprofit agencies, including religious organiza-tions, have contracted with government for the provision of social services for more than 100 years.

The Progressive Era, 1900–1930

According to Lester Salamon, secular and religious nonprofit organiza-tions utilized government funds to deliver education and social services in America even before the American Revolution.[15] For example, govern-ment funds supported Harvard and Yale universities, which were at one time Protestant religious institutions. The rationale was that religious educational institutions were serving a public purpose. Over time, many of these organizations became entirely secular.[16]

When large waves of immigrants moved to America at the turn of the twentieth century, government funding supported hospitals, and eventu-ally, private social service organizations. Unlike educational institutions and hospitals that received fees for service, private social service organiza-tions relied primarily on charitable contributions to provide services to the poor and needy. However, charitable contributions alone could not provide enough revenue to address the distress of all those who required assistance. This was the case even when organized charity drives, eventually known as United Way, were conducted on behalf of charitable organizations.[17]

As the twentieth century advanced, resource development for welfare became more organized in both the public and private sectors. As mentioned, in 1910, Catholic charity organizations established the National Conference of Catholic Charities. Its purpose, write Brown and McKeown, was to pro-mote information sharing among the many Catholic charitable institutions, and to "chart the developing relationships between Catholics and state and local governments."[18] Catholic Church leaders supported government funding of their church-sponsored social welfare efforts and worked through the National Conference of Catholic Charities to achieve such funding from the states. Coordinated community fundraising efforts, known as community chest campaigns, developed in earnest after World War I. The chests provided resources that enabled nonprofit organizations to expand.[19] Leading citizens coordinated these community-wide fundraising drives.

Public resources for the poor and needy during this period were limited to payments from local and state governments. By 1920, in spite of protests from critics who said that pensions to mothers would be too costly or would impoverish recipients, 40 states had established mothers' pension laws.[20] In addition to pensions, state and local governments provided per-diem payments or subsidies to institutions caring for neglected, dependent, and delinquent children—subsidies well below the cost of care. Governments expected the organizations to use charitable funds to make up the difference between subsidies and actual cost.

In studying state subsidies to charitable organizations throughout the United States at the beginning of the twentieth century, Frank Fetter discovered that "excepting possibly two territories and four western states, there is probably not a state in the union where some aid is not given either by the state or by counties and cities." Fetter reported that religious organizations were among the agencies that received public subsidies. He saw this as an erosion of American principles, primarily the principle of the separation of church and state. He believed that subsidies led to the corruption of government officials, weakened public institutions, created dependency among the poor, discouraged charitable giving, and fostered a lack of accountability. The issues Fetter raised foreshadowed modern concerns.[21]

The New Deal Era, 1930–1960

The Great Depression battered the lives of most Americans, and private charities did not have the resources to cope with the overwhelming need. As businesses failed and jobs were lost, private money became scarce. As Salamon reports, the New Deal changed the face of American welfare: "In establishing New Deal legislation in the 1930s, the federal government became involved in funding social services primarily by providing financial support to state and local governments to support their cash assistance programs."[22]

Leaders of Catholic charities were concerned that the government would take over what was fundamentally their role. Eventually, however, as the charity organizations were unable to care for the poor with charitable funds, Catholic charity leaders acquiesced. They endorsed the action of the federal government while insisting on a role in the new welfare arrangement. This role was based on the theory of subsidiarity as articulated by Pope Pius XI in his 1931 encyclical, *Quadragesimo Anno*. Subsidiarity meant that "nothing should be done by a higher and larger institution that cannot be done as well by a smaller and lower one."[23] The proponents of this philosophy attempted to maintain a role for local voluntary social agencies so that government would not assume all social and funding responsibilities.

By and large, New Deal initiatives were successful. President Roosevelt, bolstered by this achievement, worked for passage of the Social Security Act in 1935. The legislation mandated that state funds be used for the public administration of child welfare services. Many believed this provision threatened private agencies. "*Mandated* state participation in the financing of child-care programs would jeopardize the local funding of Catholic Charities in key states such as Pennsylvania, where the constitution prohibited the allocation of state funds to private institutions," write Brown and McKeown.[24] Eventually, language was added to the bill "that did not extend either state or federal control over private charitable institutions."[25] The matter of public payments to private institutions would therefore become a state-by-state political battle.

The enactment of New Deal legislation and the Social Security Act established the modern welfare state. Many of the services that were once the province of the nonprofit sector were now provided by government.[26] Up until that time, charitable nonprofit organizations had provided such services as health care, education, and shelter for orphans and the homeless. With the New Deal, services once considered *charity* were now considered the *rights* of the citizens of the modern welfare state. These rights, as Harold Wilensky defines them, consist of "government-protected minimum standards of income, nutrition, health, housing, and education for every citizen, assured to him as a political right, not as charity."[27]

Catholic social teaching echoes these rights in promoting the structuring of society to protect the dignity and rights of the human person, foster justice and limit or eliminate injustice, and encourage and promote the common good.[28] In the past, the voluntary sector was often described as separate from—and an alternative to—government. With the growth of government-sponsored services, these two groups began to intersect and interrelate, suggesting that the current paradigm of the separateness of the voluntary sector from government is no longer useful.

The Entitlement Era, 1960–1980

According to Marguerite Rosenthal, the major impetus to enlarge the nonprofit sector came during the 1960s, with the passage in 1962 and 1967 of amendments to the Social Security Act.[29] The 1962 amendment allowed federal participation in payment for services, allowing 75 percent reimbursement to the states; however, purchase-of-service contracts were limited to public agencies. Passage of the 1967 amendment to the Social Security Act expanded the ability of government to purchase the services of voluntary agencies, including religiously affiliated organizations. This expansion greatly enhanced resources to nonprofit organizations and enlarged the debate over whether such funding would weaken the voluntary sector. Critics were concerned that voluntary organizations would become quasi-governmental, lose their ability to advocate for the poor and vulnerable, be less flexible in developing needed services, and unable to maintain both their autonomy and distinct missions.[30] These concerns foreshadowed the development of federal agencies designed specifically to help church-related nonprofit organizations retain their identity and religious mission.[31]

Meeting the needs of the poor and vulnerable in America has resulted in public-private cooperation that includes not only direct grants and contracts from government agencies to nonprofit organizations, but also such mechanisms as third-party reimbursement, tax credits, and tax-exempt bonds. A consequence of these initiatives is less philanthropic support of the nonprofit sector, creating a spiral of greater reliance on sources of government revenues.[32]

The Retrenchment Era, 1980–1996

After five decades of unprecedented government expansion of welfare services, the 1980s saw a devolution and retrenchment of government support for welfare and an increased focus on private initiatives. Although the nonprofit sector was reduced overall, nonprofit organizations that participated in Medicaid actually saw their government funding grow. Indeed, many social services organizations realigned their services to fall into the health care market, so the organizations could participate in this funding stream.

However, most organizations in the nonprofit sector experienced considerable financial strain. Agencies were forced to turn to fee-for-service revenues and/or commercial activities. Many nonprofit organizations had to rely on increased charitable contributions to survive. Churches and other community groups were expected to be the safety net for the fallout from these policies. Although services were increased, religious organizations were in no position to fill all the service gaps that were created.

The Charitable Choice Era, 1996–Present

As the twentieth century came to a close, two initiatives—welfare reform and Charitable Choice—dominated the social welfare agenda. In

1996, Congress established the Personal Responsibility and Work Opportunity Reconciliation Act and abolished Aid to Families with Dependent Children, replacing the latter with Temporary Assistance to Needy Families. In this way, Congress dismantled programs that had provided cash assistance to poor families for more than 60 years.

The Personal Responsibility and Work Opportunity Reconciliation Act of 1996 included a provision for "Charitable Choice" (Section 104 of P.L. 104–93). Charitable Choice removes obstacles and facilitates the process that allows faith-based organizations (FBOs) to apply for government funds to provide public services. Applying for government funds puts FBOs in competition with secular providers. President George W. Bush established the Office of Faith-Based and Community Initiatives (OFCI) to (in part) assist in overcoming the perception that FBOs have to give up their religious identity if they accept government money.

Charitable Choice legislation allows FBOs to maintain their religious character. The law permits the display of religious art, symbols and texts, and the administration of personnel policies in accordance with religious beliefs. A section of Charitable Choice prohibits the use of federal funds for proselytization to guard against the use of public funds for exclusively religious activities.[33] Provisions permit the government to purchase services directly from the religious polity (a church, synagogue, or mosque). The initial legislation provided that religious groups did not have to form a secular corporation in order to establish a contractual relationship with the government. However, a subsequent amendment permits state governments to require FBOs to establish separate entities for providing government services.[34] The enactment of Charitable Choice has generated legal and policy debates related to religious coercion, free-speech rights, employment discrimination, the secularization and accountability of religious organizations, and church-state separation.

On February 5, 2009, President Barack Obama issued an executive order establishing the White House Office of Faith-Based and Neighborhood Partnerships, thus continuing the tradition of government partnership with faith-based organizations. On June 11, 2009, the Pew Forum on Religion and Public Life organized a symposium to discuss the preceding eight years of faith-based initiative under President Bush and to look ahead at challenges and opportunities for the new faith-based office.[35] The first questions posed to the director of the new White House office, Joshua Dubois, were about hiring people based on their faith tradition. Mr. Dubois indicated that the office would take a case-by-case approach to dealing with issues that arise about hiring practices.[36] While not much controversy has been reported in the press concerning President Obama's faith-based initiative, according to the Pew Forum, "policymakers and religious communities alike are still divided about the participation of faith-based organizations in the delivery of federally-funded social services."[37]

Impact of Government Funding and Institutional Theory

Recent studies of the nonprofit sector have focused on the difference between religious and secular organizations. The future of the nonprofit sector is of scholarly interest, primarily because the boundaries between public and private, nonprofit and profit, and religious and secular are becoming blurred.[38] Recent experiments in education reform—involving vouchers redeemable for education in secular, religious, or for-profit private schools—are but one example of the shifting lines of demarcation.[39] The evolution of government funding for private education is analogous to the development of government funding in the social service sector. The fear about blurred boundaries arises from the idea that nonprofit organizations could lose their distinctive character politically and legally, thus weakening society and democracy.[40]

Studies that specifically address the impact of government funding on the religious identity and mission of faith-based organizations have reached different conclusions. A number conclude that government-funded faith-based organizations have been able to maintain their religious identity and mission.[41] Others report that nonprofit faith-based organizations have lost their religious identity and mission and become like their secular counterparts.[42]

The theory of isomorphism suggests that a process of homogenization occurs between religious and secular organizations, as they interrelate over time in the same field and become increasingly alike.[43] Thus, religious organizations relating to professional, government, and nonreligious organizations would become more secular. Scott Cormode presented the case of churches imitating secular society; in particular, Protestant churches' establishment of fraternal lodges, women's associations, and institutional church activities (such as boys and girls clubs, day nurseries, and recreational activities).[44] The churches instituted these groups and activities to attract new members and adjust to the prevailing social forces of the nineteenth century. Eventually, many of these associations became entirely secular.

Similarly, the Catholic Church developed clubs and societies as part of parish life. These organizations were often fashioned around prayerful devotions and became a dominant force in Catholic life, especially for immigrants. As in Protestant churches, the influence of secular society encouraged the development of fraternal lodges. The Knights of Columbus, for example, is an organization that could eventually be found in every state of the union.

In contrasting the emergence of clubs and societies in the Protestant and Catholic churches, Cormode suggests that the Protestants "brought secular attractions to the church without converting them to religious ends," whereas the Catholics "adopted secular means but gave them religious ends."[45] He went on to suggest that the development of Catholic social groups, in which members participated in prayers and rituals that were at the heart of Catholicism, "reveal[s] the sacralizing possibilities of institutional isomorphism."[46] What an organization does with the forms it borrows and mimics from other organizations must be added to the debate about secularization.

The distinction between religious and secular has been an important element in the ongoing debate over government funding of FBOs. At the center of this debate are two issues: the separation of church and state and the belief by some that religious organizations that accept government funding have to surrender or dilute their religious identity, autonomy, and culture.[47]

According to Sheila Kennedy, a lawyer and social science researcher, the "interchangeability of 'religious,' 'sectarian,' and 'faith-based' as descriptive terms" confuses the secular-religious debate in terms of the legal and social science points of view. Kennedy continued: "There has been and is, however, enormous variation among the entities so labeled, and certain of those variations are both constitutionally significant and politically relevant to the passage of Charitable Choice."[48]

The questions of how to define faith and religion in the context of a religious social service agency such as Holy Family Institute, and who should define them, remain important and only recently have become the subject of research.[49]

Case Study of Holy Family Institute

The Holy Family Institute case study investigated the impact of government funding on the Catholic identity and mission of the organization over the course of 102 years, from 1900 to 2002. The study utilized a historical perspective and in-depth case-study methodology. The basis of this approach is the institutional model of organizational theory. The study traced the organizational structure, processes, and culture of HFI over time to discover the impact of government funding on the organization's Catholic identity and mission.

Organizational theory defines the processes that affect the culture of organizations, their belief systems, and values.[50] According to institutional theory and the process of isomorphism, some organizations are powerless to resist pressures from dominant organizational fields. For example, religious organizations whose field includes significant government funding are subject to the powerful forces of government agencies. In response, religious organizations become like government agencies or secular organizations in the social welfare field. This process of homogenization (becoming more similar to others) is called isomorphism. The HFI study demonstrated that homogenization in all aspects of organizational life is not inevitable.

Catholic identity and mission, for a Catholic social services organization, is governed by legitimate authority in the Catholic Church. To answer the research questions—(1) who defines the Catholic identity and mission of HFI, and how are such constructs measured? (2) what was the amount of government funding compared to other income sources? and (3) what were the effects of receiving government funding on the Catholic identity and mission?—I conducted document reviews of board minutes, audits, and government and United Way reports.

To learn about religious practices, values, and culture, I interviewed alumni whose aggregated period of residence at HFI was 1919–99. I also administered a questionnaire to board members and administrators in order to ascertain their view of Catholic identity and mission at the institute. In addition, I measured HFI's Catholic identity and mission by applying faith-based typologies to the data.

Establishment and Changes

Based on the institutional theory and the process of isomorphism, the various attachments and interactions an organization has with religious authority are reflections of its link to faith.[51] Holy Family Institute is related to the Sisters of the Holy Family of Nazareth, a separate organization.[52] According to canon law, once a religious order of women or men establishes a house in the diocese, it has the right to pursue its works and to own and acquire the means to do so. Religious orders are subject to the bishop in matters of doctrine and faith, but not in internal governance or works. "Each religious institute has its own charism (the specific spirit and character of the congregation). This charism is the gift of the Holy Spirit, who inspired those who founded various institutes."[53] Religious orders enjoy a great deal of autonomy in establishing apostolic works according to their own individual charism.

The First Constitutions of the Congregation of the Sisters of the Holy Family of Nazareth state that one of the primary purposes of the congregation is to "take care of the orphans, the poor and the sick, and for the love of Jesus assist them according to its means either through the Sisters or through others."[54] It is not surprising, then, that the Sisters of the Holy Family of Nazareth established an orphanage, thereby providing a family to those who have none.

The Sisters of the Holy Family of Nazareth began their apostolic service in Pittsburgh in 1895, teaching at the school of St. Stanislaus Kostka Parish. The church was, and still is, on Smallman Street in the Strip District. The bishop of the Diocese of Pittsburgh had entrusted the parish to the Congregation of the Holy Ghost, a religious order of men whose charge was to minister to Polish immigrants. Given the enormous needs of the Polish Catholic community in the parish and encouragement from the Holy Ghost Fathers, the sisters began providing housing for orphans. To this end, Mother Lauretta Lubowidzka, the American provincial (the order's leader in America), negotiated an interest-free loan of $9,000 from St. Stanislaus Church. She used it to purchase a house and land a few miles from Pittsburgh, which eventually served as the orphanage.[55]

On May 29, 1903, the Sisters of the Holy Family of Nazareth were incorporated. They named a board of directors to handle the legal affairs related to the purchase and transfer of land for the orphanage. According to Melanie DiPietro, a Sister of Charity who holds both a law degree and a doctorate in canon law, this move was not unusual.[56] In the early 1900s, congregations of religious women often conducted the affairs of the apostolate through the order's corporation. In November 1904, Fr. Caesar Tomaszewski, along with six laymen, incorporated the orphanage with the Commonwealth of Pennsylvania so that the institution could obtain state appropriations.[57] In other words, the property was titled to one corporation and a new operating corporation, the Holy Family Orphan Asylum, was created to obtain state funding.

The "purpose" clause in the 1904 articles of incorporation is very broad for an organization that cared primarily for Polish Catholic children who were referred mostly from Catholic parishes. In fact, the articles do not mention any religious purpose. The only religious suggestion, other than the biblical mandate to care for the orphan (James 1:27), is in the name of the organization.

1. The name of the Corporation is "The Orphan Asylum of the Holy Family."

2. The purpose for which the corporation is formed is the establishment of and maintenance of an Asylum for destitute orphaned children, without regard to race, nationality or religious belief, wherein such orphans may receive without charge, such care,

nurture and education as is designed not only to ameliorate their present condition, but also to fit them to become, in their maturity, patriotic useful citizens of this Commonwealth and of the United States. [58]

The sisters established the philosophy and mode of operation for the orphanage by stipulating that the rule of the Congregation of the Sisters of the Holy Family of Nazareth was paramount. [59]

Two issues are noteworthy in regard to the first five years of Holy Family's history. Both relate to the incorporation of the apostolate, initially by the Sisters of the Holy Family of Nazareth, and then by Fr. Tomaszewski and the six laymen. These acts confirmed the existence of the orphan asylum as a nonprofit charitable corporation in the eyes of the state. The incorporation by Fr. Tomaszewski and the laymen is significant because it placed the orphanage outside the legal control of either religious order, a situation that was not remedied until 39 years later.

Corporate Restructuring

On May 27, 1943, the Orphan Asylum of the Holy Family amended its charter, changing its name to Holy Family Institute. The corporation board confirmed the appointment through election. [60] In 1953, HFI directors resolved to transfer all the property to the Sisters of the Holy Family of Nazareth of Western Pennsylvania. [61] The lay board adopted new bylaws that made 15 members of the Sisters of the Holy Family of Nazareth the directors of the corporation. The new bylaws also created the Advisory Board, consisting of 12 lay members (the former Board of Directors). The restructuring gave the Sisters of the Holy Family of Nazareth ownership of the property, as well as full governance and management authority in the corporation.

After the Second Vatican Council (1962–65), the Catholic Church experienced tremendous change, including revitalization. "This Council . . . provided a theological framework for interpreting the Church's understanding of itself and its relationship with the modern world." [62] Catholic identity changed greatly, as did the identity of Catholic-related organizations. Religious orders reexamined their organizations' founding and specific missions in the church, laity assumed a larger role within the church and its institutions, and the church encouraged a more collegial style of decision making.

Among the revisions at HFI was change in the personnel base at all levels. The institute, originally staffed by Sisters of the Holy Family of Nazareth, came to employ laypeople. Staff members could be members of the Catholic Church, members of other Christian denominations, members of other religions, or have no religious affiliation. Personnel changes necessitated new structures between sponsors, board, and staff members.

These civil legal structures had to conform to canonical requirements. As a result, the incorporation of HFI (and any Catholic organization) was more complex than that of a secular nonprofit organization. The incorporation of HFI necessitated the articulation, codification, and dissemination of Catholic moral values and traditions. A Catholic identity and mission had been assumed by the original incorporators. Therefore, Catholic identity and mission had to be promoted later among board members and staff.

A 1983 revision of canon law prompted many religious orders to reexamine their organizational structures. Work by DiPietro, Cardinal Adam Maida, Nicholas Cafardi, and Elizabeth McDonough encouraged religious orders to limit membership in their corporations to the major superior and council of the religious order.[63] In 1986, HFI reorganized the Holy Family Institute Corporation. Governance changed so that only the provincial superior and her council, rather than all perpetually professed sisters in the province, served as members of the corporation with reserved powers. The professed sisters within the congregation were eligible to serve on the Board of Directors. By 1988, the Advisory Board's lay members were invited to serve on the Board of Directors.

The Sisters of the Holy Family of Nazareth subsequently amended HFI's articles of incorporation to include a statement of purpose that better reflected the institution's public-benefit services and religious identity. Amended bylaws, also adopted in 1988, included a preamble describing the organization's relationship to the Sisters of the Holy Family of Nazareth and to the Catholic Church:

> The Holy Family Institute is Catholic in origin and philosophy. This corporation shall be managed and operated (by the Members and Trustees) in accordance with the teachings, tradition, theology and Canon Law of the Roman Catholic Church. This corporation adopts as its own the traditions and charism of the Congregation of the Sisters of the Holy Family of Nazareth.[64]

Staffing and Mission Education

In the early 1980s, the leaders of the Sisters of the Holy Family of Nazareth recognized that, because of the dwindling number of new members in America, fewer sisters would be available to work at HFI as the century progressed. This realization led to the creation of a new position at HFI titled director of sponsorship. The title later became director for mission effectiveness. The main responsibility of the person in this position was to ensure the fulfillment of HFI's mission and philosophy, in the tradition of the Sisters of the Holy Family of Nazareth. A process to review and revise the mission statement to better reflect the organization's Catholic identity was created, and an ongoing educational program for all staff and board members was developed. Program topics included HFI's history, the Catholic Church, the sisters, and the sisters' charism, defined as *a particular concern for families.* A member of the Sisters of the Holy Family of Nazareth filled this position until 1990. At that point, HFI's executive director decided that all HFI administrators should share the responsibility of maintaining the institution's Catholic identity and mission. A "mission" program was designed for this purpose and was to be administered by all supervisors in the organization.

Another change was the shift to lay staffing. In 1984, a layperson became spiritual development director for the first time. The spiritual development program, then and now, meets the ecumenical needs of the children and youth in residence. Children and youth participate in Bible studies and retreats. Visiting youth groups from Catholic and Protestant churches provide regular social activities that include religious prayer. The Spiritual Development Director conducts weekly prayer services for staff.

As a function of the mission program, administrators reviewed services, policies, and processes to determine how well they reflected the "family perspective" essential to the institute's Catholic identity and mission. On the basis of this review, HFI restructured employee health benefits to include health plans for families. Outreach to the families of youth in the residential program intensified. In 1987, the agency started the first in-home family-preservation program in Allegheny County.

From the 1980s onward, mission meetings have emphasized the development of organizational culture and making managerial and governance decisions in accordance with Gospel values. The meetings encourage supervisors to recognize staff members for professional accomplishments and contributions to the organization's culture and to celebrate as a community. As another reflection of HFI's Catholic identity, all new staff members are invited to be commissioned at a ceremony conducted in the chapel, and some staff members gather routinely in the chapel for support and prayer, to celebrate a new birth, or to mourn the loss of a family member or friend.

Sources and Amounts of Revenue

The government paid HFI for its care of children as early as 1910. Government entities that purchased services included Allegheny County

Juvenile Court and the City of Pittsburgh. In 1935, Allegheny County purchased services directly rather than through the county court system.[65] By the 1960s, passage of the Social Security Act increased the availability of county grants and contracts because the act allowed the federal government to provide welfare funds to states. In Pennsylvania, the state gave the funds, through contracts and grants, to the counties. The counties allocated payments to individual agencies.

Table 1 presents HFI's sources of revenues, by percentage, during each of the eras described earlier in this chapter.

Table 1. HFI's Revenue Sources, by Era and Percentage.

Period	Era	Revenue Received by Percentage of Total				
		Charity	Church	Government	United Way	Other
1900–1929	Progressive	53.0	12.2	14.3	3.1	17.4
1930–1959	New Deal	5.5	7.1	31.6	39.8	16.0
1960–1979	Entitlement	2.8	8.6	72.9	11.7	4.1
1980–1994	Retrenchment	7.5	0.4	82.7	3.6	5.8
1995–2002	Charitable Choice	9.9	0.6	77.0	2.1	10.3

At HFI, revenues from government grants and contracts increased dramatically from 1960–79. Revenue from these contracts doubled—in some cases, quadrupled—every five years.[66] By 2002, 80 percent of HFI's $26 million annual budget was from purchase-of-service contracts with government entities or fees from public school districts.[67] And in the fiscal year ending June 30, 2009, government funding comprised 78 percent of the organization's $32 million annual budget.

With few exceptions, the amount of financial support from the Catholic Church, as a percentage of all revenue, has been relatively low compared to monies from all other sources.[68] During the New Deal Era, the amount of revenue from government sources doubled from what it had been during the Progressive Era. During the Entitlement Era, it doubled again. During the years of federal government retrenchment, institute revenue from local and state government was at its peak, 83 percent of total revenue. Salamon notes that, in 1980, a federal tax cut resulted in a 13 percent drop in revenue for social welfare.[69] Nevertheless, Holy Family Institute's government support grew dramatically in this period.

The survey Salamon conducted of nonprofit organizations shows that institutional and residential care organizations experienced a 4 percent growth in government funds during the 1980s. He suggests that this was a result of the continued growth of the federal Medicaid program.[70] While Holy Family Institute received very little Medicaid revenue in the 1980s, the organization did expand the variety of programs and services, which resulted in diversified funding. Fees from school districts, an indirect form of government funding, and new government contracts funded the new offerings.

As government funds increased, funds from the United Way and church sources decreased. During the 1980s, charitable contributions were 4.7 percent higher than they were in the previous era as a result of capital campaign fundraising. At the beginning of the Charitable Choice era, Holy Family Institute conducted another campaign to increase the agency's endowment and decrease reliance on government funding.

Alumni Interviews

My HFI study included 33 interviews with 17 men and 16 women who had lived at Holy Family Institute at some time between 1919 and 1998. The alumni helped me to construct a picture of daily activities at HFI during various decades.

In HFI's first 60 years, activities began early in the day, with the celebration of Mass. Only then did everyone eat breakfast. Chores followed, as did the learning activities that eventually became organized Catholic schooling. Each day was infused with prayers, and many days included additional prayer activities: processions, benedictions, and novenas to commemorate saints' feast days. All direct care staff members were from the order of the Sisters of the Holy Family of Nazareth. The superintendent was a sister, or a Holy Ghost or diocesan priest. This routine of life, with many overt symbols of the Catholic religion, was remarkably stable until 1960.

From that point, and as the staff consisted of a gradually fewer number of religious sisters, HFI's Catholic identity was not as apparent. In answering a question about HFI's name, one alumnus replied, "Holy Family? It's a Catholic institute, right?" Another replied, "From what I understand, back then . . . it was run by nuns . . . and they took in orphans. That's why. . . . Because the nuns, they're a holy family."

Alumni from after the 1960s more often spoke of the voluntary nature of the religious activities. They remarked that, generally, most of the youth wanted to take part. Almost all the alumni reported that exposure to religion was a source of comfort and values. Participation helped them to learn right from wrong and develop conscience, decency, and a sense of direction. Some alumni, who were in residence before the 1960s, complained that their involvement in religious practices was "overkill" (excessive).

Almost all the alumni reported that the religious exposure at Holy Family Institute had had a positive impact on them, their relationships, and their current religious practice. Most alumni reported continued participation in organized religion, although the religion in which they chose to participate was not always the religion of their childhood.

Most alumni who lived on campus before the mid-1960s remarked that funds for the institution came from residents' family members or from the "begging" that the sisters did in the community. Most were unaware of government funding. Beginning with alumni from the 1930s, most were aware of funding from the United Way or its precursors (the Red Feather organizations or the community chest). Alumni from the period after the mid-1960s mentioned funding from government agencies, such as Juvenile Court, but hardly ever mentioned payment from family members.

Board Members and Administrators Surveys

As part of this study, I developed a survey to assess board members' and administrators' perceptions of the Catholic identity and mission of Holy Family Institute. Conducted in 2002, the survey was based upon three central sources of organizational action: authority, resource dependency, and culture.[71] Overall, the responses from the survey revealed that Holy Family Institute was tied to its Catholic identity and mission in all three dimensions. The weakest tie related to resource dependency. Findings indicated that Holy Family Institute was more closely tied to secular sources of funding than to religious sources.

In general, board members and administrators agreed: HFI's name was explicitly religious, the name was central to the purpose, the institute was presented to the public as a religious organization, and it was governed by a religious entity. They were also in agreement in believing that the religious identity of Holy Family Institute had both advantages and disadvantages. Finally, they agreed that the mission statement was explicitly religious and that the public persona of Holy Family Institute was religious.

Most respondents granted that HFI's financial resources did not come from religious organizations, and only some funding came from religious individuals. They also agreed that nonreligious organizations made referrals to HFI. However, their responses suggested that although Holy Family Institute was closely tied to secular sources for financial funding, the organization received moral resources and enjoyed partnerships with religious institutions that helped HFI maintain a significant religious character.

Board members and administrators agreed that they had religious convictions as individuals, and these groups believed that their colleagues had religious convictions. Having a religious conviction was not a work requirement, but was essential to achieving the goals of the organization. Respondents believed that services to clients were provided in a personal manner and were individualized. The respondents indicated that religious activities for clients were voluntary rather than mandatory. There was a consensus of opinion in board members' and administrators' perceptions of the religiousness of key organizational dimensions related to the culture of the organization. In spite of the variety of sources of funding, Holy Family Institute had maintained its Catholic identity and mission.

Analysis of HFI's Religious Identity

To quantify religious identity and expression at HFI, I applied a scoring system related to four generic typologies that became popular with the advent of Charitable Choice. The scoring system rated organizations along a continuum from "faith saturated" (highly religious) to secular. The typologies were those created by Robert Benne, Thomas Jeavons, Stephen Monsma, and the Working Group on Human Needs and Faith-Based and Community Initiatives.[72]

According to all four typologies, prior to 1965 HFI scored as a *highly* religious, faith-saturated, orthodox institution. The typologies attribute high religiosity to an agency that:

- Hires staff according to the agency's faith commitment

- Serves clients whose religious affiliation matches that of the agency

- Makes religious activities mandatory

- Draws resources primarily from people or organizations that share its faith

The typology scores relating to the second period (1965–2002) dropped an average of 30 percent, placing HFI in the range of a *moderately* religious faith-related organization. However, the alumni interviews, and the board and administrator survey relating to the same period, told a different story. The responses testified to a continuously strong religious character. The key to understanding this paradox is to realize that the generic faith-based typologies presuppose homogeneity among American religious organizations.[73]

After 1964, the theological and social teaching of the Roman Catholic Church emphasized the need to increase ecumenical sensitivity in hiring and program outreach and to respect religious diversity and freedom. Because HFI followed this teaching, HFI lost points for religiosity, according to the generic typologies. HFI does not require staff to be Catholic and HFI's charter requires the agency to serve children without respect to religion. HFI lost more points because it does not require clients to participate in religious activities. The only way to measure an organization's religious identity is to develop a typology to define the religious nature of an organization that is based on its own theological distinction and meanings.[74]

A New Yardstick of Religious Identity

The generic typologies proved to be an unreliable means of measuring HFI's religious character because they were not specific to the religious affiliation of the agency being assessed. With the goal of offering a means to analyze the religious character of a Catholic organization, I created the Catholic Typology for Social Service Organizations (CTSSO). The CTSSO assesses religiosity according to 14 criteria that relate to authority, culture, and resources *as Catholicism defines them.*

A Catholic typology begins with an understanding of Catholic social thought. Contemporary Catholic social thought began in 1891, with the social encyclical of Pope Leo XIII, *Rerum Novarum.* This work was the first of the church's pronouncements on the social conditions of the time. The papal encyclicals and statements from the conferences of bishops reflect the foundational principles that guide Catholic social service organizations:

> *The permanent principles of the Church's social doctrine constitute the very heart of Catholic social teaching.* These are the principles of: *the dignity of the human person,* . . . which is the foundation of all the other principles and content of the Church's social doctrine; *the common good; subsidiarity;* and *solidarity.* These principles, the expression of the whole truth about man known by reason and faith, are born of "the encounter of the Gospel message and of its demands summarized in the supreme commandment of love of God and neighbour in justice with the problems emanating from the life of society."[75]

In developing the CTSSO, I also considered the work of Bernardin, DiPietro, Charles Fahey, and John Tropman.[76] The CTSSO reflects the main dimensions of the institutional model: authority, resources, and culture.

In the category of authority, items essential to a Catholic typology for social services organizations include a formal connection to the appropriate canonical entity, faithfulness to the teachings of the church, and public recognition by the local bishop.

Essential characteristics for the management of resources are accepting monies from multiple sources (including government), seeking participation and assistance from other members of the Catholic community, and adopting managerial polices and practices that achieve the just and equitable allocation of the organization's financial resources. These resources relate to employee compensation, methods of accountability, and care of material resources and the environment. The resource dimension in the Catholic typology differs from that of the generic typologies in its emphasis on *resource management*, rather than *resource dependency*.

Within the dimension of culture, essential items for a Catholic social service organization would include a critical mass of board members and administrators who intellectually and experientially understand the organization's Catholic identity and culture; application of the principle of subsidiarity in decision making; professional competency of employees and employees' commitment to working within the parameters of the religious mission and identity of the organization; services that are individualized, holistic, and respectful of dignity; a friendly environment that welcomes all and includes signs and symbols of religious identity where appropriate; a consistent expression, in oral and written communication at all levels of the organization, of Catholic identity and values; and actions that advocate a justly structured society and work to remove barriers and reform social structures that inhibit people from realizing their human and moral dignity.

If a quantitative rating system was applied to these elements of the CTSSO typology, HFI would likely score as a highly religious organization.

Conclusion

Government-religious cooperation started long before the Charitable Choice initiatives, and it will likely continue into the future. Similarly, the debate about the propriety of such cooperation has existed since government began providing monies to support citizens in need of social services. At issue is nothing less than the separation of church and state and the integrity of religious organizations that serve to protect religious values and relationships in society.

Secularization is not an inevitable consequence of government funding for Catholic social service organizations. Although its expression has evolved over the century, Catholic identity and mission at Holy Family Institute has remained intact; HFI did not substantively dilute its religious identity or mission by entering into contracts with government entities.[77] Government monies helped HFI increase the number and variety of its programs, and participation in government contracts accelerated the pace of professionalism at the institute.

In spite of the evidence that demonstrates the continuing Catholic identity and mission of Holy Family Institute, it would be naïve to conclude that the organization is immune to the forces that have led to the secularization of many social services agencies, colleges, and universities. Caring for and maintaining the mission—the soul of the organization—requires conscious commitment and work. The Sisters of the Holy Family of Nazareth have been astute in their decisions to maintain the proper canonical authority for governance of the institution and establishing a mission effectiveness and integration program.

However, the theory underlying this study suggests that the process of isomorphism that helped Holy Family Institute maintain its Catholic identity and mission can also work against it. Maintaining balance in Holy Family Institute's organizational field requires a conscious commitment to religious values, principles, and ethos, and the ability to manage competing accountability systems.

Government mandates that do not protect religious perspectives could undermine Holy Family Institute's cooperation with government to address social problems. Such mandates could undermine any other faith-based organization's cooperation with government just as easily. Government agencies have the right and responsibility to establish criteria for the delivery of social services, and they should establish them. These criteria should be applied, in a neutral fashion, to all organizations.

The HFI study revealed that government funding imposed accountability systems on Holy Family Institute, which were willingly accepted. Indeed, *any* source that supplies funds generally requires some level of accountability. Individual donors and foundations often place restrictions on their contributions and require an accounting to reveal how funds have been spent. The tensions that arise from continually meeting these standards would exist with or without government funding—and may or may not affect religious ethos. If and how government funding will affect ethos is a determination that each faith-based organization must make according to the particular requirements of that organization's faith tradition. Maintaining religious identity—and the highest degree of professional responsibility—requires close attention and strong commitment.

Caution in using generic typologies to define the religious character of any religious organization is due. Religious culture and belief and its meaning cannot be defined by arbitrary external yardsticks. Instead, institutional religious identity should be a matter of self-definition. When viewed organically and internally, an organization's religious identity and mission may be unaffected by the reporting requirements of either government or private funding agencies, even though the delivery of services conforms to professional norms. Accountability to religious authority and state mandates may not always be compatible—nor should they be. As author Stephen Carter notes, "It is vital that the religions struggle to maintain the tension between the meanings and understanding propounded by the state and the very different set of meanings and understandings that the contemplation of the ultimate frequently suggests."[78]

Accepting money from secular sources need not adversely affect the soul of any institution, religious or otherwise. While focused on the historical relationship of one particular faith-based institution and government funding, the HFI study was intended to raise awareness of the interstices of religious institutions and government funding. Much room remains for discussion, debate, and new public policy. Public policy that encourages cooperation between government and religious organizations can be an important tool to help meet the needs of the vulnerable in society, with the intention that the legitimate exercise of religious freedom is fostered and not hindered for the institution and those it is meant to serve.

Chapter
Seven

Putting Justice and Charity into Action

Empowerment for God's People

Rev. Msgr. Robert J. Vitillo
Caritas Internationalis

Putting Justice and Charity into Action

Empowerment for God's People

A simple dictionary or internet search engine survey of the term "empowerment" reveals a wide range of usage, from its earliest appearance in seventeenth-century English language to denote "investing with authority," to its more modern link to the Civil Rights movement and its employment across a broad spectrum of political, economic, and social ideologies. During preparations for its Vision 2000 initiative, Catholic Charities USA convened a group of stakeholders from its own membership, from the Catholic Campaign for Human Development, and from several community organizing networks, and mandated them to discern an appropriate meaning and application of this term within the Catholic Charities movement. As a former member of the task group, I can attest to the serious reflection and debate that transpired as we arrived at the following definition:

> Empowerment is a process of engagement that increases the ability of individuals, families, organizations, and communities to build mutually respectful relationships and bring about fundamental positive change in the conditions affecting their daily lives.[1]

Empowerment—Concepts and Actions as Described in the Word of God

If we scroll back through the pages of salvation history, we will find, at least in the opinion of this writer, that our ancestors in the faith—the patriarchs, the prophets, Jesus himself, the apostles, and the earliest members of the Christian community—possessed a firm and clear understanding of empowerment in the life of God's people, even if they did not name this term as such.

From the earliest books of the Old Testament, we learn of God's special care for the poor. The Jewish people did not restrict their understanding of God's love for the poor and powerless merely in a passive manner. They had direct proof and experience of their own ability to empower themselves. Through God's grace, Abraham and Sarah were empowered to convert their previously barren marital union into a fruitful one that gave birth to the people with whom God chose to establish his particular covenant (Genesis 15–17).

So, too, the Exodus story of Israel's liberation from slavery in Egypt was—and continues to be—recounted and reenacted by faithful Jews each year. Thus the Jewish people preserved the memory that, with God's grace and strength bestowed on the once-timid Moses, they were able to walk out of the stranglehold placed upon them by Pharaoh and begin their sweet but arduous journey toward the Promised Land (Exodus 1–40).

This same theme of both personal and community empowerment remained dominant throughout the remainder of the Old Testament. The prophet Isaiah, for example, told of God's direct promise that the cries of the poor would not be uttered in vain: "The afflicted and the needy seek water in vain, their tongues are parched with thirst. I, the Lord, will answer them; I, the God of Israel, will not forsake them" (Isaiah 41:17).

Isaiah also insists on God's desire for all people to be engaged in the empowerment of the poor and marginalized, through works of both justice and charity:

> Is this the manner of fasting I wish . . . That a man bow his head
> like a reed, and lie in sackcloth and ashes? . . . This, rather, is the
> fasting that I wish: releasing those bound unjustly, untying the
> thongs of the yoke; Setting free the oppressed, breaking every yoke;
> Sharing your bread with the hungry, sheltering the oppressed and
> the homeless; Clothing the naked when you see them, and not
> turning your back on your own. (Isaiah 58:5-7)

When God called Jeremiah to serve as his "prophet to the nations," the young man protested. "I know not how to speak; I am too young." Once again, the Almighty One inspired confidence and power in his appointee:

> Have no fear before them, because I am with you to deliver you,
> says the LORD. . . . See, I place my words in your mouth! This

day I set you over nations and over kingdoms, to root up and
to tear down, to destroy and to demolish, to build and to plant.
(Jeremiah 1:5-10)

Despite the confidence placed on his lips by the God who called him, this
prophet never was able to live out his vocation in a comfortable manner.
The people, with whom he pleaded to reform their ways and deeds and
to deal justly with their neighbors (Jeremiah 7:5), stubbornly refused to
heed God's request, to the point that God commanded Jeremiah: "You,
now, do not intercede for this people; raise not in their behalf a pleading
prayer! Do not urge me, for I will not listen to you" (Jeremiah 7:16). Yet
the prophet felt so empowered in his calling that he dared to prevail upon
the Lord: "Punish us, O Lord, but with equity, not in anger, lest you have
us dwindle away" (Jeremiah 10:24).

Luke the Evangelist tells us that Mary, even before the birth of the
Messiah and despite her sensitive condition as a single, unmarried woman
in a culture that attached little recognition to such status, empowered herself through her *fiat* expressed to the angel: "Behold, I am the handmaid
of the Lord. May it be done to me according to your word" (Luke 1:38).
Subsequently, in Mary's emotional response to the greeting of her cousin
Elizabeth, "And how does this happen to me, that the mother of my Lord
should come to me?" (Luke 1:43), Mary linked her own empowerment
with that made possible by God for all his people, especially for those
most in need, through the long-awaited birth of his son, whom she was
privileged to carry in her womb:

> My soul proclaims the greatness of the Lord; my spirit rejoices in
> God my savior. For he has looked upon his handmaid's lowliness;
> behold, from now on will all ages call me blessed. The Mighty One
> has done great things for me, and holy is his name. His mercy is
> from age to age to those who fear him. He has shown might with
> his arm, dispersed the arrogant of mind and heart. He has thrown
> down the rulers from their thrones but lifted up the lowly. The
> hungry he has filled with good things; the rich he has sent away
> empty. (Luke 1:46-53)

Again it was Luke who told us that Jesus initiated his public ministry
by proclaiming the same empowerment text already quoted from the
prophet Isaiah (Luke 4:18-19), thus eliminating any possible doubt that
Jesus' might have been a message to maintain the status quo for the rich
and powerful oppressors of the poor and vulnerable, who always were
granted priority attention within God's covenant with the Jewish people.

Jesus put into everyday action God's word spoken through the prophet Isaiah. He befriended those who were considered outcast by contemporary Jewish society. He called a tax collector, Matthew, into his inner circle of apostles (Matthew 9:9) and asked another, Zacchaeus, for a dinner invitation (Luke 19:1-10), despite the fact that respectable Jews at that time considered those engaged in such work on behalf of the Roman Empire to be traitors to their own people. He reassured the sick and disabled that neither their own sins, nor those of their parents, had caused their health problems and then called on them to wash away their scales of leprosy, to recover their vision, and to take up their mats and walk (John 9:24-34; Mark 1:14-45; Matthew 21:14-15, et al.). He treated women with more respect than usually accorded them by prevailing social and cultural norms, listened and responded to their questions about God's reign (John 4:7-10; Luke 11:38, et al.), touched and was touched by women seeking to be healed (Mark 5:21-43), was moved to action in response to Martha's affirmation that his presence may have prevented the death of her brother Lazarus (John 11:1-44), allowed Mary to wash his feet with her tears and to anoint them with precious oils (John 12:1-8), and chose to reveal himself in his risen state to the women who had remained faithful during his final agony and death (John 20:11-18; Luke 16:1-8).

While firmly admonishing his followers to respect and abide by the law, Jesus did not hesitate to challenge those who made inequitable demands on or abused others by invoking the false premise of applying the law. Thus he overturned the tables of the money changers in the temple who were taking advantage of poor pilgrims deprived of access to the special currency reserved for purchase of sacrificial animals within the confines of the temple (Matthew 21:12-13). He set aside the proscription of work on the Sabbath when his followers had need of food (Mark 2:23-28) and when those seeking his help begged to be healed of their infirmities (Luke 13:10; John 9:13, et al.). He challenged those plotting to kill him that if they destroyed the "temple" of his body, it would be "re-built" in three days (John 2:19).

Yet, despite these words and deeds of empowerment with regard to both himself and others, Jesus gave his apostles the example of washing their feet and told them to do the same with those whom they would teach and over whom they would exercise authority, because "no slave is greater than his master nor any messenger greater than the one who sent him. If you understand this, blessed are you if you do it" (John 13:1-17).

Moreover, he set limits on his followers when they attempted to chase away little children brought by their mothers to be touched by him (Luke 15–17). He reprimanded Peter for using force against the slave of the high priest at the time of his arrest (John 18:10-11). After the resurrection,

Jesus appeared to his followers, not with the vestige of an earthly king as they continued to expect and as can be seen by their question, "Lord, are you at this time going to restore the kingdom to Israel?" (Acts 1:6). He encouraged them to understand, to the contrary, that true empowerment lay in preaching the remission of sins to all the nations (Luke 24:46) and promised them that those who professed the faith and preached the good news would be able to expel demons, speak entirely new languages, handle serpents, be able to drink deadly poison without harm, and heal the sick through the imposition of hands (Luke 16:15-20).

Indeed that vision prophesied by Jesus became a reality at the feast of Pentecost: "And they were all filled with the holy Spirit and began to speak in different tongues, as the Spirit enabled them to proclaim" (Acts 2:4).

The boldness of the apostles extended far beyond words and included many cures, such as that of the man "crippled from birth" who approached Peter and John to ask for alms but received instead the ability to walk: "Peter said, 'I have neither silver nor gold, but what I do have I give you: in the name of Jesus Christ the Nazorean, walk'" (Acts 3:1-10).

This behavior of the apostles did not escape notice by those who formerly felt threatened by Jesus and now demanded explanation from the leaders of the newly emerging church: "Observing the boldness of Peter and John and perceiving them to be uneducated, ordinary men, they were amazed" (Acts 4:13).

For others, however, the empowerment demonstrated by the apostles attracted profession of faith and conversion of life:

> With great power the apostles bore witness to the resurrection of the Lord Jesus, and great favor was accorded them all. There was no needy person among them, for those who owned property or houses would sell them, bring the proceeds of the sale, and put them at the feet of the apostles, and they were distributed to each according to need. (Acts 4:33-35)

Thus we see that the vision, concept, and language of empowerment enjoy a firm foundation in both the Old and New Testaments of the Bible.

The Historical Tradition of the Church: Works of Mercy and Empowerment

During the early centuries of the Christian era, the growing and developing church did not ignore the work of charity as an essential component of the Christian community. The short treatise *Didache*, its authorship and date of its preparation not identified definitively, was accorded much importance by early church fathers and was thought to have been handed down by the apostles. Thereby it provided a prototype for early church doctrine and law.[2] In this canonical document, almsgiving was highly recommended: "Let your alms sweat in your hands, until you know to whom you should give." Further, those incapable of work were mentioned as deserving of care and service from other Christians.[3]

In his second epistle, Clement of Rome, whose papacy extended between 92 and 101 AD, taught that almsgiving and good works were necessary requirements for the remission of sin. Polycarp of Smyrna, who served as bishop in the second century, strongly recommended almsgiving in his *Epistle to the Philippians*, "that by your good works . . . you may receive praise."

From earliest times, the pleas for charity were tempered with a demand for justice. Thus St. John Chrysostom admonished:

> Not to enable the poor to share in our goods is to steal from them and deprive them of life. The goods we possess are not ours, but theirs. . . . The demands of justice must be satisfied first of all; that which is already due in justice is not to be offered as a gift of charity.[4]

From our reading of later church history, we know of the church's active tradition in the works of charity. Many of the religious orders were established on the principle of sharing the goods of this earth with the poor. In Europe and in other parts of the world, many of the first hospitals, orphanages, and schools were founded by the church to enlighten the minds of the youth and to lift the burden of suffering from those most in need. In the eighth century, Archbishop Egbert of York established an ecclesiastical rule that "bishops and priests shall set up a *hospitium*."[5]

What may be less well known but equally valid were the works of justice within our church's historical tradition. One such example may be found in the medieval practice of offering sanctuary to those who were being persecuted unjustly. The acceptability of such a practice occasionally has been debated among church leaders in modern times, yet our forebears in the Middle Ages had no problem with opening up their church buildings and monasteries to offer refuge to those forced to flee their home territories and countries in order to preserve their very lives and human dignity.

This insight of St. Vincent de Paul seemed to leave no room for hesitation among his followers to submit themselves to the power of the poor and thus to adopt a servant role *vis-à-vis* their beneficiaries:

You will find out that charity is a heavy burden to carry, heavier than the bowl of soup and the full basket. But you will keep your gentleness and your smile. It is not enough to give soup and bread. This the rich can do. You are the servant of the poor, always smiling and good-humored. They are your masters, terribly sensitive and exacting masters you will soon see . . . It is only for your love alone, that the poor will forgive you the bread you give them.[6]

Catholic Social Teaching in the Modern Era—Demand for Empowerment among the Poor and Marginalized

From the nineteenth century on, popes and bishops increasingly have articulated the right and necessity of dissolving the economic, social, and cultural bonds that keep the most needy from empowering themselves. In his watershed encyclical *Rerum Novarum*, Pope Leo XIII confronted the inhuman treatment of laborers within the laissez-faire economy of the Industrial Revolution and strongly supported the bonds of social solidarity and responsibility in the overall organization of society.[7] Pope Pius XI argued, in his encyclical *Quadragesimo Anno*, that economic activity should be subordinated to and directed toward the human welfare of all the citizens in society.[8]

In his quest for social harmony and equitable participation in society, Pope John XXIII did not ignore the needs of "those citizens of straitened fortune who are dissatisfied with their very difficult lot in life," as stated in *Ad Petri Cathedram*.[9] He assured the poor and oppressed that the church was not hostile to them but rather "cares for them as would a loving mother." He reminded Catholics that the church "preaches and inculcates a social doctrine and social norms which would eliminate every sort of injustice and produce a better and more equitable distribution of goods, if they were put into practice as they should be." Finally, he urged, "Friendly cooperation and mutual assistance among the various classes, so that all men may become in name and in fact not only free citizens of the same society but also brothers within the same family."[10]

In *Mater et Magistra*,[11] Pope John XXIII appealed for the exercise of mutual responsibility among all persons, especially in the areas of economic life and business. In another equally famous encyclical, *Pacem in Terris*, this same pontiff further characterized social responsibility as both a fundamental right and an intrinsic obligation for all persons:

> The dignity of the human person involves the right to take an active part in public affairs and to contribute one's part to the

common good of its citizens. As . . . Pius XII pointed out: "The human individual, far from being an object, a merely passive element in the social order, is in fact . . . its subject, its foundation and its end."[12]

The bishops participating at the Second Vatican Council departed from their usual methodology of introducing church documents through a list of carefully detailed, but rather abstract, theological principles. To the contrary, they recalled the church's responsibility first of "scrutinizing the signs of the times and interpreting them in the light of the Gospel." Thus they engaged in deep reflection on the issues and challenges faced by the human family during what they described in *Gaudium et Spes* as a "new stage of history," characterized by "profound and rapid changes" that have led to "a cultural and social transformation, one which has repercussions on . . . religious life as well."[13] They noted "an abundance of wealth, resources and economic power" as well as "the torment of hunger and poverty among so many in the human family." They celebrated the keen sense of freedom among men and women but lamented the bitter political, social, economic, racial, and ideological disputes in the world.[14]

At the conclusion of this social analysis, the council fathers affirmed that all persons are created "to the image of God" not as "solitary" beings, and that without others we can neither "live nor develop [our] potential."[15] They urged respect for "the fundamental rights of the person" and condemned every type of discrimination . . . as "contrary to God's intent."[16] They recognized that human freedom can be threatened equally by extreme poverty and by dependence on "too many of life's comforts" or by living "in a kind of splendid isolation."[17] They acknowledged that sincere disagreement could arise among the faithful but then called for mutual enlightenment "through honest discussion, preserving mutual charity and caring above all for the common good."[18]

In the second part of this pastoral constitution, the bishops turned their attention to areas of "universal concern." They lauded the increasing consciousness among people "that they themselves are the authors and artisans of the culture of their community"[19] and declared that "it is now possible to free most of humanity from the misery of ignorance."[20] They cautioned that economic development . . . must not be left to the judgment of a few or of groups possessing too much economic power, or of the political community alone, or of certain more powerful nations.[21] They recalled the command of the church fathers to "feed the man dying of hunger, because if you have not fed him, you have killed him," and called for the support of individuals or peoples with "the aid by which they may be able to help and develop themselves."[22]

In *Populorum Progressio*, Pope Paul VI observed with much pain and passion that:

> The injustice of certain situations cries out for God's attention. Lacking the bare necessities of life, whole nations are under the thumb of others; they cannot act on their own initiative; they cannot exercise personal responsibility; they cannot work toward a higher degree of cultural refinement or a greater participation in social and public life. They are sorely tempted to redress these insults to their human nature by violent means.[23]

He called for "organized programs designed to increase productivity . . . that should have but one aim: to serve human nature" in order to "reduce inequities, eliminate discrimination, free men from the bonds of servitude, and thus give them the capacity, in the sphere of temporal realities, to improve their lot, to further their moral growth and to develop their spiritual endowments."[24] He steadfastly affirmed that:

> Man is truly human only if he is the master of his own actions and the judge of their worth, only if he is the architect of his own progress. He must act according to his God-given nature, freely accepting its potentials and its claims upon him.[25]

In a subsequent apostolic letter titled *Octogesima Adveniens*, this same pope identified "an urgent need to re-make at the level of the street, of the neighborhood, or of the great agglomerative dwellings, the social fabric whereby man may be able to develop the needs of his personality."[26] Moreover, he strongly exhorted Christians to put into practice the social teachings of the church on the level of their daily lives:

> It is not enough to recall principles, state intentions, point to crying injustices and utter prophetic denunciations; these works will lack real weight unless they are accompanied for each individual by a livelier awareness of personal responsibility and by effective action.[27]

Through his prolific and intensive reflections on the situation of the human family, most especially on that of its most poor and vulnerable members, Pope John Paul II shed new light on the necessary empowerment of such persons as is demanded by Catholic social teaching. In his apostolic letter *Sollicitudo Rei Socialis*, he proposed the need to move beyond the individual practice of justice and charity in order to establish a genuinely empowered solidarity among all peoples:

> Positive signs in the contemporary world are the growing aware-ness of the solidarity of the poor among themselves, their efforts to support one another, and their public demonstrations on the social scene which, without recourse to violence, present their own needs and rights in the face of the inefficiency or corruption of the public authorities. By virtue of her own evangelical duty, the Church feels called to take her stand beside the poor, to discern the justice of their requests, and to help satisfy them, without losing sight of the good of groups in the context of the common good.[28]

In his 2000 World Day of Peace Message, Pope John Paul II insisted that "the advancement of the poor constitutes a great opportunity for the moral, cultural and even economic growth of all humanity." He further urged: "Let us look at the poor not as a problem, but as people who can become the principal builders of a new and more human future for ev-eryone."[29] At the close of the Jubilee Year 2000, he exhorted:

> Now is the time for a new "creativity" in charity, not only by ensur-ing that help is effective but also by "getting close" to those who suffer, so that the hand that helps is seen not as a humiliating handout but as a sharing between brothers and sisters.[30]

Pope Benedict XVI, too, has shown a keen sensitivity to the pre-requisite practice of both virtues, charity and justice, by all who dare to call themselves Christian. In his first encyclical, *Deus Caritas Est*, he acknowledged that "building a just social and civil order, wherein each person receives what is his or her due, is an essential task which every generation must take up anew." He simultaneously maintained that "the Church cannot and must not take upon herself the political battle to bring about the most just society possible" and admitted that "since it also is a most important responsibility, the Church is duty-bound to offer . . . her own specific contribution towards understanding the requirements of justice and achieving them politically." Pope Benedict discerned that the "duty to work for a just ordering of society" is "proper to the lay faithful" and appeals to them not to "relinquish their participation" in such areas but rather to "promote organically and constitutionally the *common good*." Moreover, he called upon "specific expressions of ecclesial charity," such as Catholic Charities organizations and other members of the global confederation of Caritas Internationalis, to "animate the entire lives of the lay faithful and therefore also their political activity, lived as 'social charity.'"[31]

In his second encyclical, *Spe Salvi*, the Holy Father articulated the need for an empowered and community-based approach to human development and progress, because "the right state of human affairs, the moral well-being of the world, can never be guaranteed simply through structures alone, however good they are." He maintained structures "must not marginalize human freedom" and that "even the best structures function only when the community is animated by convictions capable of motivating people to assent freely to the social order."[32]

Pope Benedict XVI focused his 2009 World Day of Peace Message on the necessary interrelationship between efforts at building peace and promoting authentic human development. He declared that in order to accord priority to the poor the human family must allow "room for an ethical approach to economics on the part of those active in the international market, an ethical approach to politics on the part of those in public office, and an ethical approach to participation capable of harnessing the contributions of civil society at local and international levels."[33] Shortly after delivering this message, and in conjunction with his first apostolic visit to Africa, the Holy Father reinforced these points within the specific context of this region:

> Friends, armed with integrity, magnanimity and compassion, you can transform this continent, freeing your people from the scourges of greed, violence and unrest and leading them along the path marked with the principles indispensable to every modern civic democracy . . . African men and women themselves, working together for the good of their communities, should be the primary agents of their own development.[34]

Also relevant as a doctrinal foundation for reflection and action by Catholic Charities USA were the writings of the United States Conference of Catholic Bishops, developed in conformity with, and during the same time period, as the papal and other magisterial documents outlined above. Of particular note in this regard is the bishops' document titled Economic Justice for All: A Pastoral Letter on Catholic Social Teaching and the U.S. Economy. In this document, the bishops focused most of their attention on the economy, as is indicated in the title; however, they also wisely recognized that no economic analysis is complete without due reflection on the social and political factors that permit access to participation in the economy. In this regard, they identified the essential need for empowered participation in such communities as follows:

> The principle of participation leads us to the conviction that the most appropriate and fundamental solutions to poverty will be those that enable people to take control of their lives. For poverty is not merely the lack of adequate financial resources. It entails a more profound kind of deprivation, a denial of full participation in the economic, social, and political life of society and an inability to influence decisions that affect one's life. It means being powerless in a way that assaults not only one's pocketbook but also one's fundamental human dignity. Therefore, we should seek solutions that enable the poor to help themselves.[35]

These same bishops urged "the Catholic laity to bring peace and justice to the world by working energetically to reclaim national concern for the common good."[36] They also maintained that young people of all social backgrounds can be empowered by the church's work of justice and service:

> The ministry of justice and service nurtures in young people a social consciousness and a commitment to a life of justice and service rooted in their faith in Jesus Christ, in the Scriptures, and in Catholic social teaching; empowers young people to work for justice by concrete efforts to address the causes of human suffering; and infuses the concepts of justice, peace, and human dignity into all ministry efforts.[37]

Far from being idealist or simplistic in their vision of the social, economic, and political challenges to be confronted in the United States and throughout the world, the bishops of this country acknowledged the struggles of those who seek to practice justice and charity and then encouraged them to respond in a hope-filled manner:

> It is too easy to be immobilized by the complexity of social problems, the feelings of exhaustion in the face of endless human needs, or the seeming powerlessness of one person to change the world. Yet one of the wonderful lessons of the Gospel is the power of the few to be leaven for many—the continuous wonder of planting small seeds from which great forests grow. By our own efforts, each of us can make the reign of God a reality. Additionally, the poor themselves have a duty to develop their own resources, to work industriously, and to contribute to the good of society.[38]

Putting Catholic Social Teaching into Action—
The Empowerment Efforts
of Major Social Ministry Structures in the United States

As Catholics in the United States prepared to cross the threshold of the third millennium, their bishops reminded them:

> Through our works of charity and justice, we . . . are challenged to put into practice the principles that we have learned from our Church's teachings and tradition. Thus, in marking the one-hundredth anniversary of contemporary Catholic social teaching, Pope John Paul II called on us to consider the social message of the Gospel as not just a "theory, but above all else a basis and a motivation for action."[39]

Let us examine, therefore, how Catholics in this country have translated teaching into action, with particular focus on the promotion of empowerment, through their association with three major social ministry structures: Catholic Charities USA, Catholic Relief Services, and The Catholic Campaign for Human Development.

Before doing so, however, it seems necessary to touch a sensitive point in the evolution of such ministry in this country—that of the charity-justice debate. In my view, we have the benefit of clear scriptural and magisterial teaching that Christians must practice both the virtues of charity and justice in the course of their faith lives. That teaching has been confirmed by the lived tradition of the church's practice during these past 2,000 years. Despite such clarity, however, a long-standing debate about charity and justice, or, more pointedly, about the relationship between the two, has raged among some Christian believers. In their book titled *The Poor Belong to Us: Catholic Charities and American Welfare*, Dorothy Brown and Elizabeth McKeown described the often acrimonious debate that unfolded between the Catholic justice advocates and the charitable practitioners during the early twentieth century. They recalled the words of Fr. Edward McGlynn, a priest from New York, who championed the oppressed laboring classes and simultaneously attacked the system of child care sponsored by his own archdiocese: "You may go on forever with hospitals and orphan asylums and St. Vincent de Paul societies, but with them you can't cure the trouble."[40] During the 1920s, disturbed that the church was sponsoring homes for working women but appeared to be slow in advocating for living wages to be paid to such women, John Cooper lamented: "How long shall we continue straining out gnats and swallowing camels? How long shall we continue tithing mint and anise and cumin and leaving the weightier things of the law? . . . Can we build up charity on the ruins of justice?"[41]

Meanwhile, Msgr. William J. Kerby, the first executive secretary of the National Conference of Catholic Charities, expressed strong concerns that charity was out of favor with progressive contemporaries who were making strident demands for fair wages, child labor laws, public health measures, and social insurance against industrial accidents. Brown and McKeown characterized Father Kerby's concerns as follows:

> By itself [the] calculus of distributive justice could not sustain the community. Justice required the foundation of charity . . . Arguing that charity provided the necessary context for the deliberate and impersonal machinery of justice, he urged his colleagues and students to create a movement that would reform the practices of charity for the sake of justice.[42]

These debates have continued to the present day. During more than 35 years of service to the church's social ministry, on diocesan, national, and global levels, I have lost count of the number of times I have been caught in the "crossfire" between the defenders of charity and the promoters of justice. Perhaps the insights of Pope Benedict XVI can shed light on this mistaken "competition":

> [The Church] cannot and must not remain on the sidelines in the fight for justice . . . The promotion of justice through efforts to bring openness of mind and will to the demands of the common good is something which concerns the Church deeply. . . . Love—*caritas*—will always prove necessary, even in the most just society. There is no ordering of the State so just that it can eliminate the need for a service of love. . . . In the end, the claim that just social structures would make works of charity superfluous masks a materialist conception of man: the mistaken notion that man can live "by bread alone" (Matthew 4:4; cf. Deuteronomy 8:3)—a conviction that demeans man and ultimately disregards all that is specifically human.[43]

Catholic Charities USA

On the occasion of the centenary celebration of Catholic Charities USA, much and well-merited attention will be accorded to this organization's heroic record of service to the poor and vulnerable in the United States. Thus I will restrict my reflections to the empowerment focus of this organization—a focus that has long-standing and deep resonance in the life of Catholic Charities. Msgr. John O'Grady, leader of the National Conference of Catholic Charities for some four decades, promoted empowerment of poor people by advocating for the passage of the Social Security Act of 1935 and for federal housing legislation. In 1951, he even helped to mobilize congressional passage, and subsequent overriding of President Truman's veto, of more liberal immigration policies in order to resettle additional persons displaced during World War II and still being held in internment camps. For that action, he received the following message from the Vatican: "God can only reward you for your noble and courageous fight. You win even in apparent defeat."[44] Such strategic successes seem to demonstrate quite well the balance between charity and justice/empowerment that always has motivated this vital movement in the church of the United States.

Few could deny, however, that the Cadre Study, conducted in the early 1970s, brought Catholic Charities several leaps forward in its determination to be an empowering organization. No longer was the work of charity to be summed up in emergency assistance and family counseling. The diocesan charity agencies were called upon by the historical document resulting from the study, titled *Toward a Renewed Catholic Charities Movement*, to expand their activities by including advocacy for just social policies and legislation and convening of people at national, diocesan, and parish levels with the ultimate goal of humanizing and transforming the social order. In a similar way, Catholic Charities workers and volunteers were urged to strike a greater balance among service provision, political activism, community education, and client empowerment. Those calling for a renewed Catholic Charities also acknowledged that these new strategies had deep theological roots:

> As an integral expression of the Church of Christ, we are charged not simply with attempts to meet human need, but with the further challenge of a reflective penetration of every expression of need as a revelation of the human condition that all share. Recognizing that such radical understanding of need and suffering cannot be achieved except through the people who most experience and express them, it is incumbent that we face the dynamic of baptism, namely, that of challenging and enabling those we serve to push their consciousness of their need and its causes to the deepest level possible.[45]

On the more practical level, this renewed approach was characterized as follows:

> In order to foster individual freedom and liberty, the spirit and programs which Catholic Charities sponsor should be of such a nature to discern, to call attention to, and to prevent the cause of bondage and oppression. Catholic Charities then must stop wishing to resolve the poverty, the misery of the oppressed by individual acts of charity alone.[46]

I still vividly remember my experiences as a young priest and social worker during those exciting, post-Cadre Study times when the diocesan Catholic Charities agency in which I served (Paterson, New Jersey) was among the first to expand its services beyond family counseling, adoptions, and emergency services, to include community organizing of public housing residents and aging persons, as well as advocacy at city, county, state, and federal levels. One such indelible memory includes the look of shock on the face of a state director of social services when she was confronted by a group of empowered senior citizens, trained by Catholic Charities in community organizing techniques, who demanded an explanation for the secretly projected cuts in the state's social assistance funding—cuts that quickly were rescinded.

The Cadre document was not the last word on empowerment within Catholic Charities; in many ways, it was only the first of such words. In its Vision 2000 Strategic Plan, Catholic Charities was called to "enhance our historical commitment to quality service by making the empowerment of those we serve, especially people who are poor and vulnerable, central to our work."[47] The Catholic Charities Empowerment Task Force, mentioned in the introduction to this article and responsible for the definition on which the reflection in this article has been based, attempted to delve even more deeply and practically into the direction set by Vision 2000. The task force identified the following principles as central to the concept of empowerment: people are the primary agents of change; empowering changes happen through participative relationships; the human person is both social and spiritual; and what affects one aspect of the person, affects the other.

The following scenario was delineated by the task force in order to assist Catholic Charities in assessing the level of empowerment employed by them in their programs and services:

> The agency itself becomes a vehicle of change and transformation where clients and communities become full partners in planning for a better, more wholesome, and respectful place to live. The lens through which it sees the world is one where power is in the partnership. In this scenario, Catholic Charities agencies and staff are not responsible for solving problems. Instead, staff engages the

individuals, families, and communities who are experiencing the difficulties in processes which are controlled by them and through which they develop their own solutions to problems.[48]

Catholic Relief Services

Through efforts to become more empowering organizations, and in a manner similar to that undertaken by Catholic Charities USA, Catholic Relief Services (CRS) and sister Caritas organizations in other parts of the world moved beyond an almost exclusive reliance on emergency relief to development-oriented interaction with people in developing countries. They began to treat those benefiting from their generosity as partners rather than as recipients. Today, within their home countries, CRS and Caritas organizations expend energy and funds to change the social policies and laws that often lead to further marginalization and victimization of the poor and vulnerable in developing countries. They facilitate efforts to increase civic participation and reconciliation in areas affected by oppression and conflict. They promote access to medications, treatment, and livelihoods for those affected by illnesses such as HIV and AIDS, tuberculosis, and malaria, all of which can constitute a swift and sure death sentence in low-income countries.[49]

During the 1990s, the leadership and staff of Catholic Relief Services boldly decided to "re-vision" its policies and programs by applying the "justice lens" of Catholic social teaching. It described this new strategy as follows:

> Building on CRS' strength from its decades of relief and development experience and its emphasis on the roots of its mission in Catholic Social Teaching, CRS country programs are starting to apply the justice lens to programming in areas such as community health, poverty lending, education, agriculture, emergency programming, civil society, and peace-building and reconciliation. . . . The justice lens calls us to analyze a multiplicity of relationships in society between and among various actors—individual, family, social group, local community, institution, nation, and human community—where we previously tended to restrict our analyses to relationships between governments and their constituents, the Church and its people, or CRS and counterparts. In this way, the lens also shapes decisions about with whom we work and the character of our efforts together. . . . While these operational partnerships take many forms, at their best, they reflect right relationships in the concept of partnership—embodying

essential principles such as respect for human dignity and people's ownership of their development process—based on shared vision, subsidiarity, openness to different perspectives, mutuality, and transparency.[50]

Catholic Campaign for Human Development

When they established the Catholic Campaign for Human Development (CCHD), the Catholic bishops of the United States were well aware of the excellent services already being provided to needy individuals and families in this country by Catholic Charities, as well as by Catholic health care and educational institutions. At the same time, the bishops were deeply moved by the racial unrest and subsequent violence resulting from the ever-widening gap between the rich and the poor—a gap often divided along racial lines—and, more proximately, from the assassination of Rev. Martin Luther King Jr. Thus, after studying the prophetic initiative launched by Cardinal John Dearden, who granted $1 million to community organizing work in the city of Detroit, the National Conference of Catholic Bishops recognized the concomitant need to invite all Catholics in the country to give more direct support to empowerment efforts initiated by groups of people living in poverty and/or who are otherwise vulnerable. The bishops believed that, by acquiring leadership skills and building strategic relationships in local communities, such empowered persons could emerge from their marginalization. These words were expressed at the initiation of the campaign:

> There is an evident need for funds . . . to be used for organized groups of white and minority poor to develop economic strength and political power in their own communities . . . We believe that this new effort can lead the People of God to a new knowledge of today's problems, a deeper understanding of the intricate forces that lead to group conflict, and a perception of some new and promising approaches that we might take in promoting a greater spirit of solidarity among those who are successful, those who have acquired some share of the nation's good, and those still trapped in poverty.[51]

During the past 40 years, both as a result of the bishops' commitment and the support of the annual CCHD collections from Catholic parishioners throughout the United States, the campaign has succeeded in offering more than $280 million in national grants for community organizing and economic development sponsored by more than 8,000 community-based, self-help groups of empowered people.[52]

These statistics do not tell the whole story, however. Much more compelling is the direct witness of the beneficiaries who proudly show off their renewed neighborhoods, now recovered from the slum landlords, drug dealers, pimps, and gangs who once terrorized them. So, too, the participants in CCHD-funded groups boast of the progress made by their children in schools benefiting from the stronger parent-teacher collaboration and expanded budgets made possible through their organizing efforts. Migrant workers claim a place at the table with the growers in order to obtain desperately needed pay increases as well as basic benefits. Local residents in inner-city areas who had lost all local supermarkets and other commercial services now are welcoming back outside merchants, and groups of poor and low-income people are hosting their own community-owned businesses. Youth and young adults are beginning to dream again—not of ways to escape the oppressive cycle of poverty by drugs or alcohol or group violence, but, to the contrary, of empowering actions to improve their surroundings and to achieve a bright new future. The life of faith and action within parishes in inner cities, suburbs, and rural areas is strengthened by the leadership development that takes place among their members when they participate in community-based, self-help groups such as those supported by CCHD.

Conclusion

The story of the Catholic Church's dedication to and engagement in the empowerment of peoples, especially of the poor and vulnerable, is as old as its roots in the Old Testament; the witness of Jesus' own life, death, and resurrection; the model of equity and equality advanced by the first Christians; the teachings that began with the Gospels and continue to this very day; and the lived tradition of the church's social ministry. Far from limiting the efforts of marginalized people to empower themselves, the church has fostered and promoted such initiatives, with the simple proviso that such efforts be rooted in respect for the dignity of the human person, in the value of the community, in the goal of the common good, and in principles of partnership and nonviolence.

As Catholic Charities USA observes its centenary milestone, it can take rightful pride in advancing the empowerment of those whom it serves as well as of communities of faith and of civil society with which it partners. May God's grace help these efforts to bear ever more abundant fruit, in accord with the following concept and strategy for integral human development as envisioned by the Catholic Church: "The ultimate purpose and content of development programs is giving people the concrete possibility to share their own lives and be protagonists of development."[53]

Chapter
Eight

Mission and Identity

How *Who We Are* Shapes *What We Do* and *How We Do It*

Rev. Fred Kammer, SJ
Jesuit Social Research Institute
Loyola University New Orleans

Mission and Identity

How *Who We Are* Shapes *What We Do* and *How We Do It*

In the mid-1980s, Catholic Community Services of Baton Rouge, the Catholic Charities agency where I first worked, approved its initial strategic plan with this mission:

> Catholic Community Services of Baton Rouge proclaims the gospel vision of Jesus Christ as its mission by serving the needs of individuals and families, especially the poorest, and working with Church and community for justice, peace, and compassion in society.

Woven through this single sentence were three roles with long and complex histories in the Catholic Charities world: "service, advocacy, and convening." Also included were strong and principled themes from Catholic social teaching—justice, peace, compassion, the importance of family, evangelization, the preferential option for the poor, and, of course, the good news of Jesus of Nazareth. Hundreds of Catholic Charities agencies and institutions had developed or would develop similar mission and vision statements whose fabric was woven from the same three core roles and similar principles.[1]

The National Conference of Catholic Charities (1910–)

The formal "mission" story for Catholic Charities USA begins in 1910 on the campus of Catholic University of America (CUA). At the invitation of Most Rev. Thomas Shahan, CUA's president, the National Conference

135

of Catholic Charities (NCCC) was founded to promote the foundation of diocesan Catholic Charities bureaus, encourage professional social work, "bring about a sense of solidarity" among those in charitable ministries, and "be the attorney for the poor." The 400 or so delegates from 24 states were predominantly laypeople, representative of women and men who had founded the many charitable institutions in various ethnic communities, members of the Society of St. Vincent de Paul, and Catholic academics and public figures concerned about the poor. President Taft hosted the closing conference ceremonies at the White House. The *Proceedings* recited the purposes as follows:

> The National Conference has been created to meet a definite situation. It aims to preserve the organic spiritual character of Catholic Charity. It aims to seek out and understand causes of dependency. It aims to take advantage of the ripest wisdom in relief and preventive work to which persons have anywhere attained, and to serve as a bond of union for the unnumbered organizations in the United States which are doing the work of Charity. It aims to become, finally, the attorney for the Poor in Modern Society, to present their point of view and defend them unto the days when social justice may secure to them their rights.[2]

In the early years of the NCCC, an intense effort—especially by Msgr. John O'Grady, executive secretary of the NCCC from 1920 to 1961—focused on developing the diocesan Catholic Charities bureau or agency as a means of organizing and professionalizing charitable works. By 1922, there were 35 central bureaus of Catholic Charities formed in cities or dioceses. By 1937 the number of bureaus had increased to 68 in 35 states.

In a way, this diocesan-level development was a focus on the service role of Catholic Charities, complemented by efforts to improve the quality of services in keeping with the newly developing field of social work. For example, in 1923 the NCCC published *A Program for Catholic Child-Caring Homes*, a work of its Conference on Religious to improve institutional standards. In 1934, The National Catholic School of Social Service was founded at Catholic University of America at the urging of the NCCC, with Msgr. O'Grady as its first dean.

The second role of Catholic Charities—advocating for a more just society—was smelted in the social and economic cauldron that was dominated by the Great Depression, the New Deal, and World War II and its aftermath. The NCCC and diocesan bureaus promoted social legislation based upon Catholic principles, and Msgr. O'Grady became a national voice on social reform. Two examples stand out. In 1935, the Social Security Act passed Congress for the first time, with strong support from the NCCC for the concept of insurance benefits based upon rights as opposed to a needs test. The act provided the framework for what are called social security benefits (for worker retirement, survivors, and dependents), workers' compensation, unemployment compensation, and social welfare (Aid to the Aged, Blind, and Disabled, now Supplemental Security Income, and Aid to Families with Dependent Children, now Temporary Assistance to Needy Families). This framework later included Medicare and Medicaid. Then, in 1949, the National Housing Act was passed with strong support from the NCCC and Msgr. O'Grady, culminating 20 years of his leadership of the Catholic community and the nation on housing.

In its third role—convening—the NCCC and local charities found common cause with a number of other social welfare organizations, child caring institutions, and other advocates for improving the quality of social services and expanding the government's responsibilities for social welfare. Among church organizations with whom the NCCC collaborated were the Society of St. Vincent de Paul, the Christ Child Society, the Association of Ladies of Charity, the National Conference of Catholic Women, and the National Catholic Welfare Conference (now the United States Conference of Catholic Bishops).

The Cadre Study (1969–1972)

In the wake of the political, social, and cultural turmoil of the 1960s, significant new civil rights and social legislation, and the momentous Catholic transformation promoted by the Second Vatican Council (1962–65), NCCC members in 1969 undertook a three-year self-study aimed at clarifying the mission of Catholic Charities agencies and the national conference. It was called the Cadre Study for the core group of charities and other Catholic leaders who spearheaded it. At the 1972 annual meeting in Miami, the NCCC membership approved the Cadre Study report *Toward a Renewed Catholic Charities Movement*, which outlined the movement's triple roles:

> *The Continuing Commitment to Service.* Catholic Charities must stand ready to serve those most in need, especially those most alienated, most oppressed, most distressed. Our credibility as Christians is established when we offer ourselves in service to individuals, to our communities, to our country, to our Church. Focus should be given to the increased services needed, to all those who remain unserved, and to the unfinished work before us.

Humanizing and Transforming the Social Order. This is based on a belief in the necessity of pursuing social justice for all and particularly for those unable to do so for themselves, which, in turn, involves effecting changes in the existing social systems. One component is that of advocacy, courageously calling attention to the root causes of poverty and oppression. Other components are those of social planning, policy development, and contributing to the shaping of social welfare legislation.

The Convening of the Christian Community and Other Concerned People. This is a process of reaching out to others to stimulate them to social awareness and to recruit them as active partners in the pursuit of the goals of the Catholic Charities movement. One method of this should be the convening of meetings and assemblies in order to discern more clearly the roots of distress and poverty and to reach decisions which enable those convened to act. This role includes reaching out to and working with the parish community to assist it in its ministry of service. It involves recruitment, consciousness raising, discernment, and action.[3]

The shorthand statement of the Cadre mission—service, advocacy, and convening—has framed the mission of the national organization to the present day.

Pope John Paul II and Catholic Charities (1987)

In his address to members of Catholic Charities USA, formerly the NCCC, at their 1987 annual meeting in San Antonio, Texas, Pope John Paul II emphasized the multiple roles of Catholic Charities in the context of Catholic social teaching. Tracing the history of charitable service back to the Scriptures, the Holy Father emphasized that the church has worked from its beginnings to carry out the teaching of Jesus about the special love of God for the poor (Matthew 25:31-46); and, citing the parable of the rich man and the poor Lazarus, he warned of the "dire consequences" of "gross disparities of wealth between nations, classes and persons." The pope emphasized the role of service in these words: "Service to those in need must take the form of direct action to relieve their anxieties, and to remove their burdens, and at the same time lead them to the dignity of self-reliance."[4] The Holy Father also underscored the advocacy or transformational role of the Catholic Charities mission. "Service to the poor also involves speaking up for them and trying to reform structures which cause or perpetuate their oppression."

In the context of global dimensions of poverty and injustice, he went on to urge the members of Catholic Charities to "see what can be done as soon as possible to purify the social structures of all society in this regard." Then, in his closing exhortation, the members heard the pope emphasize all three parts of their mission in the words, "Gather, transform, and serve!"

Vision 2000 (1993–1996)

In the mid-1990s, Catholic Charities USA undertook another multi-year, in-depth study of their mission and organization to prepare for a new millennium. Vision 2000 engaged thousands of staff, board members, clients, and volunteers in asking anew about mission, needs, and priorities. The final report, approved by the CCUSA Board of Trustees in 1996, highlighted the following vision:

> Believing in the presence of God in our midst, we proclaim the sanctity of human life and the dignity of the person by sharing in the mission of Jesus given to the Church. To this end, Catholic Charities works with individuals, families, and communities to help them meet their needs, address their issues, eliminate oppression, and build a just and compassionate society.[5]

The report then developed four strategic directions flowing from the vision statement and the convenings of Catholic Charities staff, board members, and volunteers, as well as listening sessions of the task force members with others within the church and larger society.

> *Strategic Direction I: Relating to Those We Serve.* Enhance our historical commitment to quality service by making the empowerment of those we serve, especially people who are poor and vulnerable, central to our work.
>
> *Strategic Direction II: Relating to Community.* Build an inclusive Catholic Charities which engages diverse people, organizations, and communities in transforming the structures of society that perpetuate poverty, undermine family life, and destroy communities.
>
> *Strategic Direction III: Relating to Church.* Strengthen our identity with, and relationship to, the broader Church and witness to its social mission.
>
> *Strategic Direction IV: Relating to One Another.* Build the organizational and resource capacity for people to participate in effecting the vision of Catholic Charities.[6]

The Vision 2000 report came at a time of significant challenges within a rapidly changing national environment. These challenges affected not just Catholic Charities, but all nonprofits, especially those deeply committed to the most vulnerable people. The four strategic directions built upon the three roles first enunciated in the Cadre Study—service, advocacy, and convening—but urged new commitments.

Strategic Direction I—Making Services Empowering

Strategic Direction I called for a deep and transforming focus on those served and their self-determination. This direction reflected the 25-year-old call of the Cadre Study to quality social service, self-help, and self-actualizing. There was a new insistence on empowerment of clients—especially in the face of the demographics of need in which two-thirds of those served came for emergency services, especially food and shelter.[7] This demand for emergency services particularly aggravated the challenge of making empowerment integral to Catholic Charities' services, since empowerment seemed so far from the local soup kitchen, shelter, or food bank. Yet, many agencies were developing creative ways to make even those services empowering.

But "empowerment" in Vision 2000 was broader than the individual client service. "Key Characteristics," developed in the report for each strategic direction, reminded members of powerful community-building devices and dynamics such as community organizing and economic development. For example, local offices for the Catholic Campaign for Human Development (CCHD)—the U.S. bishops' antipoverty program of community and economic development—were an integral part of the structure of about 40 percent of Catholic Charities agencies. Vision 2000 challenged them to think about CCHD as more than a program and ask how empowerment strategies could be utilized to affect overall approaches to the needs and challenges of communities. The report encouraged members to amplify community-based-and-focused services and innovative local alliances.[8]

Strategic Direction II—Confronting Societal Divisions

Strategic Direction II challenged members to confront deep societal divisions, beginning with racism, and the sinful social structures that ravage families and communities and intensify poverty. This direction clearly reflected the Cadre Study's second goal of "humanizing and transforming the social structures." But after 25 years of trying to implement that goal, this direction recognized two powerful barriers to effective action.

First was the reality and power of racism in two contexts. The internal context was within member agencies themselves, a sad fact emphasized to task force members as they met with staff and volunteers in state and regional listening sessions during the first year of the process. This was reinforced by the inadequate racial and ethnic diversity among diocesan directors of Catholic Charities and senior management and staff. The external context was the continuing reality of societal racism. Recent examples were the 1992 Los Angeles riots, the 1996 church burnings,[9] the continuing exclusion of black homeowners from white neighborhoods, and the perception that racism was only barely "masked" in debates over welfare reform and immigration. Later, in 2005, America was shocked again at racism unmasked in the aftermath of Hurricane Katrina.

The second social reality emphasized by Direction II was the existence of "sinful social structures," recognized by the church since Vatican II as critical to understanding social reality and emphasized heavily in the teachings of John Paul II and in the pastoral letters of the U.S. bishops. Catholic Charities workers knew well that many of these structures—inadequate wages and benefits, punitive and degrading welfare programs, substandard and unaffordable housing—profoundly affected family life and structure, poverty, and community quality across the nation.

The racism part of this direction seemed easier to define, and its challenge to members easier to frame in the report. Catholic Charities USA had initiated its Racial Equality Project even before the final report was approved. Interest has continued to be strong since the mid-1990s and has given rise to the development by the organization of a cultural assessment tool to assist agencies to move beyond tolerance to promoting racial and cultural diversity. It also has given rise to scholarships for increased participation of minorities in Catholic Charities USA annual gatherings and its Leadership Institute as well as a commitment to confront the intrinsic connection between racial injustice and poverty, as demonstrated in the 2008 Catholic Charities USA study *Poverty and Racism: Overlapping Threats to the Common Good.*[10]

Vision 2000 task force members acknowledged that the social change part was more difficult. They believed that racism lay at the heart of the American social question, and that confronting racism was a privileged place for entering into social change. But they also understood that beyond racism much of what this strategic direction implied was still inchoate, needing development as Catholic Charities moved into the new century. Members needed to struggle to understand complex social reality better and develop appropriate responses. There were real unknowns here; but, as Msgr. John Gilmartin of New York repeated to the task force, if Catholic Charities did not take major steps toward social change, they would have twice as many clients across the country in the not distant future.

Strategic Direction III—
Connecting to and Animating the Church

Strategic Direction III urged individual and organizational members to deepen their connection to, and animation of, the Catholic Church for the sake of the Gospel and their own mission. During the first year's listening sessions, task force members had heard this theme especially from agency directors. "How do I lead a religiously diverse staff, volunteers, and board members in a *Catholic* agency?" and "How does new lay leadership—not priests and religious; sometimes not Catholic—learn and pass on Catholic social teaching and the Catholic Charities tradition?"

First, the Vision 2000 report recognized that these too were truly complex issues, and that the challenges came from the left, the right, and the middle of the religious and political spectrum. At Catholic Charities USA, the Catholic Identity Project had already begun as another "early initiative" of Vision 2000, aiming to produce within a year or so additional focused resources to assist all its members. By 1997, Catholic Charities USA published *Who Do You Say We Are?—Perspectives on Catholic Identity in Catholic Charities*.[11] The book contained reflections from Catholic Charities veterans, canonical guidance, values and ethical principles, spirituality, and practical recommendations for implementation at the local level.

This strategic direction also focused on the church parish. It called for substantially more than parish social ministry as already practiced by many agencies. It meant reaching out to "Catholics beyond parish," e.g., in small faith communities, in the public sector, in the business community, in government, and in the professions. Catholic Charities needed to be present at what Rev. Bryan Hehir[12] called the "fault-lines" of society, where this church included both the wealthiest and most powerful as well as the poorest and least understood.

Vision 2000 urged members to promote the church's own social mission as a prophetic task drawn from Scripture and Catholic social teaching. Some members had argued that the task force should scale back the promotion of Catholic social teaching to target only those involved in Catholic Charities, but the task force explicitly rejected that argument and maintained that this responsibility should be focused on the whole church community.

Strategic Direction IV—Strengthening Our Organizations

To do all that was implied in the first three strategic directions, Strategic Direction IV made it clear that members needed to strengthen both their national organization and their local agencies. In the task force's thinking, four threshold issues faced the national organization: membership, governance, fundraising, and dues. Each of these was a difficult challenge. After extensive consultation over the first two years and a special meeting with diocesan directors of Catholic Charities in March 1996 in Kansas City, the task force developed specific proposals affecting membership, governance, and the financing of the national organization.

Similar pressing concerns faced Catholic Charities at the state and local levels. External forces challenged members to develop stronger state alliances with one another and with other voluntary organizations. Among these forces were the expansion of managed care, the block grant devolution of federal money and power to states, and recent national decisions about "regionalization" of refugee resettlement programs. To strengthen capacities and resources at the local levels meant revisiting questions of funding, volunteers, relations to parishes and other diocesan agencies, alliances with other providers, collaboration among programs, and the training and further professional development of staff, boards, and volunteers.

Ultimately, Vision 2000 called members to attend more proactively to a complex set of relationships that grew out of the special character of Catholic Charities. Edward J. Orzechowski, chairman of the Vision 2000 Task Force and executive director of Catholic Charities of the Archdiocese of Washington, DC, spelled this out in his introductory remarks to the 1996 Kansas City meeting of diocesan directors. These four Strategic Directions, he said, were really about renewing and reforming their relationships (1) with those Catholic Charities serve, (2) with the larger community, (3) with the church, and (4) with one another. Catholic charitable works had been changing ever since the first Catholic charitable foundation in New Orleans in 1727. Vision 2000 was another major marker in that history and it challenged agencies and members to refine their missions and the ways in which they served their communities and larger society.

In All Things Charity (1999)

On November 18, 1999, the week before Thanksgiving, the U.S. bishops affirmed the mission of Catholic Charities and its recent directions in a wide-ranging pastoral message titled In All Things Charity: A Pastoral Challenge for the New Millennium.[13] The document, connected to John Paul II's preparation for the Jubilee Year 2000, first rooted the work of all the church's charities in Scripture and the history of the church. It went on to challenge U.S. society to new emphases on the inextricable link between charity and justice, on global awareness, and on increased generosity and involvement in the coming millennium.

The bishops recited the accomplishments of individuals and organizations in the history of the church across the world and in the United

States. They highlighted Catholic Charities (including the Cadre report), the Society of St. Vincent de Paul, the Ladies of Charity, and others. They urged individuals, families, parishes, religious congregations, unions, and businesses to deepen their commitment to charity and justice. They also described the respective responsibilities of the voluntary sector, private sector, and public sector in working for charity and justice and in the delivery of needed social services in an era of increasing privatization.

Specifically, the bishops singled out those who made Catholic Charities a reality in this country: "We take this opportunity to extend our heartfelt gratitude and encouragement to those countless individuals who, over the years, have been engaged in Catholic Charities service at the parish, diocesan, and national levels."[14] With respect to Catholic Charities' work, the bishops recognized the need to develop professional competencies, increase leadership formation and staff and board development, respect the cultural and faith traditions of those served, and preserve and promote the Catholic roots, identity, and mission of agencies. They urged agencies to provide fair salaries and comprehensive benefits to employees and to maintain appropriate support systems for volunteers. In a spirit of ecumenism, the bishops thanked "the many staff and volunteers of other faith traditions who generously bring their own commitment to the poor and needy and thereby enrich the work of Catholic social agencies across the country."[15]

In addition, the pastoral message quoted the Vision Statement of the Vision 2000 report of Catholic Charities USA and went on to *"strongly appeal to diocesan and parish communities to support the activities and form partnerships with Catholic Charities."*[16]

Pope Benedict XVI and *Deus Caritas Est* (2005)

In the initial year of his pontificate, Pope Benedict XVI issued his first encyclical letter, *Deus Caritas Est* (God Is Love).[17] The first part, which he terms "more speculative," is a rich theological, scriptural, and spiritual essay on the mysterious love that God offers to us and its intrinsic link to human love. In the second part, Pope Benedict discusses "the ecclesial exercise of the commandment of love of neighbor" focusing on the work of charity and justice within the contemporary church. The first part contains important themes that ground the "more concrete" work of the second. These themes coalesce to make it clear that one cannot call oneself a Christian believer without an active love for one's neighbor, especially those who are poor. Benedict describes God's love for humanity as a passionate[18] and gratuitous[19] involvement in the human community, presents the Eucharist of Jesus as essentially social,[20] and explores a fascinating choice of "the great parables of Jesus."[21] The chosen parables are the rich man and Lazarus in Luke 16 (a favorite also of Pope John Paul II in addressing prosperous nations), the Good Samaritan in Luke 10, and the Last Judgment in Matthew 25. All are strongly social in character.

In part one's discussion of the two great commandments, the pope works from the first letter of John, emphasizing the "unbreakable bond between love of God and love of neighbor."[22] Through this unity, made possible in the revelation of God in Jesus, Benedict writes that, in and with God, we can love persons whom we do not like or even know. We can offer them what they need and, going beyond necessities, "give them the look of love which they crave." Without such love of neighbor, our relationship to God becomes arid, "proper," and loveless. The two commandments are "thus inseparable, they form a single commandment."[23]

Part two is titled "*Caritas*: The Practice of Love by the Church as a 'Community of Love.'" It focuses on the church's *institutional* practice of love, so we find here less of the analysis and application of Catholic social teaching to global social realities than we find in the encyclicals of John Paul II. However, Benedict does discuss both charity and justice and the relative responsibilities of laity and the institutional church. He also affirms modern Catholic social teaching from *Rerum Novarum* in 1891 to *Centesimus Annus* in 1991.[24]

Pope Benedict begins from a dual foundation: love of neighbor is a responsibility of the entire ecclesial community; and love also "needs to be organized if it is to be an ordered service to the community."[25] He traces a 2,000-year-old tradition of *diaconia*—"the ministry of charity exercised in a communitarian, orderly way"—from the deacons in the Acts of the Apostles to its fourth-century institutionalization within each Egyptian monastery to its evolution into sixth-century juridical corporations to which civil authorities entrusted grain for public distribution.[26]

Benedict notes that charitable activity on behalf of the poor and suffering was an essential part of the Church of Rome from its earliest days, highlighted in the third-century work of St. Lawrence and imitated by the emperor Julian the Apostate in the fourth century.[27] His historical survey concludes that "the Church's deepest nature is expressed in her three-fold responsibility: proclaiming the word of God (*kerygma-martyria*), celebrating the sacraments (*leitourgia*), and exercising the ministry of charity (*diakonia*)."[28] He also notes approvingly that this ministry of charity extended beyond the membership of the church to embrace—a lesson from the Good Samaritan—a "standard which imposes universal love towards the needy whom we encounter."

The church has a direct role through its charitable organizations to meet the immediate needs of suffering people. That role is always necessary, even in the most just society, because there are always people suffering, lonely, and with material needs requiring a response extending beyond the material to the care and refreshment of their souls. That direct role takes place within the context of an increasingly globalized world, featuring the ability of media to broadcast the faces of suffering to every continent and a worldwide network of assistance made possible by governmental and humanitarian organizations. For those thinking relief can be done by individuals alone, Benedict notes, "The solidarity shown by civil society thus significantly surpasses that shown by individuals."[29] Thus, the pope expresses gratitude for the many forms of cooperation existing between governments and church agencies, the work of philanthropic and charitable organizations, and the generosity of volunteers, especially the young.[30]

Finally, the pope enumerates those responsible for the church's duty of charity, including parishes and all levels of the church. He includes the responsibilities of each bishop for organizing and supporting the ministry of charity within his diocese and the need for leaders guided by faith and urged by Christ's love to do the work of charity and to embody that same love. He notes the need for deep prayer to sustain those workers in the midst of human suffering, failure, and discouragement, and emphasizes the importance of a robust faith, hope, and love.[31]

Catholic Charities USA Code of Ethics (2007)

First published in 1983 and modified only slightly thereafter, the *Catholic Charities USA Code of Ethics* recently underwent a thorough revision in light of member needs, the first encyclical of Pope Benedict, the new *Compendium of the Social Doctrine of the Church*,[32] and new and complex issues emerging for members in recent years. The new code was approved by the Board of Trustees of Catholic Charities USA on September 12, 2007. It contains significant parts dealing with the use and purpose of the code, its scriptural and theological foundations, principles of Catholic social teaching, fundamental values, and then ethical standards. In its prologue, we find the familiar 1972 tripartite mission of the Cadre:

> Catholic Charities USA, in concert with Caritas Internationalis, is committed to providing quality social services, advocating for just structures in society and working to convene the Catholic community, along with all people of good will, to provide help and create hope.[33]

Detailed sections deal with responsibilities to clients, competence of staff, and the work of volunteers, all applying to the *service* goal of Catholic Charities. Further specifics in the code, such as the sections on "Mission Engagement," "Staff Participation," and "Coalition Building," spell out the responsibilities of agencies, boards, management, and staff for *advocacy* for social justice and engagement in the wider community—*convening*.

The Scriptural and Theological Foundations for Mission

As did the 2007 *Catholic Charities USA Code of Ethics*, it is important to briefly explain how the mission of Catholic Charities fits within the larger context of Catholic social teaching, including its deep scriptural roots. That revelation begins with the nature of the human person. The new *Compendium of the Social Doctrine of the Church* puts it this way:

> *The fundamental message of Sacred Scripture proclaims that the human person is a creature of God* (cf. Ps 139:14-18), *and sees in his being in the image of God the element that characterizes and distinguishes him:* "God created man in his own image, in the image of God he created him; male and female he created them" (Gen 1:27). God places the human creature at the centre and summit of the created order.[34]

The human person is not just sacred, however, but also social. The social nature of the person is not revealed solely in the incompleteness of Adam without Eve in the narrative of Genesis, but it is revealed all through the Jewish Scriptures in the compelling story of God's love for a people—Israel—and the intimate bond that this God has with them and that they in turn have with God and with one another. The covenants of God with Israel are expressive of this intimate bond and call the people to duties of mutual justice and charity, with a special care for the poor among them whom God especially loves. The U.S. Catholic bishops, writing in their pastoral message In All Things Charity, reminded their readers of the Jewish tradition in these words:

> The Old Testament writers describe the great covenant of Sinai, which concretized the relationship of the community of Israel with God. This divine revelation illumines our understanding of the breadth and depth of charity. In the covenant, God promises steadfast love and faithfulness to the people of Israel. They, in turn, pledge to worship him alone and to direct their lives in accordance with God's will, made explicit in Israel's great legal codes. Integral to those codes is the special concern charged to the community for the widows, orphans,

and strangers who comprised God's beloved poor. While the poor remain faithful to God, they are oppressed by a combination of poverty, powerlessness, and exploitation by others. "What these groups of people have in common is their vulnerability and lack of power. They are often alone and have no protector or advocate." The poor are oppressed politically and denied a decent share in the blessings of God's creation, which are intended to be shared by all of humanity.[35]

The bishops then describe the role of the jubilee in light of this tradition of community and its responsibility for God's beloved poor:

The jubilee year (cf. Lv 25), which fell every fifty years, was meant to restore equality among all the children of Israel, "offering new possibilities to families which had lost their property and even their personal freedom." The jubilee year was proclaimed to assist those in need, to free those enslaved (often for debt), to restore property to its original owners, and to allow the poor to share fully in God's abundant blessings.[36]

Jesus in turn ushers in this new millennium, restoring right relationships among people and with their God. Justice lies at the heart of those right relationships, the jubilee year, and what we call Catholic social teaching. Quoting Jesus in the fourth chapter of Luke's Gospel, the bishops declared that "Jesus himself is the proclamation of the Great Jubilee." They went on to explain:

In the fullness of time, it is Jesus who proclaims the good news to the poor. It is Jesus who gives sight to the blind and frees the oppressed. By His words and above all by His actions, Jesus ushered in a "year of the Lord's favor," becoming in his passion and death the ransom for many.[37]

Pope Benedict's "great parables of Jesus"—the rich man and poor Lazarus, the Good Samaritan, and the Judgment scene in Matthew 25—deepen our understanding of the centrality of love and justice in the revelation of the love of God embodied in Jesus of Nazareth. Further, as Benedict emphasized, the exercise of the ministry of charity (*diakonia*) is part of the threefold responsibility of the church. Catholic social teaching also comprises a part of the proclamation of the Gospel (*kerygma-martyria*), another part of that threefold responsibility.

At this point it seems good to turn more directly to the development of Catholic social teaching, which the *Catechism of the Catholic Church* describes in these general terms:

> The Church's social teaching comprises a body of doctrine, which is articulated as the Church interprets events in the course of history, with the assistance of the Holy Spirit in light of the whole of what has been revealed by Jesus Christ.[38]

> The Church's social teaching proposes principles for reflection; it provides criteria for judgment; it gives guidelines for action.[39]

As the catechism explains, the church makes moral judgments about economic and social matters "when the fundamental rights of the person or the salvation of souls requires it."[40] These kinds of judgments go back two millennia to the earliest days of the followers of "the Way" of Jesus. The appointments of deacons, the collection promoted by St. Paul for the Christians suffering in Jerusalem, and the powerful and graphic warnings about the dangers of wealth in the Epistle of James are all early social applications of the Gospel.

In the postapostolic centuries, the writings of Cyprian, St. John Chrysostom, Origen, St. Augustine, St. Clement of Alexandria, and St. Basil warn about the dangers of wealth and the punishment for failing to give alms. The Christian community was to be generous and compassionate as they knew that their God was toward them, and they knew well the close identification that Christ had made between himself and the poor.

In the Middle Ages, while monasteries and religious congregations were notable for their organized care for orphans, widows, the elderly, the sick, and the poor, the philosophers and theologians were developing a comprehensive body of thought that married Christian values with those of the Greek, Latin, Arab, and Jewish thinkers. From these were developed the underlying concepts of both personal and social justice and the nature of the virtuous life that provided the foundations for what we now call modern Catholic social teaching.

The key building blocks in this social teaching are the encyclical or teaching letters of the popes and the documents of the Second Vatican Council and synods of bishops. Among these we might describe "the classics, moderns, and contemporaries." The two great classics were the encyclical letters of Pope Leo XIII (*Rerum Novarum* in 1891) and Pope Pius XI (*Quadragesimo Anno* in 1931), beginning in the Industrial Revolution and creating the initial framework of the church's discussion. The two moderns from Pope John XXIII (*Mater et Magistra* in 1961 and *Pacem in Terris* in 1963) heavily influenced the work of the Second Vatican Council. The council document on The Church in the Modern World (*Gaudium et Spes*, 1965) is the most authoritative achievement, beginning a 40-year wave of more contemporary reflection that has brought us to Pope Benedict's *Deus Caritas Est* in 2005.[41]

How does the scriptural tradition of justice and charity and the 2,000-year-old tradition of Catholic social teaching bear on our contemporary realities and the mission of Catholic Charities? Most commentators enunciate a series of principles of Catholic social teaching drawn from the long and complex history of the church's interface with political, social, economic, and cultural realities.[42] The *Compendium*, in a Vatican effort to be synthetic, perhaps overly so, identifies four core principles of Catholic social teaching, including extensive commentary on the four. A short description of each is taken from the *Compendium*:

> 1. **Human dignity**: *A just society can become a reality only when it is based on respect of the transcendent dignity of the human person. The person represents the ultimate end of society, by which it is ordered to the person:* "Hence, the social order and its development must invariably work to the benefit of the human person, since the order of things is to be subordinate to the order of persons, not the other way around."[43]

> 2. **The common good**: *The principle of the common good, to which every aspect of social life must be related if it is to attain its fullest meaning, stems from the dignity, unity and equality of all people.* According to its primary and broadly accepted sense, *the common good* indicates "the sum total of social conditions which allow people, either as groups or as individuals, to reach their fulfillment more fully and more easily."

> *The common good does not consist in the simple sum of the particular goods of each subject of a social entity. Belonging to everyone and to each person, it is and remains "common," because it is indivisible and because only together is it possible to attain it, increase it and safeguard its effectiveness, with regard also to the future.*[44]

> 3. **Subsidiarity**: It is impossible to promote the dignity of the person without showing concern for the family, groups, associations, local territorial realities; in short, for that aggregate of economic, social, cultural, sports-oriented, recreational, professional and political expressions to which people spontaneously give life and which make it possible for them to achieve effective social growth. . . .

> *On the basis of this principle, all societies of a superior order must adopt attitudes of help* ("subsidium")*—therefore of support, promotion, development . . . with respect to lower order societies. . . .*

> *The principle of subsidiarity protects people from abuses by higher-level social authority and calls on these same authorities to help individuals*

and intermediate groups to fulfill their duties. This principle is imperative because every person, family and intermediate group has something original to offer to the community.[45]

4. **Solidarity**: *Solidarity highlights in a particular way the intrinsic social nature of the human person, the equality of all in dignity and rights and the common path of individuals and peoples towards an ever more committed unity.* . . . *In the presence of the phenomenon of interdependence and its constant expansion, however, there persist in every part of the world stark inequalities between developed and developing countries,* inequalities stoked also by various forms of exploitation, oppression and corruption that have a negative influence on the internal and international life of many States. *The acceleration of interdependence between persons and peoples needs to be accompanied by equally intense efforts on the ethical-social plane,* in order to avoid the dangerous consequences of perpetrating injustice on a global scale.[46]

As the *Catholic Charities USA Code of Ethics* explains, the values and work of Catholic Charities are in keeping with the principles of Catholic social teaching and promote them in society. In terms of human dignity, Catholic Charities works to affirm and respect the dignity of each person and to promote their rights and duties. Catholic Charities promotes the common good in its efforts to help all people to access what they need in society to reach their fulfillment, to encourage all persons to work for the rights of all the community, and in their advocacy for justice within society. Catholic Charities, in keeping with the principle of subsidiarity, encourages decision making by all those capable of doing so, participation by those affected by decisions, and empowerment of those most in need. Further expressions of subsidiarity occur in the participation of Catholic Charities in the public discourse about charity and justice, especially for those with little or no voice of their own, and in their own work as an "intermediate group" in providing services in society, including partnerships with government at all levels. Insofar as solidarity is concerned, Catholic Charities embodies the special concern for the poor in its priorities for the most needy, in the emphasis on participation by those served in agency decision making, and in advocacy for and with those most in need in public discourse.[47]

The Catholic Identity of Catholic Charities

Across this nation there are hundreds of independent organizations, involving thousands of programs, which make up the Catholic Charities network. In 2008, 64,458 staff, 6,352 board members, and 239,794 volunteers served 8.5 million people (unduplicated).[48] They were the face and hands and heart of Catholic Charities. Despite the incredible variety of people of many faiths (and none) who make Catholic Charities a reality, certain essentials shape the agencies as *Catholic* Charities. Ten of them stand out.[49] They are drawn from the history of the mission of Catholic Charities sketched out above and in earlier chapters of this volume, from authoritative documents of the Catholic Church, and from the experiences of Catholic Charities agencies.

First, this ministry is rooted in the Scriptures. In the Jewish Scriptures, at the heart of the biblical concept of *justice* was the care of the widow, orphan, and the stranger. The Jewish people had a special responsibility to respond to their needs, and this justice was the gauge of whether they understood their relationships to God and one another. Ironically, the contemporary work of Catholic Charities worldwide continues to focus primarily on the same groups who comprised the biblical *anawim*: poor women; poor children; and those marginalized because, literally, they are foreign workers, immigrants, and refugees, or they are racially different, or they have a disability, HIV/AIDS, or some other condition that sets them apart. How these people are treated tests every society's justice and the common understanding that we are all children of one God who is passionately concerned about the least among us. Jesus taught this tradition as well. In the famous judgment scene in Matthew 25, one of Pope Benedict's "great parables," Jesus tells his followers that the world will be judged by how they treat him—found among the hungry, homeless, sick, imprisoned, and poor.

Second, this ministry has been an integral part of the Catholic Church for 2,000 years. As we have seen, beginning with the appointment of the deacons in the apostolic church, the ministry of justice was inaugurated in the community—poor widows and children were cared for. As Pope Benedict pointed out, this ministry was institutionalized in the Egyptian monasteries of the fourth century, then in corporate ecclesial structures of the sixth century entrusted by government with the means to assist the poor.

In the great monasteries of the first millennium, monastic communities of men and women took care of orphans, the sick, the elderly, travelers, and the poor. From the monasteries, this ministry was carried later by women and men religious back into the cities where orphanages, homes for the sick and elderly, hospices, and many other centers for health and social services were established. Still later, lay and religious associations such as those begun by St. Vincent de Paul expanded and deepened this work. Many other great saints were known for their ministries to the poor and vulnerable: St. Francis of Assisi, St. Clare, St. Peter Claver, St. Catherine of Siena, St. Martin de Porres, St. Ignatius of Loyola, and St. Elizabeth Ann Seton.

These traditions came to the New World to become part of the institutional and parish life of the Catholic Church here. The first such foundation was the orphanage, home for "women of ill repute," school, and health care facility begun by the Ursuline Sisters in New Orleans in 1727. By 1900, over 800 Catholic charitable institutions existed in the United States. Now, Catholic Charities staff and volunteers, serving almost eight million persons a year, care for infants with fetal alcohol syndrome, sponsor group homes for persons with mental disabilities, provide apartments for the elderly, resettle refugees, counsel troubled families, offer hospice to persons with HIV/AIDS, feed hungry families, and shelter the homeless.

Third, Catholic Charities promotes the sanctity of human life and the dignity of the human person. The ultimate rationale for these services is belief in the sanctity of the human person and the dignity of human life, the underlying foundation for all Catholic social teaching. This is reflected, for example, in adoption services that are among the most traditional and the care for the sick and the elderly that is a hallmark of the work of Catholic Charities. While society may exclude some people because they are sick, disabled, poor, or racially different, Catholic Charities reaches out to them, respecting their human dignity. While many may reject people because they are in prison or undocumented, Catholic Charities works to enhance their dignity, improve their lives, and meet their needs. Jesus Christ excluded no one from his healing touch and was known for his fellowship meals with tax collectors and sinners.

Because of the theological and philosophical traditions of this faith community, at the heart of which are human sanctity and dignity, Catholic Charities has certain values and ethical standards that shape its work and are set out in the *Code of Ethics*, discussed earlier. Among these values is the preferential concern for the poor articulated by Pope John Paul II and so many others. This is played out in the nature of agency services, the locations of their offices, the use of sliding fee scales, and advocacy for social justice.

Fourth, Catholic Charities is authorized to exercise its ministry by the diocesan bishop. Whether founded by a diocese, parish, religious congregation, or lay activists, Catholic charitable works and institutions root their formal Catholic identity in relationship to the church and the diocesan bishop. As emphasized by Pope Benedict in his encyclical on charity, the bishop is charged in church teaching and canon law with responsibility for the apostolate within diocesan confines and with a special charge to care for the poor. However organized in terms of canon and civil law, Catholic Charities has responsibilities to operate consistently with the teachings and values of the church and in line with the ecclesial responsibility of the bishop.

Fifth, Catholic Charities respects the religious beliefs of those they serve. Many people are surprised to learn that Catholic Charities serves people of all faiths and none. Most agencies do not keep statistics on the religious affiliation of those coming to them. This is not an accident of history or a result of receiving funding from the United Way or government entities. Instead, it reflects a determined position to serve the entire community, a custom going back as far as the fourth century and, in this country, to the Ursuline Sisters in New Orleans in 1727. Again, in the pattern of Christ Jesus, the agencies' response is to families and persons in need—hungry, homeless, depressed, troubled, frail—regardless of beliefs. We see this in Jesus' own ministry, where he cured the daughter of the Canaanite woman in Matthew 15 and the centurion's servant in Luke 7. Pope Benedict emphasized this in discussing the Good Samaritan and its message of universal love.

This decidedly ecumenical approach is very Roman Catholic. It reflects our respect for human dignity, religious liberty, and the ecumenical sensitivity promoted at Vatican II. Many people come to Catholic Charities for particular needs: a hot meal, a safe place to stay, a voucher for prescription medicine, resettlement in a new nation, and resources to rebuild after a natural disaster. They do not seek or need religious proselytizing, nor would staff members and volunteers offer it. It would be more than strange to preach Catholic beliefs to a devout Muslim family being resettled from Bosnia, a Buddhist Vietnamese grandmother coming to a Catholic Charities senior center, a Baptist elder to whom volunteers deliver a meal at home, or a Lutheran father entering a job-training program. Agencies are Catholic precisely in their respect for others' religious beliefs. As Pope John Paul II told the members meeting in San Antonio in 1986, "For your long and persevering service—creative and courageous, and blind to the distinctions of race or religion—you will hear Jesus' words of gratitude, 'You did it for me.'"

Ten years later, Pope John Paul addressed the Pontifical Council Cor Unum on the role of charitable activity worldwide. Charitable activity is an eloquent means of Catholic evangelization because it witnesses to a spirit of giving and of communion inspired by God who created all men and women, the pope said. But, he continued, the primary motivation for Catholic giving is to serve Christ in the poor and suffering and to promote the justice, peace, and development worthy of God's children.

Actions of aid, relief, and assistance should be conducted in a spirit of service and free giving for the benefit of all persons without the ulterior motive of eventual tutelage or proselytism.[50] Pope Benedict was equally explicit in his encyclical on love: "Charity, furthermore, cannot be used as a means of engaging in what is nowadays considered proselytism. Love is free; it is not practiced as a way of achieving other ends."[51]

The love of God is to be shown in the work of Catholic Charities, not imposed as a condition for housing, food, or counseling services. For a variety of reasons, however, Catholic Charities also may sponsor particular programs for the Catholic community, including marriage preparation, parish outreach, Catholic school counseling, or other more specific services. These are usually funded by the Church, primarily for Catholics, and with more explicitly Catholic content.

Sixth, Catholic Charities recognizes that some services require attention to the physical, mental, *and spiritual* needs of those they serve. In some services, it is appropriate and necessary to recognize and respond to the physical, mental, and spiritual needs of those served. Addiction treatment programs, marriage and family counseling, grief ministries, and other services attend to all the integrated facets of human beings. Catholic Charities does this in many ways consistent with its respect for the individual's religious beliefs. For example, twelve-step programs have a distinctive spiritual component essential to their success. Homeless shelters often provide opportunities for sharing faith and hope, prayer of all kinds, and expressions of belief in a higher power. Senior centers and residences may provide opportunities for chaplaincy services of various denominations, depending on the desires of those served. Finally, marriage and family counseling often must include the spiritual beliefs and values of those involved and how those beliefs help or hinder movement towards healing within the family.

Pope Benedict underscores this openness to the spiritual in all charitable services by emphasizing the concern of love for the whole person. Often, he says, no matter what the need in question, people crave "the look of love" because of their interior desire for a sign of love, of concern.[52] John Paul II had made a similar point in his 1987 San Antonio address to Catholic Charities USA when he declared, "No institution can by itself replace the human heart, human compassion, human love or human

initiative, when it is a question of dealing with the sufferings of others."
The deepest cause of their suffering may well be "the very absence of
God," wrote Pope Benedict. The church's charitable activity, then, does not
impose religion, but remains open to communicate God's love in deeds:

> Those who practice charity in the Church's name will never seek to
> impose the Church's faith upon others. They realize that a pure and
> generous love is the best witness to the God in whom we believe and
> by whom we are driven to love. A Christian knows when it is time to
> speak of God and when it is better to say nothing and let love alone
> speak. He knows that God is love (cf. *1 Jn* 4:8) and that God's pres-
> ence is felt at the very time when the only thing we do is to love.[53]

St. Francis of Assisi is said to have made the same point to his followers
when he urged, "Preach the Gospel, if necessary use words."

**Seventh, Catholic Charities have a special relationship to the
Catholic diocese and to Catholic parishes.** In over half of U.S. dioceses, Catholic Charities agencies have formal programs through which
the agency seeks to support and encourage the parish in its ministry to
the community and its needs.[54] In many others this parish relationship
also exists, although more informally. In this capacity, agencies assist parishioners in the exercise of their baptismal commitment to the poor and
needy.[55] Agencies provide professional resources, training, support, and
encouragement to parish-based ministries such as food pantries, outreach
to the frail elderly, community organizing, legislative networks for social
justice, and action for global solidarity and peace. By so doing, agencies
help pastors and parishes to form caring faith communities. These efforts
in turn expand agencies' own ministry through the hands and hearts of
many thousands of parishioners. They even enlist parishes and parishioners in joint ventures such as community-wide soup kitchens, sponsorship
of refugee families, and prison visitations. The U.S. bishops, writing In All
Things Charity, urged parish leaders and members to develop links with
diocesan Catholic Charities agencies and encouraged agencies to reach
out to parishes to support their social concern activities.[56]

Catholic Charities also cooperates with diocesan leadership by operating or collaborating with diocesan offices and programs, funded largely
by the church. These might include the Catholic Campaign for Human
Development antipoverty program, family life and respect life programs,
youth organizations, offices for African-American or Hispanic-American
Catholics, Catholic Relief Services, the St. Vincent de Paul Society, and

justice and peace offices. In so doing, Catholic Charities assists the Catholic Church in carrying out other related aspects of the church's ministry within and to the wider community and helps fulfill their own mission to serve people in need, advocate for a just society, and bring people together to solve community problems.

Eighth, Catholic Charities works in active partnership with other religiously sponsored charities and with the civic community. Reflecting the teaching of the Second Vatican Council and an even longer experience with practical ecumenism, Catholic Charities expresses the willingness and responsibility of the Catholic Church to work hand in hand with other religions and other people of goodwill to serve community needs. They often support community-wide fundraising for the benefit of Catholic Charities, charities sponsored by other churches, and other nonprofit organizations, such as those conducted by the United Way. They build coalitions to address emerging community needs by developing new collaborative responses, community education, and combined advocacy before public and private forums. The U.S. bishops have encouraged such activities and partnerships:

> Voluntary organizations play an important part in our collective efforts to promote the common good, protect human life, reach out to people in need, and work for a more just and compassionate society.
>
> Parishes, diocesan organizations, and Catholic charity and justice organizations should take every reasonable opportunity to work with such associations as well as with those organizations sponsored by other faith communities.[57]

The bishops also urged collaboration with the private sector where businesses, corporations, and unions could play a strong role in promoting jobs with decent wages, providing volunteers and financial support, and supporting charities with technical assistance, business skills, and capital.[58] Pope Benedict urged charity workers to "work in harmony with other organizations in serving various forms of need, but in a way that respects what is distinctive about the service which Christ requested of his disciples."[59]

Ninth, Catholic Charities supports an active public-private partnership with government at all levels. The church has a strong tradition of teaching about government responsibilities to promote the common good and protect the least among us, and the responsibilities of Catholics as citizens and taxpayers to support those roles and actively participate in civic life. In his encyclical, Pope Benedict taught that "the just ordering of society and the State is a central responsibility of politics." In fulfilling this responsibility, "justice is both the aim and the intrinsic criterion of all politics."[60] The church's role here is the formation of consciences and education about the "authentic requirements of justice" in the civic realm in which everyone has a duty: "Building a just social and civil order, wherein each person receives what is his or her due, is an essential task which every generation must take up anew."[61] The church does not replace the state, but has a duty to promote justice in the public dialogue.

An additional relationship exists between church and state, Benedict wrote, whereby there has been "the growth of many forms of cooperation between State and Church agencies."[62] In keeping with subsidiarity, government should encourage various forms of subsidiary organizations such as Catholic Charities, who bring their own strong mission, resources, and volunteers to serve the needs of the public. In many cases, government provides financial resources that are far beyond the wherewithal of private charities, which in turn bring to bear the human and spiritual resources that are unavailable to government.

Two instances come to mind. One is income support, often to the elderly, disabled, and needy families, a role for which only government has the resources. The U.S. bishops explain:

> As a result of the Great Depression, which lasted from 1929 to 1941, it became evident to people of the United States that only the government could develop resources to ensure regular income support for aged, disabled, or otherwise needy families. It has accomplished this by establishing such vehicles as Social Security; retirement, disability, and survivors' programs; unemployment compensation; workers' compensation; food stamps; and dependent children programs. No private charity has the resources, for example, to provide steady monthly support to families without adequate income.[63]

The *Compendium* describes such redistribution of income under the heading of social justice and pursuit of authentic well-being within a country.[64] Charities cannot replace this governmental function—basic income support—but they often provide additional financial and in-kind support (food, clothing, a rent payment) when government income support is inadequate for family needs (which is all too often) and in times of crisis for families otherwise able to support themselves.

The second area of complementarity between government and voluntary agencies such as Catholic Charities is in providing needed social services. In the light of these teachings, Catholic Charities has sought and accepted partnerships with cities, counties, states, and the federal government in which they receive government funding for services to the wider community that they judge to be consistent with their missions. These payments may take the form of contracts to deliver foster care to vulnerable youth, health care for individuals paid for by Medicaid, and government funding of construction such as housing. Government provides funding; and agencies bring additional funding, volunteers, efficiency, values, credibility, and dedication to community service and needy families. As the U.S. bishops explain approvingly:

> The U.S. government has also provided funding for needed social services by purchasing service contracts and providing other funding for nonprofit agencies. These agencies, in turn, have provided hands-on care by trained staff, enrichment of volunteers, private fund raising, and dedicated commitment to deliver the services to children, families, elders, and people with disabilities. This pluralism has been an essential characteristic of twentieth-century social service delivery in the United States. Pluralism in public programs is strengthened and made more genuine when individuals can choose to receive social services through a variety of providers, including religiously affiliated social service organizations.[65]

What is true of the federal government is also true of states and localities, either with federal funding delivered through block grants and other means or with separate state or local funds.

Tenth, Catholic Charities blends advocacy for those in need and public education about social justice with service to individuals, families, and communities in need. Throughout the last century, the Catholic Church has been increasingly outspoken about the need for social, economic, and political change. This change is consistent with the obligations of social justice in order to meet the needs of the entire community, with a special concern for the poor. This complements the duties of individuals to reach out to the needy in charity and justice.

Catholic Charities, consistent with the Vatican and the bishops, makes working for a more just society an integral part of its mission. It is not enough to feed more hungry families; Catholic Charities also must ask why so much hunger persists in this wealthy nation and how that condition might be changed by individual, community, business, and government action. Thus, local Catholic Charities include advocacy, empowerment, and work for justice as intrinsic parts of its mission of caring for needy individuals, families, and communities. In taking this position, Catholic Charities agencies understand the evangelical connection between justice and charity:

> In his apostolic exhortation *The Church in America (Ecclesia in America)*, Pope John Paul II clearly presents the Christian responsibility to ensure that charity and justice result in individual actions and work for systemic change. We Christians must "reflect the attitude of Jesus, who came to 'proclaim Good News to the poor' (Lk 4:18). . . . This constant dedication to the poor and disadvantaged emerges in the Church's social teaching, which ceaselessly invites the Christian community to a commitment to overcome every form of exploitation and oppression. It is a question not only of alleviating the most serious and urgent needs through individual actions here and there, but of uncovering the roots of evil and proposing initiatives to make social, political and economic structures more just and fraternal."[66]

This connection has been a part of the history of Catholic Charities USA from its founding in 1910, promoted consistently in the recommendations of the Cadre Study and Vision 2000, and contained in the mission of the national organization and the requirements of various editions of its *Code of Ethics*.

Conclusion

The mission and identity of Catholic Charities are extremely complex realities. They have roots stretching back into the Scriptures, dimensions that shape their corporate structures and partnerships within the church and in civil society, and demands that place them in the streets with the very poor, in the boardrooms of corporate America, in the pews of the neighborhood parish, and in the halls of Congress and state legislatures. Living up to this mission and fleshing out the fullness of Catholic identity are a daily challenge for Catholic Charities agencies and their staff, boards, and volunteers.

Chapter
Nine

Catholic Charities

Safeguarding and Advancing the Church's Presence in the World

Rev. Msgr. Kevin Sullivan
The Catholic Charities
of the Archdiocese of New York

Catholic Charities

Safeguarding and Advancing the Church's Presence in the World

Few argue against charity. Along with motherhood and apple pie, charity receives almost universal approbation from both secularists and religionists.[1] In such diverse places as St. Paul's letter to the Corinthians (love is the greatest), and the U.S. tax code (the deductibility of charitable contributions), charity emerges in a privileged place. However, we must admit a few naysayers. On the one hand, some don't want to "baby" people with too much charity. Others equate charity with a condescending attitude that disrespects the recipients' dignity. Yet on the whole, charity's approval numbers remain extremely high, particularly among Catholics. National polls consistently rank concern for the poor as among their highest priorities. One fairly recent poll that asked Catholics what was most important to their faith produced a noteworthy result. Concern for the poor was in a virtual tie with belief in the resurrection of Jesus as the top priority for the faith of American Catholics.[2] I suspect this may be why the Catholic Church's organized work of helping people in the United States has consistently been called Catholic Charities.[3]

From the perspective of the Catholic Church, the staying power of the title Catholic Charities is a good thing, but it does come with a challenge: that we communicate *charity* in its fullest Christian sense, rooted in the biblical understanding of love. The failure to do so gives legitimacy to some of the "charity naysayers," who can point to examples that undermine the genuine meaning of Christian charity.

However, understood in its full sense, charity is an essential part of the identity of the Christian and must be practiced both by individual

Christians and collectively by the community of the church. In other words, without charity the Christian and the church are in danger of being marginalized and the church's sacraments and teaching compromised. In the same way, Catholic Charities is compromised without the sacraments and teachings of the church. Making this case has become much easier by the compelling argument of Pope Benedict XVI in the first encyclical of his papacy, *Deus Caritas Est.*

Building upon this foundation, I would like to make the further case that Catholic Charities is the fulfillment of the church's responsibility to practice collective charity in faithfulness to the Gospel. Were there not Catholic Charities, then the Catholic Church would be required to create Catholic Charities in order to be authentic to its identity as the Church of Jesus Christ. In developing this case, I will touch on four interrelated areas:

1. Individual charity and the communal work of Catholic Charities are essential and constitutive elements of the biblical teaching of Jesus and the Catholic Church at all levels.

2. The scope of Christian charity, both individually and communally (Catholic Charities), needs to be based upon a more traditional, comprehensive biblical understanding of charity (*caritas*) as *agape* or Christian love, which includes both justice and charity. Because the English word *charity* has limiting denotations and connotations, this point needs to be repeated.

3. The human rights tradition of the church, most fundamentally the dignity of the human person as expressed in the encyclical of John XXIII, *Pacem in Terris*, provides concrete direction for the focus of Catholic Charities work. It serves as a safeguard against certain narrow understandings of charity that are common in secular parlance.

4. The programs and services of Catholic Charities throughout the United States can be overlaid upon this human rights tradition of the church to identify areas for growth and development for addressing the broad range of basic human needs.

Illustrations of the Work of Charity

Before developing the four interrelated areas, I would like to root this thesis in the concrete history of the church and the lives of real Catholics by presenting four nineteenth-century examples from the church in New

York. These historical examples include an immigrant slave, women religious, parish laity, and a New York archdiocesan priest. These examples show that fervent Catholics with different callings in diverse circumstances demonstrated the ministry of charity to be at the heart of their individual priestly, religious, or lay Christian vocations. The church, in various ways, has recognized these individuals as serving as inspiration for generations of Catholics who followed them. In these examples, it is also instructive to point out that these individual or small group ministries of charity blossomed into large communal works of charity that have subsequently been embraced by entire religious communities and the Archdiocese of New York. These examples have been replicated many times over across the United States and throughout the world.

Let us consider an immigrant slave. Pierre Toussaint, brought to New York from Haiti, became known for his extraordinary loyalty and charity. Freed as a young man after the death of his owner, he used the wealth he earned as a hairdresser of great skill and repute to provide charity for those in need. As a daily communicant at St. Patrick's Old Cathedral in the early 1800s, Pierre Toussaint developed a relationship with Sister Mary Elizabeth Boyle and the Sisters of Charity. This relationship led him to become a major benefactor in developing and sustaining their initial orphanages. A few decades later, the work would grow into the establishment in 1857 of the New York Foundling Hospital as a haven for homeless and abandoned children. Today, the New York Foundling Hospital is among the largest and most respected Catholic Charities agencies, serving thousands of children and families each year throughout New York City and in Puerto Rico. Pierre Toussaint exemplifies a dedicated Catholic with deep spirituality for whom both individual and communal charity were an integral part of his Catholic Christian vocation.

Let us recall one particular group of women religious. Sister Mary Ann Sammon, a young Irish immigrant inspired by the life of St. Dominic, walked the streets of the Lower East Side of New York City gathering orphaned and homeless children and taking them to her cloistered Dominican convent. The number of children needing care continued to grow and in 1868, Sister Mary Ann and a few Dominican sisters brought nine little girls out of the poverty and overcrowding of New York City to a rural suburb some 30 miles away in Blauvelt, New York. This mission of caring began what is now, over 150 years later, St. Dominic's Home. More than 800 staff members continue the legacy of the Blauvelt Dominican Sisters by caring for more than 2,000 children, adolescents, adults, and families through their services and programs in the Bronx and the lower Hudson Valley, New York.[4]

Let us turn to a dedicated parish-based group of laity. Toward the very end of the nineteenth century, children were being transported across country in trains and placed in large institutions. In addition, rampant sectarian disputes were impacting the care of orphaned and neglected children. Thomas Mulry and the laymen of the St. Vincent de Paul Society saw the need for recruiting Catholic foster homes for the placement of children. Through their efforts, the Catholic Home Bureau was established in 1898 as the first foster home agency in the nation. In 1909, Thomas Mulry and Edmund Butler of Catholic Home Bureau attended the first White House conference on children to marshal government support and planning for protection of children across the nation. Today, over a century later, more than 1,100 abused or neglected children and youth are in foster care under the Catholic Guardian Society and Home Bureau.[5]

Let us look at a sexton of St. Mary's Church, John Drumgoole, who began to shelter homeless children on Grand Street in Lower Manhattan in the mid-nineteenth century. Ordained a priest of the Archdiocese of New York in 1868 at the then advanced age of 52, Fr. Drumgoole never lost sight of his goal to help children. The conditions in New York for children had not improved, and many young Catholic children were being sent to the Midwest to work as farm laborers. One response to this crisis was the Vincentians' founding of the Newsboys' Home on Warren Street, which later came under Fr. Drumgoole's leadership and became known as the Mission of the Immaculate Virgin. And yet, Fr. Drumgoole felt that the general environment of the city at the time was a great threat to younger children, so he sought out a more rural setting on Staten Island. There, he founded the mission's farm at Mount Loretto, which housed almost 2,000 children. This residence of the mission remains, no longer as a foster care agency but a multiservice agency serving children and adults on Staten Island.[6]

These four examples concretize and authenticate the theological and theoretical aspiration that the church's charitable work is central to its ministry. The work of charity is intrinsic to the mission of the church. Every vocation, religious, lay, or clergy, needs to see charity, not only as an essential part of their vocations as individuals, but may also legitimately make this "organized work of charity" the primary focus of their vocations. Remembering, understanding, and appreciating the central role that individual and collective charity has had in the lives of prominent Catholics provide a critical safeguard for the church to continue to engage in communal charity at the center of its mission. Even as acute challenges arise to both financial and human resources, the work of charity is part of every Christian vocation and has as legitimate a call on the church's human and financial resources as the preaching of the Word and the celebration of the sacraments.[7]

Charity—Essential for the Individual Christian and the Church Community

The Gospel message of Jesus affirms the practice of charity as essential for the individual Christian disciple and for the community of disciples, the church. Establishing the centrality of charity in the Gospel is not a difficult task and might seem self-evident and unnecessary to many. Yet sometimes, the obvious merits attention and reiteration lest we fail to understand how foundational the concept of charity is to the Gospel. Establishing charity as central does not push aside other essential realities— death and resurrection, law and grace, word and sacrament. The challenge is to affirm that the great mysteries of our faith *and* charity are both at the center of the Christian dispensation. Once the centrality of charity is recognized, then its far-reaching implications must be considered.

Four key passages from the New Testament undeniably place charity at the center of the Gospel message of Jesus: the letter of James, the first letter of John, the parable of the Good Samaritan from Luke's Gospel, and the Last Judgment scene from Matthew's Gospel.[8] The first two chapters of the letter of James most directly draw the connection between religion, care, faith, and love:

> Religion that is pure and undefiled before God and the Father is this: to care for orphans and widows in their affliction and to keep oneself unstained by the world. (James 1:27)

> What good is it, my brothers, if someone says he has faith but does not have works? Can that faith save him? If a brother or sister has nothing to wear and has no food for the day, and one of you says to them, "Go in peace, keep warm, and eat well," but you do not give them the necessities of the body, what good is it? So also faith of itself, if it does not have works, is dead. (James 2:14-17)

The first letter of John poignantly draws the connection between the sacrificial love of God for us and the disciples' requirement to practice love:

> The way we came to know love was that he laid down his life for us; so we ought to lay down our lives for our brothers. If someone who has worldly means sees a brother in need and refuses him compassion, how can the love of God remain in him? Children, let us love not in word or speech but in deed and truth. (1 John 3:16-18)

The parable of the Good Samaritan from Luke's Gospel extends the mandate to love one's neighbor beyond well-established and accepted human boundaries and divisions. The parable is Jesus' response to a follow-up question from a legal scholar attempting to justify himself. Jesus affirms the scholar's articulation of the dual command to love God totally and love neighbor as oneself as the way to eternal life. The legal scholar then wants to know, "Who is my neighbor?" and receives the answer of the parable of the Good Samaritan. It is likely that the expansive definition of neighbor that Jesus introduces provides little comfort to his questioner.

> Jesus replied, "A man fell victim to robbers as he went down from Jerusalem to Jericho. They stripped and beat him and went off leaving him half-dead. A priest happened to be going down that road, but when he saw him, he passed by on the opposite side. Likewise a Levite came to the place, and when he saw him, he passed by on the opposite side. But a Samaritan traveler who came upon him was moved with compassion at the sight. He approached the victim, poured oil and wine over his wounds and bandaged them. Then he lifted him up on his own animal, took him to an inn and cared for him. The next day he took out two silver coins and gave them to the innkeeper with the instruction, 'Take care of him. If you spend more than what I have given you, I shall repay you on my way back.' Which of these three, in your opinion, was neighbor to the robbers' victim?" He answered, "The one who treated him with mercy." Jesus said to him, "Go and do likewise." (Luke 10:29-37)

The ominous Last Judgment scene from Matthew's Gospel makes patently clear that how one treats those in need is tantamount to how one treats God. After separating the "sheep," the righteous, on his right hand from the "goats," the unrighteous, on his left hand, Jesus says to those on his right:

> Come, you who are blessed by my Father. Inherit the kingdom prepared for you from the foundation of the world. For I was hungry and you gave me food, I was thirsty and you gave me drink, a stranger and you welcomed me, naked and you clothed me, ill and you cared for me, in prison and you visited me. . . . Amen, I say to you, whatever you did for one of these least brothers of mine, you did for me. (excerpted from Matthew 25:31-46)

These four New Testament passages leave little doubt that love and service are expected of the disciple who wishes to remain faithful to Jesus.

Some 2,000 years later, the first encyclical of Pope Benedict XVI, *Deus Caritas Est*, presents a compelling and straightforward case for both individual and collective charity as central to the life of the Christian disciple and also the community of disciples, the church. Three excerpts from the second part of this encyclical on the biblical mandate of love capture the essence of the encyclical's teaching on the role of charity in the church:

> The Church cannot neglect the service of charity any more than she can neglect the Sacraments and the Word.
>
> Love for widows and orphans, prisoners, and the sick and needy of every kind, is as essential to her as the ministry of the sacraments and preaching of the Gospel.
>
> Love of neighbor, grounded in the love of God, is first and foremost a responsibility for each individual member of the faithful, but it is also a responsibility for the entire ecclesial community at every level: from the local community to the particular Church and to the Church universal in its entirety. As a community, the Church must practice love. Love thus needs to be organized if it is to be an ordered service to the community.[9]

Deus Caritas Est is perhaps the clearest affirmation in the entire modern corpus of Catholic social teaching, from Leo XIII's *Rerum Novarum* in 1891 to John Paul II's *Centesimus Annus* in 1991, of the essential place that the social ministry of charity plays in the church. Benedict makes two fundamental points with far-reaching ramifications: (1) charity and service are as essential to the church as the Mass and the Bible and (2) charity and service are obligations both of individuals and the community of the church.

Let me draw out the second point, the obligation of communal charity, with a comparison to private prayer and the Eucharist that will indicate how strong this teaching is. Today, a number of people, including Catholics, say, "Why do I need to go to church when I can pray on my own?" They maintain that the private practice of one's religion, particularly when it comes to prayer, is sufficient. While many might not like this, few would dispute this as an accurate description of the current state of affairs. However, such an approach has no significant support in orthodox church teaching and practice. The Eucharist, our communal act of worship, not private devotion, is at the center of the church's life. The church has made participation in the weekly Sunday Eucharist the norm for Catholics and has enshrined this in church law. The communal celebration of the Eucharist is at the center of the religious life of practicing Catholics.

Pope Benedict teaches that the same is true of the individual and communal practice of charity. Individual virtue and individual acts of charity are not sufficient. The church as a whole, and at all levels, must exercise communal acts of charity. To remain orthodox, Catholicism needs, as a community of faith, to engage in organized acts of charity. This is precisely what Catholic Charities does. Catholic Charities fulfills the church's obligation to communally exercise the service of charity as an ecclesial community.

In reflecting on the centrality of charity in the ministry of Jesus in the Gospels, the church developed charity as one of the three theological virtues, along with faith and hope. The virtue of charity draws directly from the Scriptures, where it is defined as "the virtue by which we love God above all things for his own sake, and our neighbor as ourselves for the love of God."[10] The *Catechism of the Catholic Church* describes virtue as such:

> A virtue is traditionally described as a habitual and firm disposition to do the good. It allows the person not only to perform good acts, but also to give the best of himself or herself. The virtuous person tends toward the good with all his sensory and spiritual powers; he pursues the good and chooses it in concrete actions.[11]
>
> Human virtues acquired by education, by deliberate acts and by a perseverance ever renewed in repeated efforts are purified and elevated by divine grace. With God's help, they forge character and give facility in the practice of the good. The virtuous man is happy to practice them.[12]

The development of virtue—the habit of doing good—is a safeguard for us as individuals to ensure that we do the right thing even when we may not be all that enthusiastic about doing so. An era that values freedom and choice for every individual action may underestimate the importance of virtue. However, most would admit that many decisions and actions flow from predispositions to act in certain ways. Virtue is the predisposition to act in a positive way. The virtue of charity predisposes us in diverse circumstances "to love God above all and our neighbors as ourselves."

By analogy, I suggest that institutions and organizations[13] play a very similar role in the life of the community of faith as virtues do in the life of the individuals. Institutions and organizations facilitate the doing of good by the community. By one standard definition, "organizations are made up of groups of individuals bound together by some common purpose to achieve certain objectives."[14] The institution of the parish ensures that the Eucharist is celebrated and the sacraments received. The Catholic school and religious education programs ensure that the faith is taught and passed on to the next generation.

Catholic Charities exists as an institution to ensure that the church as a community practices the love mandated by the Gospel, so clearly articulated by Benedict XVI in *Deus Caritas Est*. Its existence safeguards the church from turning in on itself, especially in those moments when it is tempted toward narcissism and other threats.

The presence of virtue in a person does not guarantee that in every situation the right decision will be made and the correct action done; however, it is a powerful help in that direction. So too, the existence of a good institution does not guarantee correct action, however, it is a powerful help. When the community of the church is mandated by our belief to engage in some particular communal activity, the establishment of good institutions and organizations fosters the faithful in the carrying out of that mandate. To fulfill its obligation to engage in the service of charity at every ecclesial level, the church needs institutions to safeguard the fulfillment of this mandate. Catholic Charities is the ecclesial institution that protects this component of the church's mission. If there were no Catholic Charities, the church would have to establish such an institution in order to remain faithful and orthodox.

Charity, *Caritas*, *Agape*—Understanding "Charity"

In the previous section, I proposed that Catholic Charities as an institution is essential to the church's faithful fulfillment of its mission. Now let us consider how its mission and mandate should be properly understood. Put simply, what activities should Catholic Charities undertake?[15]

The word *charities* in its title creates a significant impediment to correctly understanding the breadth of the work and mission of Catholic Charities. While serving as a recognizable and important brand name for these church organizations, the word *charities* can limit and even mislead from a proper understanding of the mandate of Catholic Charities.

The English word *charity* both denotes and connotes something that is optional: "a voluntary giving of money or other help to those in need." To do something out of charity connotes an optional kindness, not an obligation. It can also suggest, at times, condescension toward the person who is the object of the giving.

To overcome these limitations, we need to broaden our perspective beyond the borders of the United States and the English language. In many countries throughout the world, the church's organized charitable activity is called by its Latin root, *caritas*. *Caritas* is a common Latin translation of the Vulgate uses for the Greek biblical term *agape*.[16] And, *agape*, both as a noun and verb, is the common word that the Gospels use to describe the love that Jesus taught was central to his teaching and to the lives of his disciples.[17]

Christian charity rooted in the Scriptures is not optional and it can never be condescending. St. Vincent de Paul is attributed with a poignant phrase that captures the danger of charity apart from the deeper understanding of biblical love: "It is for your love alone that the poor will forgive you for the bread that you give them." Catholic Charities must take the breadth and depth of its charitable mission and mandate from this broader understanding of love—*caritas* or *agape*—that is rooted in the New Testament and the central teaching of Jesus.

This understanding is congruent with the theological virtue of charity that seeks the good of the other and calls the believer to both love God above all and to love one's neighbor as one's self. This love cannot be condescending for it would require being condescending toward one's self. In addition, it cannot be optional for individual Christians nor for the community of Christians, the church, because it is mandated by Jesus and sums up the law and the prophets.

When we understand the English word charity as the biblical *agape*, we can then confront another obstacle in appreciating the proper scope of the mission of Catholic Charities—the false divide between charity, in its narrower English sense of a voluntary giving to individuals in need, and justice, both in the sense of an obligation of helping individuals in need and also working for a more just and compassionate society. This biblically rooted Christian love mandates seeking the good of the other as we would seek our own good. Inevitably, seeking the good of many involves working toward a just ordering of society so that basic human needs are met and rights are respected.

Perhaps the clearest and most quoted affirmation that working for justice constitutes part of the mission of the church is that of the 1971 World Synod of Bishops: "Action on behalf of justice and participation in the transformation of the world fully appears to us as a constitutive dimension of the preaching of the gospel."[18] The oft-quoted 1971 statement about the importance of working for justice needs to be incorporated into Catholic Charities' work in fulfilling the biblical demand to love one's neighbor. The neighbor whom the Bible insists we love is a person made in the image and likeness of God. As such, this person is owed certain things by his or her very nature. We call these *rights*. The founding documents of this nation even affirm that we are "endowed by our Creator with certain inalienable rights." When these rights are not respected or able to be exercised, the human person is not living as intended by the God in whose image and likeness he or she is made. This quite simply is the meaning of injustice—the world out of the order established by the Creator. Seeking to correct these disorders, to work for a just ordering of the world, must be part of loving one's neighbor, both for individual Christians and for every level of the community of the church.

If a just situation is one in which the world is correctly ordered so that each person's rights are respected and able to be exercised and one's responsibilities fulfilled, then a core demand of love is to work for this just world. It therefore follows that the mission of the agency of the church charged to fulfill the command of love, Catholic Charities, must include working for justice. How could such an agency not seek to ensure that the basic human rights of individuals are respected and able to be exercised?

Work for justice often involves interaction with various other institutions of society, in particular, business and government—sometimes in collaboration, sometimes in opposition. Such efforts are ongoing and complex and often encounter simplistic political and ecclesial ideologies. The church should not be seduced by these interactions to merely mirror corporations or political parties. To resist these temptations, church efforts must remain rooted in the mandate of Christian love to seek the good of others.

The Catholic Human Rights Tradition— Safeguarding the Understanding of Charity

As we more adequately and comprehensively understand the concept of biblical charity to include that of justice, we are drawn to explore the church's human rights tradition. John XXIII, in his encyclical *Pacem in Terris*, provides the clearest articulation of this aspect of the church's social teaching. In recent years, Catholic Charities has increasingly reflected upon the Catholic social teaching as part of its mission. I suggest that this trend might be further enhanced by a more intentional and explicit focus on the human rights emphasis of this teaching as foundational to its mission, which would provide a strong rudder to help Catholic Charities avoid being driven off course by the often volatile winds of political and ecclesiastical correctness.

The humans rights tradition of the church provides a critically important safeguard to ensure that we understand that our teaching on the sanctity of human life, from conception until death, is part of the same tradition that undergirds our responsibility to feed the hungry and shelter the homeless, to visit the imprisoned and to support the physically and emotionally challenged. All flow from our fundamental understanding of the dignity of the human person and the rights that are essential to the human person.[19]

However, despite its roots in the church's long-standing natural law tradition, for many years, a human rights framework was downplayed in church teaching because of the antireligious ideologies associated with its major proponents, not the least of which were the architects of the French and Russian Revolutions. In addition, there has always been caution in applying aspects of this tradition to the internal workings of the church. Regrettably, this impeded the use of this tradition to more fully guide church institutions such as Catholic Charities.

Fortunately, a new era in the church's human rights tradition began almost 50 years ago when John XXIII put human rights at the center of the church's social teaching. On April 11, 1963, in his encyclical *Pacem in Terris*, John XXIII wrote to Catholics and all people of goodwill, calling for common efforts to establish universal peace in truth, justice, charity, and liberty. He affirmed the church's support for fostering human rights that closely paralleled the 1948 *Universal Declaration of Human Rights* of the United Nations.

The critical teachings from *Pacem in Terris* can be found in its first few sections. John XXIII begins his encyclical by asserting that peace on earth can only be established by diligently observing the order established by God. He then asserts that God created man in his own image and likeness, stamping the proper order on man's inmost nature that clearly points toward how he should act toward his fellows in society. Man's very nature, made in the image and likeness of God, generates the laws that must be followed to establish the proper order on the earth. The rights and duties that each individual has flow directly from the fundamental understanding that each individual is truly a person with intelligence and free will.[20]

From this fundamental understanding of the human person, John XXIII then presents a list of basic human rights that must be respected for a person to live out the dignity stamped in his very nature. I will focus on those most relevant for this consideration. John XXIII begins with the basic right to life and then quickly affirms the rights necessary to the proper development of life:

- the right to food, clothing, and shelter
- the right to medical care and necessary social services
- the right to be looked after in case of illness, disability stemming from work, widowhood, enforced unemployment, or whenever through no fault of his or her own one is deprived of the means of livelihood

- the right to receive a good general education and technical or pro-fessional training consistent with educational development in his own country

- the right to found a family, emphasizing the family as the primary unit of society and that the right to support and educate children belongs primarily to parents

- the right to have the opportunity to work and the right to exercise personal initiative in the work one does

- the right to receive a sufficient wage that allows a worker and his family a standard of living consistent with human dignity

- the right to own private property, with such ownership entailing a social responsibility

- the right to freedom of movement and residence *within* one's own state and the *permission* to emigrate to other countries when there are just reasons.[21]

Almost a half century later, most of these articulated rights are familiar to us. In attempting to join in partnership with others of good will in building more just societies, it is critical that most of these same human rights are articulated in the United Nations' *Universal Declaration of Human Rights*. However, as the articulated teaching of the church, they provide a compelling rationale and basis to set the agenda for Catholic Charities as an essential instrument of the church's service of love to others.

I propose that this human rights tradition, most clearly articulated by John XXIII in *Pacem in Terris* and reaffirmed and expanded in subsequent teachings, should form the basic content of Catholic Charities' agenda in carrying out the church's social mission of love in the world. What is essential to the dignity of the human person must have the highest priority in the work of Catholic Charities.

The mission of Catholic Charities should be understood to include the fuller sense of *caritas* or Christian love or, using the biblical term, *agape*. Therefore the attention that Catholic Charities must give to human rights is twofold: (1) it must engage in work that promotes human rights and their exercise when they are not present in society—from the protection of life itself and also what is necessary for the proper development of life; and (2) it must seek to compassionately and respectfully provide needed help to alleviate the pain and suffering that occurs when those rights are not respected or able to be exercised.

Allow me to illustrate this twofold thrust by applying the prism of the church's human rights tradition to a concrete example of "charity" familiar to most people: feeding the hungry. Recent surveys of Catholic Charities agencies throughout the United States show that emergency food programs are among the most common Catholic Charities programs and operate in almost every community throughout the country.[22]

Pacem in Terris affirms the right to food, and yet in New York City alone, surveys indicate that this right is not assured every month for hundreds of thousands of people. For this reason, Catholic Charities operates and supports with grants, in-kind food donations, and administrative support more than 50 community-based and parish pantries and soup kitchens, which provide more than five million meals each year to Catholics and non-Catholics alike in the New York metropolitan area. At the same time, Catholic Charities social service staff and volunteers at many of these food programs also provide additional necessary social services. One specific service is screening those coming to food pantries to see if they qualify for food stamps. Food stamps would enable them to feed their families without having to line up at a food pantry.

Furthermore, social workers also help families to obtain the work skills and jobs needed to provide for their families' needs on their own. This is not an easy task given the obstacles that many people using food pantries face. Educational deficiencies and housing instability are often present, and the residual and cumulative effects of prior poor choices often add another obstacle. Yet our teaching concerning the dignity of the human person requires that our agenda include not merely feeding the hungry but enabling the hungry to feed themselves.

However, focusing exclusively on the individual or even the individual family is incomplete because there are numerous societal factors that impact a family's ability to feed itself. Part of Catholic Charities' mission is to pay attention to this social context and identify what either impedes or promotes the exercise of human rights, in this case the right to food. Our agenda must seek to reduce what impedes the exercise of human rights and increase what promotes their exercise.

The example of hunger and food illustrates this. If there is not a sufficient food stamp program, a family cannot take the first step away from a food pantry toward food stamps. If there are no adequate job training programs, then the potential breadwinner is hindered in moving toward independence. If there are no jobs, then all the training in the world won't produce a living wage.

The agenda of Catholic Charities then must look to the social environment and policies that either hinder or promote the exercise of human rights by those we serve. For this reason, integral to the mission of Catholic Charities, properly understood, is building a society that is both just and compassionate. These flow from our fundamental belief that each person is made in the image of God and that embedded in the very nature of the human person are inalienable rights and responsibilities.

Note the important balance and richness that focusing on the church's human rights tradition provides. Catholic Charities must act with compassion to feed the hungry when a basic human right is lacking: a person does not have enough food to eat. Yet the person must be helped and, if necessary, challenged to exercise responsibility for themselves to increase their self-sufficiency as befits their human dignity. In addition, societal issues must be addressed to ensure that there is adequate training and sufficient job opportunities so that individuals can exercise their responsibility and right to work.

To understand the twofold thrust of Catholic Charities, compassionately dealing with the lack of basic human rights and furthering the exercise of these rights, it is critical to realize where we are presently situated in the history of salvation. The central mystery of Christian salvation is the death and resurrection of Jesus Christ. *Now* is the "in-between time," after the resurrection, yet before the fulfillment of God's kingdom in heaven. Two things follow. First, the proper order, although restored, has not been completely established, and thus, for our consideration, human rights will not be fully respected and exercised. Humanity will not be entirely fulfilled until Jesus comes again and the kingdom is fully established. The role of Catholic Charities is to provide compassionate care to humankind in its partially fulfilled state. Second, we are not helpless. We are called and empowered to advance the proper order of the world, even though the kingdom of peace and justice will only be fully realized when Jesus comes again. Therefore, in addition to binding up the wounds of compromised humanity, the responsibility of Catholic Charities is also to advance the kingdom and point out the injustices—i.e., the lack of human rights—and to work toward creating a more justly ordered world. Catholic Charities does this realistically, understanding that we will never completely eradicate injustice and that the task of binding up wounds will be necessary until that day when Jesus comes again.

In his second encyclical, *Spe Salvi*, Pope Benedict XVI clearly articulates this perspective: "The kingdom of the good will never be definitively established in this world." And then immediately adds, "Yet, every generation must also make its own contribution to establishing convincing structures of freedom and of the good." Pope Benedict XVI affirms once more what is perhaps the central theme of this article: "Love of God leads to participation in the justice and generosity of God toward others." Given the extent of disorder and injustice in the world, even with hope, work for justice is daunting. Without hope, one can be overwhelmed and paralyzed.[23]

The church's human rights tradition provides Catholic Charities with a twofold agenda, with one complementing the other: compassion and justice. To deny either is to fall into a position that endangers an orthodox understanding of the cross and resurrection and the place of the ecclesial community founded by the blood of the Lamb, which awaits in active hope the fulfillment of his kingdom of justice and peace and love.

The Work of Catholic Charities and the Church's Human Rights Tradition

In this final section, I propose a very simple and rudimentary approach to using the church's human rights agenda to assess and guide Catholic Charities' work. This approach takes the human rights articulated by the church, particularly in *Pacem in Terris*,[24] and looks to the actual work of Catholic Charities agencies to assess how the scope of their services and activities compares. In addition, this approach also assesses whether these services and activities focus on alleviating the pain and hurt caused by the lack of human rights or concentrate on advancing the exercise of these rights.

As previously discussed, *Pacem in Terris* lays out a list of basic human rights addressing basic needs and care, family, necessary medical and social services, work, education, property, and migration.

Now let us spell out the scope of services that Catholic Charities agencies across the United States reported in the Catholic Charities USA 2008 Annual Survey.[25] Catholic Charities agencies reported delivering, not in equal amounts, the following services and programs: food, social services, health-related services, clothing, financial assistance, pregnancy services, housing, educational enrichment, Headstart, community organizing and economic development, housing, job development, child abuse prevention services, family mediation and preservation, and immigration services.

A cursory comparison of Catholic Charities' scope of services with the basic human rights set forth in *Pacem in Terris* confirms a strong overlap between the two lists. Further, the scope of Catholic Charities activities also indicates that many agencies are engaged in organizing and developing activities that promote and extend human rights. However, this is not the entire story. A further look reveals that certain services and activities are much more prevalent than others. For example, Catholic Charities agencies are strongly committed to food programs, with the majority of agencies operating such programs. At the same time, many fewer agencies report running programs related to jobs and work. Similarly, while a number of agencies operate housing services and programs, many more provide family support services.

The Catholic Charities USA Annual Survey provides a glimpse as to how one might correlate the human rights tradition of the church to the work of Catholic Charities throughout the country. We might be able to glimpse a bit more by looking in depth at one agency.[26] Hence, I would like to look at the work of The Catholic Charities of the Archdiocese of New York, particularly at its mission and vision statements and its articulation of five broad categories of services. First, let us look at the mission and vision statements:

> The Catholic Charities of the Archdiocese of New York seeks to uphold the dignity of each person as made in the image of God by serving the basic needs of the poor, troubled, frail and oppressed of all religions. We collaborate with parishes and Catholic and non-Catholic partners to build a compassionate and just society. Through a network of administered, sponsored and affiliated agencies, Catholics Charities delivers, coordinates and advocates for quality human services and programs touching almost every human need.[27]

This mission statement affirms that (1) we seek to uphold the dignity of the human person as made in the image of God, (2) we collaborate to build a compassionate and just society, and (3) we advocate for services that touch almost every human need. The vision statement further explores what we seek to do:

> Catholic Charities helps solve the problems of New Yorkers in need—non-Catholics and Catholics alike. The neglected child, the homeless family and the hungry senior are among those for whom we provide help and create hope. We rebuild lives and touch almost every human need promptly, locally, day in and day out, and always with compassion and dignity. Catholic Charities helps your neighbors as you would like to be helped if your family were in need.[28]

Some of the language in the mission and vision statements explicitly echoes the church's human rights tradition, for example, "upholding the dignity of the human person as made in the image of God." Another phrase, "to build a compassionate and just society," articulates the twofold agenda of Catholic Charities to help those who are in need and lack basic necessities and also to work for a better ordering of society so that those needs might lessen. The phrase "rebuilding lives" communicates that those helped by Catholic Charities are not to be left in a dependent position but helped to live in greater wholeness. The final phrase of the vision statement, "helping neighbors as you would like to be helped," draws on the very familiar biblical mandate: "Love your neighbor as yourself."

This mission and vision articulation is reflected in Catholic Charities' scope of work. Catholic Charities in New York specifies its services into five categories: protecting and nurturing children and youth, feeding the hungry and sheltering the homeless, strengthening families and resolving crises, supporting the physically and emotionally challenged, and welcoming and integrating immigrants and refugees. Each of these areas of services is related to one or more human rights affirmed in *Pacem in Terris*.[29]

> *Protecting and nurturing children and youth.* The rights of children to general education, technical professional training, and support are affirmed with the clear understanding that the responsibility to ensure this belongs primarily to the parents. Catholic Charities programs often step in when parental responsibilities falter and children are in danger of having their basic rights neglected or abused.

> *Feeding the hungry and sheltering the homeless.* The right to food and shelter is clearly authenticated by the provision of 5.3 million meals and the provision and preservation of shelter, temporary and permanent housing, to more than 10,000 people annually.

> *Strengthening families and resolving crises.* The provision of social services, counseling, financial assistance, and job training and placement to more than 50,000 individuals annually correlates to the right to necessary social services and care when there is enforced unemployment and a family is deprived of their livelihood.

> *Supporting the physically and emotionally challenged.* Residences, support services, and early intervention for those with mental illnesses and developmental disabilities affirm the right to receive care in situations that result from illness or disability.

> *Welcoming and integrating immigrants and refugees.* Providing timely and accurate information, preventing exploitation, reuniting families, and finding legal work for immigrants and refugees affirms the right to migrate for a just cause.

Reviewing the scope of services of Catholic Charities throughout the United States and in the Archdiocese of New York demonstrates a correlation with the church's articulated human rights tradition. However, as any good social scientist will remind us, "correlation does not equal causality." And the logician will caution not to conclude, *"post hoc ergo propter hoc."* My own experience suggests that while the correlation exists, it may be more by happenstance and intuition rather than through an explicit attention to the church's human rights tradition. I suggest that there would be great value for Catholic Charities agencies in paying greater attention to this human rights tradition. It would be a very valuable prism to guide the assessment of current services and also to evaluate opportunities to expand.

Programs developed by Catholic Charities should be linked to advancing the dignity of the person as made in the image and likeness of God and furthering one or more basic human rights, not on the whim of an administrator, a benefactor, or the latest fad. In addition, the public policy advocacy agenda of Catholic Charities should give highest priority to advancing programs and policies to protect, preserve, or promote the exercise of these human rights including housing, food, work, families, immigration, work, education, and, above all, life itself from conception to death.

In conclusion, let me summarize five points I have tried to make:

1. The mandate of love for the Christian is rooted in, and central to, the teaching of Jesus in the New Testament.

2. The teaching and tradition of the church clearly articulates and demonstrates that the practice of Christian love must be both individual acts and organized communal activities of the church at all levels.

3. Catholic Charities, under various names, is the essential and primary instrument for the church remaining orthodox and faithful to its teaching, tradition, and responsibility to practice and carry out its communal ecclesial charitable activities.

4. The English word *charity* is misleading and too constrictive. Catholic Charities needs to comprehend the scope of its mission from the Latin word *caritas*, a translation of the biblical word *agape*. Catholic Charities' mission is to carry out the Christian love of neighbor as self.

5. This broad mandate of Christian love is best concretized when the work of Catholic Charities is rooted in the church's human rights teaching, perhaps best and most succinctly articulated in John XXIII's encyclical *Pacem in Terris*. This tradition helps to focus the

work of Catholic Charities on those areas that need our attention and twofold action: compassionate help because basic human rights, such as food and shelter, are not present; and action for a more just ordering of society so that these basic human rights may be respected and more fully exercised.

Conclusion

Developing the correct set of programs and establishing the right advocacy agenda to support the church's teaching on fundamental human rights is not an easy or clear-cut task. Applying an articulated human right to the development and carrying out of concrete programs and policies will always require prudential judgments and allow for various approaches. As well, the human rights teaching of the church, in this "in-between time," after the resurrection and before the fullness of the kingdom, will always challenge Catholic Charities to do more in its mission of compassionate and just neighborly love. The depth and breadth of this teaching and the challenge of concretizing it in actual programs and policies will always compel Catholic Charities to examine where it is falling short and what still remains to be done.

The human rights teaching will always be broader and deeper than the most extensive set of programs or the most ambitious advocacy agenda. Jesus preached a kingdom that would always lie ahead of the actual practice and life of the community of disciples, a kingdom that would always be calling them to further his message. In theological terms, the church is harbinger of the kingdom—not the kingdom itself. Similarly, Catholic Charities, in its dual role of compassionately meeting human needs and advocating for a more just society, is the church's harbinger of the justice of God's kingdom. Its work will never fully realize the justice of the kingdom. The kingdom's justice will always be greater, and call Catholic Charities to further faithfulness in guarding the integrity of the tradition and greater creativity and effectiveness in advancing the church's communal love for the world. Paying faithful attention to the church's human rights tradition will help keep Catholic Charities both relevant and vital until the fullness of the kingdom comes.

Appendix

Catholic Charities in the Last Four Decades

A Statistical Overview

Mary Gautier and Mark Gray
Center for Applied Research in the Apostolate

Catholic Charities
in the Last Four Decades

A Statistical Overview

In the early 1970s, the National Conference of Catholic Charities undertook a self-study aimed at renewing, strengthening, and restructuring the Catholic Charities movement. The study, known as the Cadre Study, was carried out over a three-year period and a formal report was presented to and approved by the members of the National Conference at the Annual Meeting in October 1972.

The purpose of that study was to assist the National Conference in changing its structure in response to changes in the church, in the aftermath of the Second Vatican Council, and in the federal government, with the great increase of public welfare and poverty programs in the 1960s. The National Conference declared a need to restructure to facilitate greater participation of its members in the Conference and to increase the involvement of the clients that they serve—the people who are involved at the grass-roots level, including people who are otherwise disenfranchised in society.

The National Conference of Catholic Charities, at that time, consisted of roughly 500 agencies, 1,000 institutions, and a multitude of other programs operating within 140 dioceses. The final report of the Cadre Study, *Toward a Renewed Catholic Charities Movement*, characterized their work at that time as such:

> Together, they touched the lives of millions of people every year. Their object was to provide services to all, but they found themselves engrossed in child welfare and family service programs,

much of which was devoted too often to a middle-class constituency . . . A study of the NCCC indicated the need to re-enter the areas of advocacy, social action, polity development, and planning, in concert with and on behalf of the poor in our society.[1]

"Capability to Know" System

Just as it helped the National Conference to recognize that it needed to reach out further to include the poor more fully in its work, the Cadre Study also produced

> a growing realization of what was meant by a *national* organization—a realization that the NCCC must not only provide certain services for its affiliates, not just help them with their programs and activities, but also bring them together with a national identity and as a national force. This was accompanied by the realization of the great potential of the Catholic Charities system, and of its character as a Movement, rather than simply an organization.[2]

The study report went on to describe the means to implement the preliminary recommendations for restructuring the National Conference of Catholic Charities. One of the recommendations was to realign and strengthen the national office. This national office would include programs for convening of concerned people, for developing a "Capability to Know" system, for greater legislative impact, for program consultation capability, for a coordinated Catholic Charities appeal, for membership development, and for adding other professional and office staff in the national office.

What the Cadre report envisioned as a "Capability to Know" system is what eventually became the Annual Survey. The study described the need as follows:

> The new thrust is based on the premise that the newly-convened people will have necessary information and analysis of issues and facts to judge and act. The Associate Directors, the Regional Conveners, and the local Directors need the informational backup to enable them to provide leadership and direction to the new thrust. Presently, there is no central bank of knowledge about what the Church is doing in the field of human services. A nationwide profile of Catholic Charities is needed. In short, much-needed research and collection of data need to be undertaken.[3]

Three years later, the NCCC published a report titled *Renewal in Catholic Charities: A Report on the Implementation of the Study of the National Conference of Catholic Charities*. The report examined each of the steps toward renewal suggested by the Cadre Study report and approved by the National Conference. It also described the action steps for implementing the "Capability to Know" system as follows:

> A statistical reporting system for Catholic Charities has been started. This is the first of its kind. The first report has been published, giving the number of persons served by Catholic Charities, the various types of programs conducted, the number of workers, and the amount of money expended. Already, this has been useful in planning programs, in interpreting the work of Catholic Charities, and in providing a greater sense of collaboration and unity among those engaged in Catholic Charities programs.[4]

The Annual Survey

In 1975, the second annual statistical report of the National Conference of Catholic Charities was published as the NCCC Report, 1974. Each year thereafter, Catholic Charities has published an annual report of the data collected in this statistical reporting system. For many years, the Annual Survey was administered by the National Conference, later named Catholic Charities USA. In 2002, however, the Center for Applied Research in the Apostolate (CARA) at Georgetown University assumed responsibility for the Annual Survey. Since that time, CARA and Catholic Charities USA have worked together to collect the annual data from all CCUSA member agencies and affiliates in an online format that is easy to use, stable over time, and able to produce the highest quality usable data for all involved.

In this article, we examine the data from each of the Annual Reports between 1975 and 2007 and describe some of the important trends. This analysis is based on the information provided by responding agencies and affiliates each year. This empirical overview of Catholic Charities services and programs over the last four decades provides a portrait of Catholic Charities services and how these have changed over time.

The Trends

One of the best indicators of the effect of Catholic Charities' efforts is the value over time of the services provided to people in need. The value of services provided is measured by the total amount that Catholic

Charities agencies report as program expenditures in the annual surveys. These amounts exclude agency expenditures related to fundraising and overhead. As shown in figure 1 below, both in absolute terms and controlling for inflation, the value of services provided by Catholic Charities agencies and affiliates has risen steadily over time. In 1974, the value of all services provided was $361 million (valued at $1.6 billion in today's dollars). As of 2007, the value of these services had increased to $3.2 billion. Thus, after accounting for change in the value of the dollar (i.e., inflation), the total value of services provided by Catholic Charities agencies and affiliates has more than doubled (increasing by 113 percent) in the last 30 years. On average, the value of services has grown each year by $80 million of today's dollars.

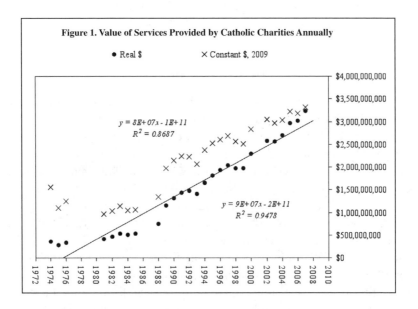

Figure 1. Value of Services Provided by Catholic Charities Annually

It would be reasonable to expect that the value of services provided by Catholic Charities would increase over time as the population of the United States grew. However, this growth in services has outpaced population growth. One way to measure this is to divide the value of services by the total population, resulting in a measure of services per capita. In the 1970s, the annual value of services provided, in today's dollars, was equivalent to an average of $6.04 for every resident of the United States.[1] Since 2000, this average has increased to $10.54 per resident.

As shown in figure 2, the number of client services provided annually by Catholic Charities has risen steadily over time, with peaks in the early

1990s and mid 2000s.[6] In 1979, Catholic Charities provided services to approximately 2.5 million people, which corresponds to approximately 11 persons receiving services for every 1,000 residents of the United States. By comparison, in 2007, 13.9 million individuals received assistance from Catholic Charities or approximately 46 persons per 1,000 residents of the United States. The largest number of persons served in any one year was in 1991, when 14.4 million people received services from Catholic Charities. This means that approximately 48.5 persons out of every 1,000 U.S. residents received services from Catholic Charities during 1991—a year in which the United States economy was in recession and the GDP (gross domestic product) contracted by -0.2 percent.

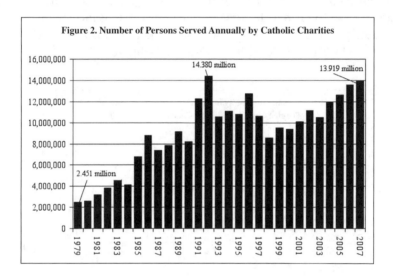

Figure 2. Number of Persons Served Annually by Catholic Charities

Macroeconomic Indicators

At first glance, the number of persons served by Catholic Charities appears not to be greatly influenced by changes in macroeconomic indicators. Catholic Charities efforts do not systematically surge and wane with the ups and downs of the business cycle. For example, the number of persons served is actually negatively related to the misery index (Pearson's R = -.772). The misery index, created by economist Arthur Okun, is simply the sum of the unemployment rate and the inflation rate.[7] It is intended to measure the economic pain felt by consumers. However, the lack of correlation with the business cycle is more a function of Catholic Charities not reducing its services during "good" economic times. Even during the good times there are still many people in need of assistance. It is also the case that many of the services provided by Catholic Charities agencies are not directly related to immediate economic needs (e.g., education, health/dental services, addiction treatment, counseling, adoption services, etc.). The data do show, however, that Catholic Charities generally serves more people with more services (as measured by the value of services provided) in the worst of economic times.

More subtly, the number of persons served by Catholic Charities is related to trends in income inequality in the United States. In 1974, families earning the highest income in the country (the top 20 percent of earners) earned 488 percent more than the lowest income families (the bottom 20 percent of earners). In 2007, this gap had widened to 708 percent.[8] Catholic Charities serves more individuals as income inequality between the wealthiest in America and the poorest increases (Pearson's R = +.831). This relationship is presented in figure 3.

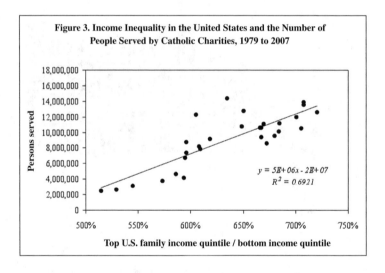

Figure 3. Income Inequality in the United States and the Number of People Served by Catholic Charities, 1979 to 2007

Per Person Services Provided

As figure 4 shows, since 1981 the value of services provided per person served by Catholic Charities has ranged from just more than $150 per person to over $300 per person in today's dollars.[9] Variations from year to year are due to a number of factors. Some variation occurs because the number of Catholic Charities member agencies varies from year to year and not every Catholic Charities agency responds to the survey in every year.[10] Other variations may be related to the types of services that were needed or to the amount of funding that was available for programs. For example, some of the increase in the value of services per person in 2003 is related to the increased amount of federal funding available at that time for providing services to families and survivors of the September 11, 2001, attacks. Similarly, in years in which more funding is made available for affordable housing, the per capita value of services provided may be higher than in years when fewer programs for affordable housing are funded.

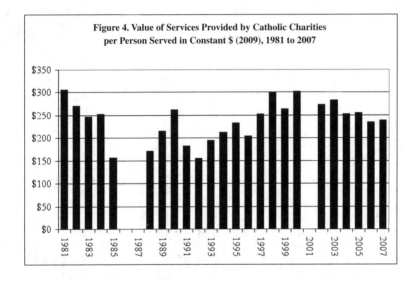

In 2007, the value of services provided per person served was $238. In the peak year, 1981, the value of services provided per person was $307 (in current dollars). This peak year occurred during a recession, in which unemployment measured 7.6 percent (compared to 4.6 percent unemployment in 2007).[11]

During periods of economic instability, in the early 1990s and again in the last two years, the share of services provided by Catholic Charities that are dedicated to emergency or short-term needs (e.g., emergency shelter, food, etc.) has risen relative to those services that are dedicated to ongoing social services (e.g., adoption, education, etc.). During the recession in 1991 and 1992, Catholic Charities agencies and affiliates provided emergency services to more than two people for every one person that received other social services. In 2006 and 2007, this ratio of emergency services relative to other social services began to approach 2:1 again, after approaching near parity in the late 1990s.

Agency Staff, Board Members, and Volunteers

The expanding efforts of Catholic Charities are not only reflected in the value of services provided or the number of persons assisted. The growth of Catholic Charities is also evident in the number of programs, affiliates, and agencies in the United States along with the number of staff, board members, and volunteers working within these institutions.

The number of people working and volunteering for Catholic Charities in the United States has grown from an average of more than 87,000 in the 1970s to an average of more than 277,000 since 2000. Since 2006, the number of Catholic Charities personnel (i.e., board members, paid staff, and volunteers) has exceeded 300,000. These trends are shown in figure 5.

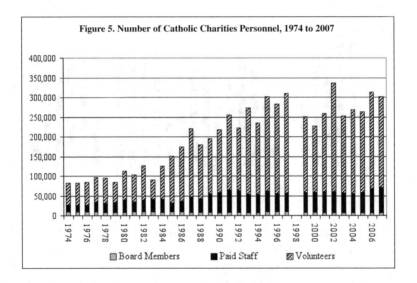

Figure 5. Number of Catholic Charities Personnel, 1974 to 2007

In particular, the number of volunteers has grown the most since the 1970s, more than tripling in size (an increase of 308 percent between 1974 and 2007). On average, Catholic Charities agencies increased their number of volunteers by 6,300 each year since 1974.

Nationally, Catholic Charities member agencies and affiliates have also added more than 1,200 paid staff members each year since 1974, growing from a staff size of more than 17,600 in 1974 to more than 64,800 in 2007 (an increase of 268 percent). Board members are the only category of Catholic Charities personnel that has decreased in number over this time period. In 2007, there were 27 percent fewer board members than there were in 1974. The number of board members peaked in 1975 at 9,720 and in 1997 at 9,638. In 2007, Catholic Charities agencies and affiliates reported 6,342 board members, compared to 8,931 in 1974.

The number of persons served for each person working or volunteering for Catholic Charities has ranged from 23 in 1980 to 65 in 1992. The peak in 1992 followed a recession year of negative economic growth in the United States (1991) and occurred during a year where unemployment measured 7.5 percent. In 2007, 46 persons were served for every person working or volunteering for Catholic Charities.

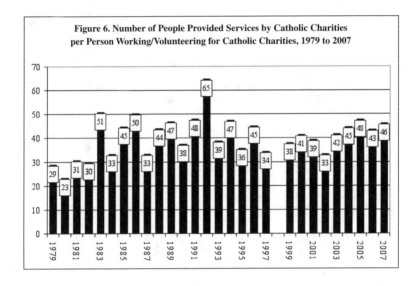

Figure 6. Number of People Provided Services by Catholic Charities per Person Working/Volunteering for Catholic Charities, 1979 to 2007

The most striking trend in this figure is how little change there has been over time. Since the early 1980s, between 30 and 50 people received services from Catholic Charities for each person working or volunteering for Catholic Charities. Obviously, Catholic Charities agencies have developed efficiencies of scale as they provide more services to more people over time. Comparing figure 6 to figure 5, one can see that Catholic Charities agencies have managed to do this, in part, by enlisting more and more volunteers to help meet the needs of a steadily increasing number of persons.

Income as a Percentage of Expenditure

In nearly every year since the beginning of the Annual Survey, Catholic Charities has accomplished its work without running a budget deficit. Since 1976 (the first year in which these data are available in the Annual Reports), only four Annual Reports show expenditures exceeding income by 1 percent or more, as presented in figure 7 below. These deficits occurred in 1976, 1981, 1987, and 1990.

Since 2000, income has averaged 103 percent of expenditures. In 2007, Catholic Charities expenditures totaled $3.690 million and its income was $3.885 million (105 percent of expenditures).

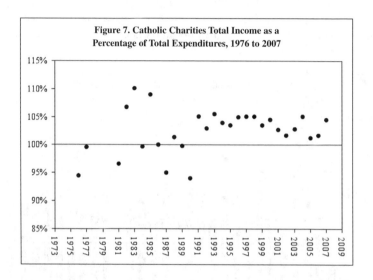

Figure 7. Catholic Charities Total Income as a Percentage of Total Expenditures, 1976 to 2007

Conclusion

What is past may be prologue. At the time of this report, data collection for the 2008 Annual Survey is underway. If the trends of the last four decades are an indicator of the future, the 2008 Annual Report will likely show that Catholic Charities is doing more now than ever. After all, the data show that Catholic Charities member agencies and affiliates are most active during times of economic recession and periods of higher income inequality, such as the recession of 2008 and 2009. The "Capability to Know" system that was envisioned by the National Conference of Catholic Charities has proven to be a valuable tool for demonstrating the effectiveness of Catholic Charities member agencies and affiliates in responding to the needs of the poor and disadvantaged during good times and bad. Future data collections and reports will continue to reflect and document these efforts.

Notes

Chapter One: Introduction

1. "Pastoral Letter," issued by the Second Plenary Council of Baltimore, Oct. 21, 1866, in *Pastoral Letters of the Catholic Bishops of the United States*, ed. Hugh J. Nolan, 4 vols. (Washington, DC: The National Conference of Catholic Bishops), I:199–200.

2. Margaret Tucker, "Cross Currents in Catholic Charities," *Catholic Charities Review* 6 (March 1922): 73–80.

3. John Paul II, The Poor Have a Privileged Place in Christ, address to the Catholic Charities USA Annual Meeting, Sept. 13, 1987, San Antonio, TX. Reprinted under "To Spread Christian Love," *Charities USA* 32, no. 2 (Second Quarter 2005): 20–23.

Chapter Three:
Theology, Social Teaching, and Catholic Charities

1. I wish to reference two earlier articles of mine that use the reference points of Leo XIII, Vatican II, and John Paul II to analyze Catholic social teaching; there is some use of the material on Leo XIII in this chapter, but the present essay has a broader purpose than the other two. Cf. "Catholic Social Teaching: Content, Character and Challenges," in *Rerum Novarum: A Symposium Celebrating 100 Years of Catholic Social Thought*, ed. Ronald F. Duska (Lewiston, NY: Edwin Mellon Press, 1991), 1–20; and "The Social Role of the Church: Leo XIII, Vatican II and John Paul," in *Catholic Social Thought and the New World Order*, ed. Oliver F. Williams and John W. Houck (Notre Dame, IN: University of Notre Dame, 1993), 29–50.

2. Eamon Duffy, *Saints and Sinners: A History of the Popes* (New Haven, CT: Yale University Press, 1997), 236.

3. Oskar Köhler, "The World Plan of Leo XIII: Goals and Methods," in *History of the Church*, vol. IX, *The Church in the Industrial Age*, ed. Hubert Jedin (New York: Crossroads Publishing Co., 1981), 3–25; Joseph N. Moody, "The Church and the New Forces in Western Europe and Italy," in *Church and Society: Catholic Social and Political Thought and Movements 1789–1950*, ed. Joseph N. Moody (New York: Arts Inc., 1953), 21–92. See Hehir articles cited above.

4. Duffy, *Saints and Sinners*, 236.

5. Gerald McCool, *The Neo-Thomists* (Milwaukee, WI: Marquette University Press, 1994), 1.

6. Charles Curran, *The Catholic Moral Tradition Today* (Washington, DC: Georgetown University Press, 1999), x.

7. John Courtney Murray, "Leo XIII on Church and State: The General Structure of the Controversy," *Theological Studies* 14 (1953): 8.

8. Köhler, "The World Plan of Leo XIII," 6.

9. Köhler, "The World Plan of Leo XIII," 25.

10. John Paul II, *Centesimus Annus*, in *Catholic Social Thought: The Documentary Heritage*, ed. David J. O'Brien and Thomas A. Shannon (Maryknoll, NY: Orbis Books, 1992), 439. All references to encyclicals are taken from this volume, with title and page number cited.

11. David O'Brien, "A Century of Catholic Social Teaching," in *One Hundred Years: Celebration and Challenge*, ed. John A. Coleman, SJ (New York: Orbis Books, 1991), 16–17.

12. Dorothy M. Brown and Elizabeth McKeown, *The Poor Belong To Us: Catholic Charities and American Welfare* (Cambridge, MA: Harvard University Press, 1997).

13. Donald P. Gavin, *The National Conference of Catholic Charities 1910–1960* (Milwaukee, WI: Bruce Press, 1962), 27.

14. Ibid., 27.

15. For in-depth commentary on the key texts of the council, see John H. Miller, ed., *Vatican II: An Inter-Faith Appraisal* (Notre Dame, IN: University of Notre Dame Press, 1966); and Richard P. McBrien, "Vatican Council II," in *Encyclopedia of Catholicism*, ed. McBrien (New York: Harper Collins Publishers, 1995), 1299–1306.

16. Austin Flannery, ed., *Vatican Council II: The Conciliar and Post-Conciliar Documents*, revised edition (Northport, NY: Costello Publishing Company, 1996); *Lumen Gentium* 350–426; *Gaudium et Spes* 903–1001.

17. Mark McGrath, "The Constitution on the Church in the Modern World," in *Vatican II: An Inter-Faith Appraisal*, ed. John H. Miller (Notre Dame, IN: University of Notre Dame Press, 1966), 398–99.

18. *Gaudium et Spes* 40–42, in Flannery, 939–43.

19. John Courtney Murray, "The Issue of Church and State at Vatican II," in *Theological Studies* 27 (1966): 201–4.

20. *Gaudium et Spes* 39, in Flannery, 938.

21. *Gaudium et Spes* 42, in Flannery, 942.

22. *Dignitatis Humanae* 2–8, in Flannery, 800.

23. Catholic Charities USA, *Cadre Study: Toward a Renewed Catholic Charities Movement* (Alexandria, VA: Catholic Charities USA, 1992).

24. For assessments of the papacy of John Paul II, see George H. Williams, *The Mind of John Paul II: Origins of His Thought and Action* (New York: The Seabury Press, 1981); George Weigel, *Witness To Hope: The Biography of John Paul II* (New York: Harper Collins Publishers Inc., 1999); Eamon Duffy, *Saints and Sinners* (New Haven, CT: Yale University Press, 1997), 282–92.

25. Benedict XVI, *Deus Caritas Est* 22.

26. See Jean-Yves Calvez and Jacques Perrin, *The Church and Social Justice: The Social Teaching of the Popes from Leo XIII to Pius XII (1878–1958)* (Chicago, IL: Henry Regnery Company, 1961), 162–73.

27. Benedict XVI, *Deus Caritas Est* 29.

28. Ibid., 28.

29. Ibid., 31.

30. Ibid., 28.

31. Ibid., 28.

32. John Paul II, *Centesimus Annus* 15, 48, in *Catholic Social Thought: The Documentary Heritage*, ed. David J. O'Brien and Thomas A. Shannon (Maryknoll, NY: Orbis Books, 1992), 450–51, 475–76.

Chapter Four: The Rise of Professionalization

1. William J. Kerby, *The Social Mission of Charity: A Study of Points of View in Catholic Charities* (New York: The MacMillan Company, 1921); John O'Grady, *Catholic Charities in the United States: History and Problems* (Washington, DC: National Conference of Catholic Charities, 1931).

2. Harold L. Wilensky, "The Professionalization of Everyone?" *The American Journal of Sociology* 70, no. 2 (1964): 137–58.

3. Walter I. Trattner, *From Poor Law to Welfare State: A History of Social Welfare in the United States* (New York: The Free Press, 1999), 89.

4. Amos Warner, *American Charities: A Study in Philanthropy and Economics*, Crowell's Library of Economics and Politics (New York: Thomas Y. Crowell, 1894), 377.

5. Trattner, *From Poor Law to Welfare State*, 92.

6. Elizabeth W. Dumez, *Celebrating Social Work: Faces and Voices of the Formative Years* (Arlington, VA: Council on Social Work Education, 2003).

7. Trattner, *From Poor Law to Welfare State*, 237.

8. Donald P. Gavin, *The National Conference of Catholic Charities: 1910–1960* (Milwaukee: Catholic Life Publications, 1962), 46–65.

9. Trattner, *From Poor Law to Welfare State*, 113.

10. Kerby, *The Social Mission of Charity*, 163.

11. Marguerite T. Boylan, *Social Welfare in the Catholic Church: Organization and Planning through Diocesan Bureaus* (New York: Columbia University Press, 1941), 3.

12. Trattner, *From Poor Law to Welfare State*, 121.

13. C. Joseph Nuesse, *The Catholic University of America: A Centennial History* (Washington, DC: The Catholic University of America Press, 1990).

14. O'Grady, *Catholic Charities in the United States*, 430.

15. Gavin, *The National Conference of Catholic Charities*, 17.

16. M. Vincentia Joseph and Ann P. Conrad, *Practice Theory and Skill Development for Supervision in the Helping Professions: A Resource Book for Staff Development* (Hyattsville, MD: PEN Press, 1983); Carlton Munson, *Social Work Supervision: Classic Statements and Critical Issues* (New York: The Free Press, 1979).

17. Trattner, *From Poor Law to Welfare State*, 238.

18. Ibid., 233–52; O'Grady, *Catholic Charities in the United States*, 434–35.

19. Trattner, *From Poor Law to Welfare State*, 239.

20. Ibid., 240–41.

21. Gavin, *The National Conference of Catholic Charities*, 56.

22. Kerby, *The Social Mission of Charity*, 168.

23. Lucian L. Lauerman, *Catholic Education for Social Work*, Studies in Sociology, vol. 9, 12–13 (Washington, DC: The Catholic University of America, 1945).

24. Ibid., 31; O'Grady, *Catholic Charities in the United States*, 434.

25. Loretto R. Lawler, *Full Circle: A Story of the National Catholic School of Social Service* (Washington, DC: The Catholic University of America Press, 1951), 35.

26. Nuesse, *The Catholic University of America*, 178.

27. Michael Williams, *American Catholics in the War* (Washington, DC: National Catholic War Council, 1921).

28. Lawler, *Full Circle*, 17.

29. Dorothy M. Brown and Elizabeth McKeown, *The Poor Belong to Us: Catholic Charities and American Welfare* (Cambridge, MA: Harvard University Press, 1997), 5.

30. Nuesse, *The Catholic University of America*, 268.

31. Lawler, *Full Circle*, 188–95; Nuesse, *The Catholic University of America*, 179–80.

32. http://www.answers.com/topic/catholic-charities-usa, retrieved July 4, 2009.

33. Council on Social Work Education, *Educational Policy and Accreditation Standards* (Alexandria, VA: Council on Social Work Education, 2008).

34. National Association of Social Workers, *Code of Ethics* (Washington, DC: National Association of Social Workers, 1996, revised 2008).

35. *Catholic Charities USA 2008 Annual Survey* (Alexandria, VA: Catholic Charities USA, 2009).

36. Irwin Epstein, "Organizational Careers, Professionalization, and Social Worker Radicalism," *Social Service Review* 44, no. 2 (1970): 123–31.

37. Carol H. Meyer, *Social Work Practice* (New York: Columbia University Press, 1976).

38. Harry Specht, *Unfaithful Angels: How Social Work Has Abandoned its Mission* (New York: The Free Press, 1993).

39. Meyer, *Social Work Practice*, 1976; Carel Germain and Alex Gitterman, *The Life Model of Social Work Practice* (New York: Columbia University Press, 1980); Dennis Saleeby, *The Strengths Perspective in Social Work Practice* (New York: Longman Press, 1992).

40. Laura R. Bronstein, "A Model for Interdisciplinary Collaboration," *Social Work* 48, no. 3 (2003): 297–306.

41. National Conference of Catholic Charities, *Toward a Renewed Catholic Charities Movement* (Washington, DC: National Conference of Catholic Charities, 1972).

42. See chapter 5 in this work about parish social ministry.

43. *Catholic Charities USA 2008 Annual Survey* (Alexandria, VA: Catholic Charities USA, 2009).

44. Ibid.

45. Sheila M. Brommel, "The Council on Accreditation for Children and Family Services: A Historical Analysis," (unpublished doctoral dissertation, University of Minnesota, 2006), 200.

46. Benedict XVI, *Deus Caritas Est*, 31.

Chapter Five: The Parish Comes Full Circle and Beyond

1. Donald P. Gavin, *The National Conference of Catholic Charities: 1910–1960* (Milwaukee: Catholic Life Publications, 1962), 101.

2. David J. O'Brien, *The American Parish: Community for People, an Historical Perspective*, Pastoral Ministry Series (Washington, DC: National Conference of Catholic Charities, undated), 6–11.

3. John O'Grady, *The Catholic Church and the Destitute* (New York: The Macmillan Co., 1929), 123.

4. Ibid., 123.

5. John O'Grady, *The Catholic Church in the United States: History and Problems* (Washington, DC: National Conference of Catholic Charities, 1931), 318.

6. Ibid., 319–24.

7. O'Grady, *The Catholic Church and the Destitute*, 122.

8. Gavin, *The National Conference of Catholic Charities*, 3.

9. O'Grady, *The Catholic Church and the Destitute*, 124–25; for more details on the relationship between social work and the St. Vincent de Paul Society and Catholic Charities, see chapter 4 in this book.

10. Gavin, *The National Conference of Catholic Charities*, 5.

11. O'Grady, *The Catholic Church in the United States*, 426.

12. Ibid., 427.

13. Ibid., 360.

14. Ibid., 358–59.

15. Ibid., 358.

16. Ibid., 359–60.

17. John J. Harbrecht, *The Lay Apostolate* (St. Louis: B. Herder Books, 1929), 428–29.

18. Ibid., 171–72.

19. O'Grady, *The Catholic Church and the Destitute*, 131–32.

20. Gavin, *The National Conference of Catholic Charities*, 7.

21. Ibid., 21–22.

22. O'Brien, *The American Parish*, 16; John McCarthy, "Parish and Social Ministry: A Sign of Hope," *America* 146 (1980): 34–37; for more details on the professionalization of Catholic Charities, see chapter 4.

23. Joseph H. Fichter, "The Structure of Parochial Societies," *The American Ecclesiastical Review* 127 (November 1952): 358–59.

24. Carol H. Meyer, *Social Work Practice* (New York: The Free Press, 1970).

25. Karl Rahner, "The New Image of the Church," in *Theological Investigations*, vol. 10 (New York: Herder and Herder, 1973), 11.

26. Karl Rahner, "Practical Theology and Social Work in the Church," in *Theological Investigations*, vol. 10 (New York: Herder and Herder, 1973), 267–68.

27. M. Vincentia Joseph, "Parallel Structures for Parish Social Ministry: A Challenge to Catholic Charities," *Charities USA* 8, no. 6 (1981): 9.

28. Ena Guidarelli, "A Return to the Parish," *Catholic Charities Review* 52 (April 1968): 12–16.

29. See the following articles in *Catholic Charities Review* 54 (December 1970): Richard W. Bateman, "A Team Approach to Parish and Community Development," 3–4; Harold Jones, "Direct Service in the Parish: A Parishioner's Perspective," 19–20; Elaine Lowry, "Organizing the Inner-city Parish Community," 9–12; Theodore S. Rowan, "The Urban Parish," 15–18; Susan D. Shubin, "The Team and its Approach," 5–8; See also Richard B. Miller, "Meanwhile Back at the Parish," *Catholic Charities Review* 54 (January 1971): 3–10.

30. M. Vincentia Joseph and Carla Pryzbilla, "Preparation for New Ministries: A Futuristic View," *Review for Religious* 36 (November 1977): 852.

31. Gavin, *The National Conference of Catholic Charities*, 40–41.

32. *Toward a Renewed Catholic Charities Movement: A Study of the National Conference of Catholic Charities* (Washington, DC: National Conference of Catholic Charities, 1972): 92–93.

33. Ibid., 83.

34. Ibid., 8.

35. Ibid., 8–9.

36. *Families and Family-institution Transactions in Child Development: An Analysis of the Family Research Program of HEW's Administration for Children, Youth and Families* (Nashville, TN: U.S. Department of Health, Education, and Welfare, 1978), 75.

37. Peter L. Berger and Richard J. Neuhaus, *To Empower People: The Role of Mediating Structures in Public Policy* (Washington, DC: American Enterprise Institute for Public Policy, 1977), 6.

38. *Agenda for Action* (Washington, DC: National Conference of Catholic Charities, 1978), 3–12.

39. Jerome B. Ernst, *Parish Outreach: Building Community through Service and Actions* (Washington, DC: National Conference of Catholic Charities, 1977); *Parish Outreach Review* 1 (Winter 1976); Parish Social Ministry Advisory Committee, *Parish Social Ministry: A Vision and Resource* (Washington, DC: National Conference of Catholic Charities, 1979).

40. Philip Murnion, "The Complex Task of the Parish," *Origins* 8 (December 1978): 434–41.

41. Donna M. Preston, "A modality for parish service units," *Catholic Charities Review* 58 (April 1973): 17–20.

42. Vincent Mainelli, "The Parish Community Becoming: Theological Reflections," *Social Thought* 1, no. 2 (1975): 11–27

43. Thomas P. Sweetser, "Parish an Community: A Sociological Perspective," *Social Thought* 1, no. 2 (1975): 29–42.

44. M. Vincentia Joseph, "The Parish as a Social Service and Social Action Center: An Ecological Systems Approach," *Social Thought* 1, no. 2 (1975): 43–59.

45. Edward M. Conway, "The Diocesan Social Service Agency in a Parish Centered Program of Social Service and Social Action: Addressing Problems of System Management," *Social Thought* 1, no. 2 (1975): 61–76.

46. Raymond Fox, "CAPE: A Brooklyn Catholic Charities Effort," *Social Thought* 1, no. 2 (1975): 77–86.

47. Lawrence G. Lauter, "The St. Vincent de Paul Society in Today's Modern Parish," *Social Thought* 1, no. 2 (1975): 87–100.

48. M. Vincentia Joseph, "Parish Outreach: The Washington Experience," Part 1, *Charities USA* 3, no. 7 (1975): 6; Part 2, *Charities USA* 3, no. 8 (1975): 11–14.

49. M. Vincentia Joseph and Ann P. Conrad, *National Trends in Parish Social Ministry: A Study of Parish Programs Affiliated with Catholic Charities Agencies* (Washington, DC: National Conference of Catholic Charities, 1977).

50. Ibid., 7–8.

51. Ibid., 28.

52. Jerome B. Ernst, "From Parish Outreach to Parish Social Ministry: Building the Parish Community," *Social Thought* 8, no. 2 (1982): 38–39.

53. M. Vincentia Joseph, "The Developmental Process of Parish Social Ministries: A Decade of Experience," *Social Thought* 8, no. 2 (1982): 37.

54. Ibid., 22–34.

55. Stephanie K. Teff, *Organizing for Aging with Parish Social Ministry* (Washington, DC: National Conference of Catholic Charities, 1982).

56. Ann P. Conrad and M. Vincentia Joseph, *Parish-Centered Volunteer Programs: A Handbook for Socio-Pastoral Ministries at the Parish Level* (Silver Spring, MD: PEN Press, 1982); M. Vincentia Joseph, *The Parish as a Ministering Community: Social Ministries in the Local Church Community. A Resource Book of Human Services and Social Action in the Parish-Neighborhood Community* (Silver Spring, MD: PEN Press, 1976, 1982, 1988).

57. National Conference of Catholic Bishops, Committee on the Parish, *The Parish: A People, A Mission, A Structure* (Washington, DC: United States Catholic Conference, 1982).

58. National Conference of Catholic Bishops, Committee on the Parish, *Parish Self-Study Guide* (Washington, DC: United States Catholic Conference, 1982).

59. Institute for Pastoral and Social Ministry and Center for the Study of Contemporary Society of the University of Notre Dame, *Notre Dame Study of Parish Life* (Indiana: University of Notre Dame Press, 1984), 5

60. Steven H. Gratto, "To Live the Beatitudes: Parish Social Ministry in the Teaching of John Paul II," *Social Thought* 13, no. 2 and 3 (1987): 39.

61. Ibid., 43.

62. John Holland, "John Paul II on the Laity in Society: The Spiritual Transformation of Modern Culture," *Social Thought* 13, no. 2 and 3 (1987): 87.

63. "Twenty Years of Building Community: Parish Social Ministry and Catholic Charities. An Interview with Bishop Sullivan," *Charities USA* 21, no. 3 (1994): 4.

64. Ibid., 5.

65. John D. Gilmartin, "Let's Become Risk Taking People," *Charities USA* 21, no. 3 (1994): 9–10.

66. *Providing Help, Creating Hope: The Parish Social Ministry Section* (Alexandria, VA: Catholic Charities USA, undated); "Success for Sections," *Charities USA* 28, no. 1 (2001): 16–17.

67. Tom Ulrich, *Parish Social Ministry: Strategies for Success* (Notre Dame, IN: Ave Maria Press, 2001).

68. *Vision 2000* (Alexandria, VA: Catholic Charities USA, 1997); the focus of *Vision 2000* is on strategic directions for Catholic Charities for the twenty-first century.

Chapter Six: Common Ground for the Common Good

1. Dorothy M. Brown and Elizabeth McKeown, *The Poor Belong to Us: Catholic Charities and American Welfare* (Cambridge, MA: Harvard University Press, 1997).

2. Robert Benne, *Quality with Soul: How Six Premier Colleges and Universities Keep Faith with their Religious Traditions* (Grand Rapids, MI: Eerdmans, 2001).

3. Catholic Charities USA, "The Catholic Charities Network at a Glance"; retrieved August 13, 2009, from www.catholiccharitiesusa.org.

4. Joseph Bernardin, "Catholic Identity: Resolving Conflicting Expectations," in *The Future of Catholic Institutional Ministries*, ed. C. J. Fahey and M. A. Lewis (New York: Third Age Center, Fordham University, 1992), 75–84.

5. Brown and McKeown, *The Poor Belong to Us*.

6. Mary J. Oates, *The Catholic Philanthropic Tradition in America* (Bloomington, IN: Indiana University Press, 1995).

7. Brown and McKeown, *The Poor Belong to Us*.

8. Personal communication of author with Rev. Larry Snyder, president of Catholic Charities USA, August 18, 2009.

9. Austin Flannery, ed., *Vatican Council II: The Conciliar and Post Conciliar Documents* (Northport, NY: Costello, 1996).

10. Charles J. Fahey, "The 'Catholic' in Catholic Charities," in *Who Do You Say We Are? Perspectives on Catholic Identity in Catholic Charities*, ed. J. Leitch (Alexandria, VA: Catholic Charities USA, 1997), 15–23.

11. Mark Chaves, "Religious Congregations and Welfare Reform: Who Will Take Advantage of 'Charitable Choice?'" *American Sociological Review* 64, no. 6 (1999): 836–46; Stephen V. Monsma, *When Sacred and Secular Mix: Religious Nonprofit Organizations and Public Money* (Lanham, MD: Rowman & Littlefield Press, 1996); F. Ellen Netting, "Secular and Religious Funding of Church-related Agencies," *Social Service Review* 56, no. 4 (1982): 586–604; Steven R. Smith and Michael R. Sosin, "The Varieties of Faith-related Agencies," *Public Administration Review* 61, no. 6 (2001): 651–70; and James Vanderwoerd, "How Faith-Based Social Service Organizations Manage Secular Pressures Associated With Government Funding," *Nonprofit Management & Leadership* 14, no. 3 (2004): 239–62.

12. Paul J. DiMaggio, "The Relevance of Organization Theory to the Study of Religion," in *Sacred Companies: Organizational Aspects of Religion and Religious Aspects of Organizations*, ed. Nicholas J. Demerath III, Peter D. Hall, Terry Schmitt, and Rhys H. Williams (New York: Oxford University Press, 1998), 7–23.

13. Steven R. Smith and Michael Lipsky, *Nonprofits for Hire: The Welfare State in the Age of Contracting* (Cambridge, MA: Harvard University Press, 1993).

14. Linda Yankoski, "The Soul of the Matter: The Impact of Government Funding on the Catholic Identity and Mission of Holy Family Institute" (unpublished doctoral dissertation, Duquesne University, 2003).

15. Lester M. Salamon, *Partners in Public Service* (Baltimore: Johns Hopkins University Press, 1995).

16. George Marsden, *The Soul of the American University: From Protestant Establishment to Established Nonbelief* (New York: Oxford University Press, 1994).

17. Wendy W. Blome, "The Relationship Between Public and Private Social Service Agencies: Competition or Cooperation in the 1990's?" *Social Thought* 16, no. 4 (1990): 24–35.

18. Brown and McKeown, *The Poor Belong to Us.*

19. Blome, "The Relationship Between Public and Private Social Service Agencies"; Brown and McKeown, *The Poor Belong to Us.*

20. Brown and McKeown, *The Poor Belong to Us.*

21. Frank Fetter, "The Subsidizing of Private Charities," *American Journal of Sociology* 7, no. 3 (1901): 359–85.

22. Salamon, *Partners in Public Service.*

23. Brown and McKeown, *The Poor Belong to Us.*

24. Ibid.

25. Ibid.

26. Bernard J. Coughlin, *Church and State in Social Welfare* (New York: Columbia University Press, 1965).

27. Harold L. Wilensky, *The Welfare State and Equality: Structural and Ideological Roots of Public Expenditures* (Berkeley, CA: University of California Press, 1975).

28. Marcos McGrath, "One Hundred Years of Catholic Social Teaching in the Western Hemisphere," *Social Thought* 17, no. 2 (1991): 18–24.

29. Marguerite G. Rosenthal, "Public or Private Children's Services? Privatization in Retrospect," *Social Service Review* 74, no. 2 (2000): 281–305.

30. Ralph M. Kramer, "An Analysis of Policy Issues in Relationships between Governmental and Voluntary Welfare Agencies" (unpublished doctoral dissertation, University of California, 1964).

31. Personal Responsibility and Work Opportunity Reconciliation Act of 1996, Pub.L. No. 104–93 [H.R. 3734, 104th Cong., 2nd Sess.].

32. Kirsten A. Grønbjerg and Steven R. Smith, "Nonprofit Organizations and Public Policies in the Delivery of Human Services" in *Philanthropy and the Nonprofit Sector in a Changing America*, ed. Charles T. Clotfelter and Thomas Ehrlich (Bloomington, IN: Indiana University Press, 1999), 139–72.

33. Vernadette R. Broyles, "The Faith-based Initiative, Charitable Choice, and Protecting the Free Speech Rights of Faith-based Organizations," *Harvard Journal of Law & Public Policy* 26, no. 1 (2003): 315–53.

34. www.cpjustice.org/charitablechoice/guide.

35. www.pewtrusts.org/news_room_detail.aspx?id=53806.

36. Jun 11, 2009, Transcript: Government Partnerships With Faith-Based Organizations—Looking Back, Moving Forward, Pew Research Center.

204 *Catholic Charities USA*

37. www.pewforum.org/

38. Martha Minow, "Partners, not Rivals? Redrawing the Lines between Public and Non-profit and Profit, and Secular and Religious," *Boston University Law Review* 80 (2000): 1061; Salamon, *Partners in Public Service*; and Smith and Lipsky, *Nonprofits for Hire.*

39. Minow, "Partners, not Rivals?"

40. Minow, "Partners, not Rivals?"; Monsma, *When Sacred and Secular Mix*; Salamon, *Partners in Public Service*; *Nonprofit Management & Leadership* 14, no. 3 (Spring 2004).

41. Benne, *Quality with Soul*; G. R. Bolduc, "A Study of the Impact of Government Participation on the Program Planning and Delivery of Catholic Social Services" (unpublished doctoral dissertation, The Catholic University of America, 1994); Coughlin, *Church and State in Social Welfare*; Monsma, *When Sacred and Secular Mix.*

42. Peter L. Berger and Richard N. Neuhaus, *To Empower People: The Role of Mediating Structures in Public Policy* (Washington, DC: American Enterprise Institute for Public Policy Research, 1977); James Burtchaell, *The Dying of the Light: The Disengagement of Colleges and Universities from their Churches* (Grand Rapids, MI: Eerdmans, 1998); Kirsten A. Grønbjerg, "Transaction Costs in Social Service Contracting: Lessons from the USA," in *The Contract Culture in Public Services: Studies in Britain, Europe, and the USA*, ed. Perri 6 and Jeremy Kendall (Brookfield, VT: Arena, 1997), 99–118; Thomas H. Jeavons, *When the Bottom Line is Faithfulness: Management of Christian Social Service Organizations* (Bloomington, IN: Indiana University Press, 1994); Marsden, *The Soul of the American University*; Smith and Lipsky, *Nonprofits for Hire.*

43. Harry S. Stout and D. Scott Cormode, "Institutions and the Story of American Religion: A Sketch of a Synthesis," in *Sacred Companies*, 62–78.

44. D. Scott Cormode, "Does Institutional Isomorphism Imply Secularization? Churches and Secular Voluntary Associations in the Turn-of-the-Century City," in *Sacred Companies*, 116–31.

45. Ibid.

46. Ibid.

47. Berger and Neuhaus, *To Empower People.*

48. Sheila S. Kennedy, *Privatization and Prayer: The Challenge of Charitable Choice*, retrieved June 18, 2002, from http://ccr.urbancenter.iupui.edu/PDFs/publications/Privatization%20and%20Prayer.pdf.

49. Vanderwoerd, "How Faith-Based Social Service Organizations"; Yankoski, "The Soul of the Matter."

50. DiMaggio, *The Relevance of Organization Theory*; Paul J. DiMaggio and Walter W. Powell, "The Iron Cage Revisited: Institutional Isomorphism and Collective Rationality in Organizational Fields," *American Sociological Review* 48, no. 2 (1983): 147–60; Clifford Geertz, *The Interpretation of Cultures* (New York: Basic Books, 1973); W. Richard Scott, *Institutions and Organizations* (Thousand Oaks, CA: Sage Publications, 1995).

51. Smith and Sosin, "The Varieties of Faith-related Agencies."

52. Flannery, *Vatican Council II.*

53. *Code of Canon Law: Latin-English Edition, New English Translation*, trans. Canon Law Society of America (Washington, DC: Canon Law Society of America, 1999); Adam J. Maida and Nicholas P. Cafardi, *Church Property, Church Finances, and Church-Related Corporations: A Canon-Law Handbook* (St. Louis, MO: Catholic Health Association of the United States, 1984), 45.

54. First Constitutions of the Congregation of the Sisters of the Holy Family of Nazareth, Congregation of the Sisters of the Holy Family of Nazareth Archives, 1887–90, Rome, Italy.

55. Letters from Mother Mary Lauretta Lubowidzka to Frances Siedliska, trans. Sister D. Ciuzycki, Congregation of the Sisters of the Holy Family of Nazareth Archives, 1898–1900, Rome, Italy.

56. Personal communication, January 26, 2003.

57. "Statement" [a financial statement with accompanying notes], signed by Father Caesar Tomaszewski, Mother Mary Lauretta Lubowidzka, and Rev. C. M. Hegerich, October 13, 1905, Sisters of the Holy Family of Nazareth of Western Pennsylvania Archives, Westview, PA.

58. Bylaws of The Orphan Asylum of the Holy Family, November 7, 1904, Holy Family Institute Archives (Series 1, Box 1, Folder 1), Emsworth, PA.

59. "Statement," Sisters of the Holy Family of Nazareth of Western Pennsylvania Archives.

60. Minutes of the meeting of the Board of Directors of Holy Family Institute, January 25, 1945, Holy Family Institute Archives (Series 4, Binder 1), Emsworth, PA.

61. Bylaws of the Advisory Board of Holy Family Institute, January 29, 1953, Holy Family Institute Archives (Series 2, Box 1), Emsworth, PA.

62. Maureen Cleary, "The Management Dilemmas in Catholic Human Service Organizations (health, welfare, and education) in Australia" (unpublished doctoral dissertation, University of Technology, 2001).

63. Melanie DiPietro, *Acts of the Colloquium: Public Ecclesiastical Juridic Persons and their Civilly Incorporated Apostolates in the Catholic Church in the U.S.A.—Canonical-civil Aspects* (Pittsburgh, PA: Pontifical University of Saint Thomas Aquinas and Duquesne University School of Law, 1998); Maida and Cafardi, *Church Property*; Elizabeth McDonough, *Religious in the 1983 Code: New Approaches to the New Law* (Chicago: Franciscan Herald Press, 1985).

64. Amended and Restated Bylaws of Holy Family Institute, 1998, Holy Family Institute Archives (Series 1, Box 1, Folder 21), Emsworth, PA.

65. Annual Report of the Holy Family Institute for the Year 1935, Holy Family Institute Archives (Series 13, Subseries 1, Box 1, Folder 3), Emsworth, PA.

66. Yankoski, "The Soul of the Matter."

67. Audit Report, 2002, Holy Family Institute Archives (Series 13, Subseries 1, Box 1), Emsworth, PA.

68. Yankoski, "The Soul of the Matter."

69. Salamon, *Partners in Public Service.*

70. Ibid.

71. DiMaggio and Powell, *The Iron Cage Revisited*; Scott, *Institutions and Organizations*; and Smith and Sosin, *The Varieties of Faith-related Agencies.*

72. Benne, *Quality with Soul*; Thomas H. Jeavons, "Identifying Characteristics of 'Religious' Organizations: Exploratory Proposal," in *Sacred Companies*, 79–95; Monsma, *When Sacred and Secular Mix*; and Working Group on Human Needs and Faith-Based and Community Initiatives, *Finding Common Ground: 29 Recommendations of the Working Group on Human Needs and Faith-Based and Community Initiatives*, retrieved April 15, 2002, from http://working-group.org.

73. Jeavons, "Identifying Characteristics."

74. Melanie DiPietro and Gregg S. Behr, *Framing the Facts: Wordsmiths, Wordmongers, and the Establishment Clause* [white paper] (Pittsburgh, PA: Buchanan Ingersoll Professional Corporation, 2002).

75. http://www.vatican.va/roman_curia/pontifical_councils/justpeace/documents/rc_pc_justpeace_doc_20060526_compendio-dott-soc_en.html#I.%20MEANING%20AND%20UNITY

76. Bernardin, "Catholic Identity: Resolving Conflicting Expectations"; Melanie DiPietro "Organizational Overview," in *Who Do You Say We Are? Perspectives on Catholic Identity in Catholic Charities*, ed. Jo-Ann Leitch (Alexandria, VA: Catholic Charities USA, 1997), 25–42; Fahey, "The 'Catholic' in Catholic Charities"; and John E. Tropman, *The Catholic Ethic and the Spirit of Community* (Washington, DC: Georgetown University Press, 2002).

77. Yankoski, "The Soul of the Matter."

78. Stephen L. Carter, *The Culture of Disbelief: How American Law and Politics Trivialize Religious Devotion* (New York: HarperCollins, 1993).

Chapter Seven: Putting Justice and Charity into Action

1. Catholic Charities USA, *A Catholic Charities Framework for Empowerment* (Alexandria, VA: Catholic Charities USA, 1998).

2. http://www.catholic.org/encyclopedia/view.php?id=3843.

3. *Didache*, chapter 1; http://www.earlychristianwritings.com/text/didache-roberts.html

4. St. John Chrysostom, *Hom.* In *Lazaro* 2,5: 48, 992 and *Apostolican Acuositatem*, 8§5, as cited in *Catechism of the Catholic Church* (Washington, DC: United States Conference of Catholic Bishops, 1994), 2446.

5. *The Pontifical of Egbert, Archbishop of York*, http://www.archive.org/stream/pontificalegbert27surtuoft/pontificalegbert27surtuoft_djvu.txt.

6. St. Vincent de Paul, *Common Rule* (1658), XI, 1.

7. Leo XIII, *Rerum Novarum*, 1891, http://www.vatican.va/holy_father/leo_xiii/encyclicals/documents/hf_l-xiii_enc_15051891_rerum-novarum_en.html.

8. Pius XI, *Quadragesimo Anno*, 1931, http://www.vatican.va/holy_father/pius_xi/encyclicals/documents/hf_p-xi_enc_19310515_quadragesimo-anno_en.html,

9. John XXIII, *Ad Petri Cathedram*, 1959, 127, http://www.vatican.va/holy_father/john_xxiii/encyclicals/documents/hf_j-xxiii_enc_29061959_ad-petri_en.html.

10. Ibid., 128.

11. John XXIII, *Mater Et Magistra*, 1961, http://www.vatican.va/holy_father/john_xxiii/encyclicals/documents/hf_j-xxiii_enc_15051961_mater_en.html.

12. John XXIII, *Pacem In Terris*, 1963, 26, http://www.vatican.va/holy_father/john_xxiii/encyclicals/documents/hf_j-xxiii_enc _11041963_pacem_en.html.

13. *Gaudium et Spes*, 1965, 4, http://www.vatican.va/archive/hist_councils/ii_vatican_council/documents/vat-ii_cons_19651207_gaudiu...5/19/2004.

14. Ibid., 4–5.

15. Ibid., 12.

16. Ibid., 29.

17. Ibid., 31.

18. Ibid., 43.

19. Ibid., 55.

20. Ibid., 60.

21. Ibid., 65.

22. Ibid., 69.

23. Paul VI, *Populorum Progressio*, 1967, 30, http://www.vatican.va/holy_father/paul_vi/encyclicals/documents/hf_p-vi_enc_ 26031967_populorum_en.html.

24. Ibid., 34.

25. Ibid.

26. Paul VI, *Octagesima Adveniens*, 1971, 11, www.vatican.va/holy_father/paul_vi/apost_letters/documents/hf_p-vi_apl_ 19710514_octogesima-adveniens_en.html.

27. Ibid., 48.

28. John Paul II, *Sollicitudo Rei Socialis*, 1987, 39, http://www.vatican.va/holy_father/john_paul_ii/encyclicals/documents/hf_jp-ii_enc_30121987_sollicitudo-rei-socialis_en.html.

29. John Paul II, "Message of His Holiness Pope John Paul II for the Celebration of the World Day of Peace," 2000, http://www.vatican.va/holy_father/john_paul_ii/messages/peace/documents/hf_jp-ii_mes_08121999_xxxiii-world-day-for-peace_en.html.

30. John Paul II, "Novo Millennio Ineunte," 2000, 50, http://www.vatican.va/holy_father/john_paul_ii/apost_letters/documents/hf_jp-ii_apl_20010106_novo-millennio-ineunte_en.html.

31. Benedict XVI, *Deus Caritas Est*, 2005, 28–29, http://www.vatican.va/holy_father/benedict_xvi/encyclicals/documents/hf_ben-xvi_enc_20051225_deus-caritas-est_en.html.

32. Benedict XVI, *Spe Salvi*, 2007, 24, http://www.vatican.va/holy_father/benedict_xvi/encyclicals/documents/hf_ben-xvi_enc_20071130_spe-salvi_en.html.

33. Benedict XVI, "Message of Pope Benedict XVI for the Celebration of the World Day of Peace," 2009, 12, http://www.vatican.va/holy_father/benedict_xvi/messages/peace/documents/hf_ben-xvi_mes_20081208_xlii-world-day-peace_en.html.

34. Address of Pope Benedict XVI During Meeting with Political and Civil Authorities and the Diplomatic Corps, Presidential Palace, Luanda, Angola, March 20, 2009, http://www.vatican.va/holy_father/benedict_xvi/speeches/2009/march/documents/hf_ben-xvi_spe_20090320_autorita-civili_en.html.

35. National Conference of Catholic Bishops, Economic Justice for All: A Pastoral Letter on Catholic Social Teaching and the U.S. Economy (Washington, DC:

National Conference of Catholic Bishops, 1986), 188, http://www.usccb.org/sdwp/international/EconomicJusticeforAll.pdf.

36. National Conference of Catholic Bishops, Called and Gifted for the Third Millennium: A Statement of the National Conference of Catholic Bishops on the Thirtieth Anniversary of the Decree on the Apostolate of the Laity and the Fifteenth Anniversary of Called and Gifted (Washington, DC: National Conference of Catholic Bishops, 1995).

37. United States Conference of Catholic Bishops, Renewing the Vision: A Framework for Catholic Youth Ministry (Washington, DC: United States Conference of Catholic Bishops, 1997).

38. United States Conference of Catholic Bishops, In All Things Charity: A Pastoral Challenge for the New Millennium (Washington, DC: United States Conference of Catholic Bishops, 1999).

39. Ibid.

40. Dorothy Brown and Elizabeth McKeown, *The Poor Belong to Us: Catholic Charities and American Welfare* (Cambridge, MA: Harvard University Press, 1997), 30.

41. Ibid., 38.

42. Ibid., 64.

43. Benedict XVI, *Deus Caritas Est* 29.

44. "Hoover's Profile: Catholic Charities USA," http://www.answers.com/topic/catholic-charities-usa.

45. Catholic Charities USA, *Cadre Study: Toward a Renewed Catholic Charities Movement* (Alexandria, VA: Catholic Charities USA, 1992).

46. Ibid.

47. Catholic Charities USA, *Vision 2000* (Alexandria, VA: Catholic Charities USA, 1997).

48. Catholic Charities USA, *A Catholic Charities Framework for Empowerment* (Alexandria, VA: Catholic Charities USA, 1998).

49. Adapted from Robert J. Vitillo, "*Gaudium et Spes*: Influences of Vatican II's Pastoral Constitution," *Origins* 34, no. 39 (March 2005): 623.

50. Catholic Relief Services, *Applying the Justice Lens to Programming* (Baltimore, MD: Catholic Relief Services, 1998), http://crs.org/publications/showpdf.cfm?pdf_id=88.

51. National Conference of Catholic Bishops, *Declaration to Establish the Catholic Crusade Against Poverty* (Washington, DC: National Conference of Catholic Bishops, 1969).

52. Catholic Campaign for Human Development, *Annual Report 2006–2007* (Washington, DC: Catholic Campaign for Human Development, 2007), http://www.usccb.org/cchd/CCHD%20AR%2006-07.pdf.

53. Celestino Migliore, address to the Economic and Social Council, 47th Session of the Commission for Social Development, New York, February 5, 2009,

Chapter Eight: Mission and Identity

1. This chapter is adapted and abridged, with permission, from chapters 1 and 2 of my Catholic Charities centennial commentary: *Faith. Works. Wonders.—An*

Insider's Guide to Catholic Charities (Eugene, OR: Wipf and Stock Publishers, 2009).

2. *Proceedings* of the first annual meeting of the National Conference of Catholic Charities, September 25–28, 1910, quoted in *Toward a Renewed Catholic Charities Movement: A Study of the National Conference of Catholic Charities* (Alexandria, VA: National Conference of Catholic Charities, 1972), 63.

3. *Toward a Renewed Catholic Charities Movement*, 100.

4. Pope John Paul II, The Poor Have a Privileged Place in Christ, address to the Annual Meeting of Catholic Charities USA, September 13, 1987; reprinted under title, "To Spread Christian Love," *Charities USA* 14, no. 9 (December 1987): 7–12.

5. *Vision 2000* (Alexandria, VA: Catholic Charities USA, 1997), 7.

6. Ibid., 9.

7. *The Catholic Charities USA 1995 Annual Survey* indicated that of 10.8 million people served in the year prior to the completion of Vision 2000, 7.2 million had come to Catholic Charities agencies for emergency services, primarily food; Patrice Flynn, *Catholic Charities USA 1995 Annual Survey: National Findings* (Alexandria, VA: Catholic Charities USA, 1996), 1.

8. See chapter 7 in this book by Msgr. Robert Vitillo on empowerment in Catholic Charities.

9. William Booth, "In Church Fires, a Pattern but No Conspiracy," *Washington Post* (June 19, 1996): A1. This article reported on 37 suspicious fires at black churches during the previous 18 months, approval by the U.S. House of Representatives of legislation making it easier for federal officials to prosecute, and President Clinton's request to Congress for $12 million for investigations.

10. *Poverty and Racism: Overlapping Threats to the Common Good* (Alexandria, VA: Catholic Charities USA, 2008).

11. *Who Do You Say We Are?—Perspectives on Catholic Identity in Catholic Charities*, ed. J. Leitch (Alexandria, VA: Catholic Charities USA, 1997).

12. Rev. Bryan J. Hehir was president and CEO of Catholic Charities USA from 2001 to 2003.

13. Chaired by Bishop Joseph M. Sullivan of Brooklyn, the ad hoc writing committee for the pastoral message consisted of Bishops Edwin M. Conway of Chicago; Nicholas A. Di Marzio of Camden, NJ; Howard Hubbard of Albany, NY; Ricardo Ramirez, CSB, of Las Cruces, NM; and John H. Ricard, SSJ, of Pensacola-Tallahassee, FL. Msgr. Robert J. Vitillo of the Catholic Campaign for Human Development was the lead staff member for the pastoral message. Many Catholic Charities staff and volunteers had an opportunity to make suggestions in the process of the development of the pastoral message.

14. In All Things Charity: A Pastoral Challenge for the New Millennium (Washington, DC: United States Catholic Conference, 1999), 30.

15. Ibid., 31.

16. Ibid., emphasis in original. Further, the bishops endorsed the work of the Catholic Campaign for Human Development, USCC Migration and Refugee Services, the USCC Department of Social Development and World Peace, and Catholic Relief Services.

17. Pope Benedict XVI, *Deus Caritas Est*, 2005.

18. Ibid., 9.

19. Ibid., 10.

20. Ibid., 14.

21. Ibid., 15.

22. Ibid., 16.

23. Ibid., 18.

24. Ibid., 27.

25. Ibid., 20.

26. Ibid., 23.

27. Ibid., 24.

28. Ibid., 25.

29. Ibid., 30.

30. Ibid.

31. Ibid., 35–39.

32. Pontifical Council for Justice and Peace, *Compendium of the Social Doctrine of the Church* (Libreria Editrice Vaticana, 2004).

33. *Catholic Charities USA Code of Ethics* (Alexandria, VA: Catholic Charities USA, 2007), 2.

34. Pontifical Council for Justice and Peace, *Compendium*, 108; italics original to text.

35. In All Things Charity, 12, quoting from Economic Justice for All (Washington, DC: United States Catholic Conference, 1986), 38.

36. Ibid., 13, quoting from Pope John Paul II in *Tertio Millennio Adveniente* 13.

37. Ibid., 14.

38. *Catechism of the Catholic Church*, 2422.

39. Ibid., 2423.

40. Ibid., 2420, quoting Vatican II's *Gaudium et Spes*, 1965, 76, section 5.

41. Subsequent to the completion of this article, Pope Benedict XVI published his encyclical *Caritas in Veritate* (2009), confirming the tradition of modern Catholic social teaching and applying it more broadly to integral human development in the context of a globalizing world.

42. For example, (1) Economist William J. Byron, SJ, writing in *America* on October 31, 1998 [vol. 179, no. 13] offered "ten building blocks of Catholic social teaching." (2) In a recent book, theologian Thomas Massaro, SJ, offers nine themes around which to organize the key texts within the tradition. Cf. *Living Justice: Catholic Social Teaching in Action* (Franklin, WI: Sheed and Ward, 2000). (3) The bishops of the United States also have worked to develop summaries of major themes from Catholic social teaching. Their efforts also demonstrate how summaries can evolve over time, as Catholic social teaching itself evolves. In 1991, on the hundredth anniversary of *Rerum Novarum*, the bishops wrote a short pastoral message (*A Century of Social Teaching: A Common Heritage, A Continuing Challenge*) in which they highlighted the following six themes from the tradition: the life and dignity of the human person; the rights and responsibilities of the human person;

the call to family, community, and participation; the dignity of work and the rights of workers; the option for the poor and vulnerable; and solidarity. Seven years later, in a new document on the teaching of Catholic social teaching, the bishops reiterated the above six themes, but added a seventh: care for God's creation. (4) In *Doing Faithjustice: An Introduction to Catholic Social Thought* (Mahwah, NJ: Paulist Press, 1991, 1992, 2004), I identified 26 "key ideas" that occur in the first 100 years of modern Catholic social teaching—from *Rerum Novarum* to *Centesimus Annus.* The fact that there are so many is an indication of the richness of the tradition and the inadequacy of any short list of principles or values to be drawn from now over a century of this line of Catholic thought.

43. Pontifical Council of Peace and Justice, *Compendium*, 132, quoting from Vatican Council II, *Gaudium et Spes* 26; italics original to text.

44. Ibid., 164, quoting from *Gaudium et Spes* 26.

45. Ibid., 185–87.

46. Ibid., 192.

47. See discussion on how Catholic Charities implements these principles in the *Catholic Charities USA Code of Ethics*, part II.

48. *Catholic Charities USA 2008 Annual Survey* (Alexandria, VA: Catholic Charities USA, 2009).

49. This section is adapted and updated from my article, "10 Ways Catholic Charities are Catholic," *Charities USA* 25, no. 1 (First Quarter, 1998).

50. Catholic News Service, reporting on Pope John Paul II's address to the Pontifical Council "Cor Unum," April 18, 1997.

51. *Deus Caritas Est* 31(c).

52. Ibid., 18.

53. Ibid., 3(c).

54. The *Catholic Charities USA 2008 Annual Survey* reports that 142 of 171 agencies participated in the survey and reported that 1,723 full-time and 71 part-time staff were involved in Parish Social Ministry.

55. See *Communities of Salt and Light*, National Conference of Catholic Bishops, 1993, and *Called to Global Solidarity*, 1998, in which the bishops call upon parishes to exercise their baptismal social responsibility.

56. In All Things Charity, 23.

57. Ibid., 36–37.

58. Ibid., 37.

59. *Deus Caritas Est* 34.

60. Ibid., 28(a).

61. Ibid.

62. Ibid., 38(b).

63. In All Things Charity, 38–39.

64. Pontifical Council for Peace and Justice, *Compendium*, 303.

65. In All Things Charity, 39.

66. Ibid., 17, citing Pope John Paul II, *Ecclesia in America*, 1999, 18.

Chapter Nine: Catholic Charities

1. This chapter is a revised version of the 2007 Monsignor George Bardes Chair in Social Justice Lecture given at St. Joseph's Seminary, Yonkers, NY, on December 5, 2007.

2. William V. D'Antonio, Dean Hoge, Mary Gautier, and James D. Davidson, *American Catholics Today: New Realities of Their Faith and Their Church* (Lanham, MD: Rowman & Littlefield Publishers, Inc., 2007).

3. Some dioceses have adopted other titles such as Catholic Social Services or Catholic Community Services. However, in the overwhelming number of cases, Catholic Charities remains the title for the principal charitable agency in each diocese. The scope of this chapter includes, but is not limited to, these. Throughout this chapter, the name "Catholic Charities" is generally used as shorthand to refer to the range of organized charitable activities carried out under Catholic auspices. Often these have a name that includes neither the word *Catholic* nor *Charities*, but rather that of "Our Lady," or a saint or a religious community. The Archdiocese of New York exemplifies this in the formal name for its Catholic Charities, established in 1917: "The Catholic Charities of the Archdiocese of New York." The word *the* has been an important part of this title because it communicates that there are multiple Catholic charitable endeavors undertaken by various ecclesial communities within this federation of agencies.

4. Taken from the web sites of the Blauvelt Dominican Sisters, www.opblauvelt.org, and of St. Dominic's Home, www.stdominicshome.org.

5. Taken from the web site of the Catholic Guardian Society and Home Bureau, www.cgshb.org. In 2006, the Catholic Home Bureau merged with another Catholic Charities agency, the Catholic Guardian Society, to form one agency, the Catholic Guardian Society and Home Bureau.

6. Taken from the web site of the Mission of the Immaculate Virgin, www.mountloretto.org.

7. Pope Benedict XVI, *Deus Caritas Est* 25. "The Church cannot neglect the service of charity any more than she can neglect the Sacraments and the Word."

8. In presenting a selective set of texts, I am aware of the exegetical warning that one can prove almost anything from the Scriptures if you are allowed to choose your own texts. I admit these texts are not exhaustive, yet I believe they are representative and provide a strong foundation for the hypothesis that charity is at the heart of the message.

9. *Deus Caritas Est*, 2005, 20, 22.

10. *Catechism of the Catholic Church*, 1022.

11. Ibid., 1803.

12. Ibid., 1810.

13. Unless stated otherwise, the adjective "good" is implied in front of the word "institution." "Bad" institutions are the communal parallel to individual "vices."

14. Geoffrey M. Hodgson, "What Are Institutions?" *Journal of Economic Issues* 40, no. 1 (March 2006). I use this description from Hodgson because it is fairly standard. Hodgson himself carefully distinguishes between institutions and orga-

nizations. While recognizing the importance of these distinctions in some contexts, in this article I use them interchangeably.

15. In exploring this, it is again important to suggest a framework that transcends any one concretization of a particular Catholic Charities agency or program. This framework should be applicable, with apt adaptations, to all Catholic Charities agencies.

16. The case being made does not rest upon strict transitive logic, i.e., charity equals *caritas* and *caritas* equals *agape*; therefore Catholic Charities equals Catholic *agape*. Language is too complex to make such an absolute straightforward case. However, by pointing out the problems with the English word *charity* and showing its roots in the Latin word *caritas*, which is also translated as "love," one immediately broadens consideration of the scope of Catholic Charities. That *caritas* can serve as an acceptable translation of the Greek biblical work *agape* in the Vulgate further draws us to see to root the work of Catholic Charities in the type and scope of love and service taught by Jesus and written about in the letter to the earliest Christian communities. I include two examples: 1 Corinthians 13:13: "So faith, hope, love [*agape/caritas*] remain, these three, but the greatest of these is love [*agape/caritas*]"; and 1 John 3:17: "If someone has worldly means sees a brother in need and refuses him compassion, how can the love [*agape /caritas*] of God remain in him?"

17. John P. Meier, "A Marginal Jew, Rethinking the Historical Jesus," in *Love and Law*, vol. IV (New Haven, CT: Yale University Press, 2009), 478–646. The author provides a comprehensive and tightly focused consideration of "the love commandments of Jesus" in the New Testament and warns against simplification and harmonization based upon centuries of conflating texts. At the same time, without claiming the author supports the following conclusion, I would say that the chapter does provide a solid foundation for rooting the biblical mandate of love in the teachings of Jesus and this mandate as going beyond mere emotions and feelings to concretely doing good for the neighbor. Furthermore, the traditional boundaries of neighbor are broadened to include anyone in need. As a mandate it cannot be optional and since it is the parallel with self-love, it cannot be condescending.

18. World Synod of Bishops, Justice in the World, 1971.

19. Recognizing this communal foundation does not mean that every right is exactly the same, enjoys exactly the same priority, and admits of the same specificity in its exercise.

20. Pope John XXIII, *Pacem in Terris*, 1963, 1, 3, 5–7.

21. Ibid., 11, 13, 15–22, 25. Teachings in the subsequent half-century developed the permission to emigrate into a right when the circumstances warrant, insisting on a reciprocal responsibility to generosity on the part of receiving countries. The *Catechism of the Catholic Church*, 2211, articulates the "right to emigrate" in the context of discussing the rights that the political community needs to protect to honor the family.

22. *Catholic Charities USA 2008 Annual Survey* (Alexandria, VA: Catholic Charites USA, 2009).

23. Benedict XVI, *Spe Salvi*, 2007, 24–25, 28.

24. The human rights tradition of the church is more extensive than *Pacem in Terris*. However, this encyclical serves as a helpful synopsis of the fundamental human rights that the church recognizes. For the purposes of this chapter, it provides a very useful guide. Others might well develop a more extensive approach using a variety of sources.

25. *Catholic Charities USA 2008 Annual Survey*; the survey instrument itself provides a great deal of information. However, the need to capture data across a very broad and diverse group of agencies and services means that much detail and specificity is not captured. As a result, the use of the survey must be illustrative and suggestive rather than definitive. Further research targeting the correlation between Catholic Charities services and human rights in church teaching would need to be designed to explore this topic in depth.

26. As executive director of The Catholic Charities of the Archdiocese of New York, I am able to use a wealth of data and information to explore this in more depth with one agency.

27. Mission Statement of The Catholic Charities of the Archdiocese of New York, retrieved from www.catholiccharitiesny.org on December 7, 2009.

28. Vision Statement of The Catholic Charities of the Archdiocese of New York, retrieved from www.catholiccharitiesny.org on December 7, 2009.

29. Briefly relating these categories of services to rights articulated in *Pacem in Terris* is meant to demonstrate a clear connection with the church's articulated human rights teaching. However, this is not an exhaustive presentation. Other church documents further develop the teaching in *Pacem in Terris*.

Appendix: Catholic Charities in the Last Four Decades

1. *Toward a Renewed Catholic Charities Movement: A Study of the National Conference of Catholic Charities* (Washington, DC: National Conference of Catholic Charities, 1972), 3.

2. Ibid.

3. Ibid., 41.

4. *Renewal in Catholic Charities: A Report on the Implementation of the Study of the National Conference of Catholic Charities* (Washington, DC: National Conference of Catholic Charities, 1975), 8.

5. The estimated number of U.S. residents as reported by the U.S. Census Bureau.

6. The Annual Reports began providing estimates for unduplicated clients in 2000. These estimates are not reported here as data are not available for previous years. The unduplicated estimate accounts for the fact that some individuals receive services in more than one service area (e.g., housing and food).

7. The misery index peaked in 1980 at 20.8 and was the subject of debate among the presidential candidates in that election year. The index declined from that peak primarily through greater efforts by the Federal Reserve to control inflation by adjusting interest rates. At the time of this report this index measured 8.1.

8. The peak year of difference between the highest and lowest income families is 2005, at 720 percent.

9. The range of years shown in the figure was determined by the availability of data. Years with no bars indicate years when the Annual Report did not present data for the value of services provided.

10. Response to the Catholic Charities Annual Survey typically ranges from approximately two-thirds to four-fifths of all Catholic Charities member agencies and affiliates. Since 2002, CARA has worked to improve the response rate and has used previous year responses to impute missing data from non-responding agencies.

11. Although the U.S. economy grew in 1981 at an annualized rate of 2.5 percent, the economy had contracted in 1980 (-0.2 percent). Also, the economic growth rates in the second and fourth quarters of 1981 were -3.1 percent and -4.8 percent, respectively.

Index